D0649461

"The Theatre We Worked For"

The Triumvirate (*clockwise from lower left:* Robert Edmond Jones, Eugene O'Neill, and Kenneth Macgowan), as seen by Miguel Covarrubias.

"The Theatre We Worked For"

THE LETTERS OF EUGENE O'NEILL

TO KENNETH MACGOWAN

Edited by Jackson R. Bryer,
   with the assistance of Ruth M. Alvarez
With introductory essays
   by Travis Bogard

NEW HAVEN AND LONDON
YALE UNIVERSITY PRESS

Published with assistance from the foundation
established in memory of Amasa Stone Mather
of the Class of 1907, Yale College.

Designed by Sally Harris
and set in Garamond type by P&M Typesetting, Inc.
Printed in the United States of America by
The Murray Printing Co., Westford, Mass.

Library of Congress Cataloging in Publication Data

O'Neill, Eugene, 1888–1953.
    The theatre we worked for.
    Includes index.
    1. O'Neill, Eugene, 1888–1953—Correspondence.
2. Macgowan, Kenneth, 1888–1963. 3. Dramatists,
American—20th century—Correspondence. I. Macgowan,
Kenneth, 1888–1962. II. Bryer, Jackson R.
III. Bogard, Travis. IV. Title.
PS3529.N5Z494   1981   812'.52 [B]   81-2997
ISBN 0-300-02583-1   AACR2

10   9   8   7   6   5   4   3   2   1

Contents

Illustrations

Preface

This volume includes all surviving correspondence between Eugene O'Neill and Kenneth Macgowan, essentially a one-sided correspondence, since most of Macgowan's letters and telegrams to O'Neill have disappeared. O'Neill's letters, however, make clear the nature of the relationship between the two men and the kind of theatre they strove to create. It is as a documenting of that relationship—between America's greatest playwright and an important director-producer-dramatic critic who shared his ideals and hopes for a truly "new" and exciting American theatre—that we intend this book. It is not just a collection of letters; the letters form only part of the story, a story told also in the four introductory essays. Not all—or even many—of the letters can stand independently as brilliant specimens of epistolary style. Some are little more than routine exchanges between friends and business associates. But all are significant in illuminating the unique bond formed between these two men with a common vision of what the American theatre could and must be. As such, we view this volume as providing material for a better understanding of O'Neill and his career, of Macgowan (who until now has been an inexplicably shadowy figure in recent dramatic histories), and of a seminal period in the development of the American theatre. Accordingly, to round out the picture, we have added a few letters bearing on the O'Neill–Macgowan relationship from persons other than the two principals—Agnes Boulton O'Neill, Carlotta Monterey O'Neill, Edna Macgowan, and Harry Weinberger, O'Neill's lawyer. We hope that the letters and the introductory essays, together, tell more fully than previous accounts the story of this friendship and of the theatre these two remarkable men worked for.

In providing footnotes for the correspondence, we have tried to steer a middle course between providing maximum information and merely giving sketchy identifications. Thus, persons, places, and events have been identified only once, except in a few cases when a subsequent appearance occurs considerably later in the volume. Birth and death dates are provided only for major theatrical figures. We have not tried to anticipate the audience for this book either by identifying only the most obscure theatrical personages or by footnoting every name or title mentioned in the correspondence; we hope the volume will attract both specialists and general readers. While we also hope that the reader will read the introductory essays preceding the letters, we have footnoted references in the letters that are explained in the essays as well.

The following abbreviations describing physical form have been utilized in the headings: TLS, typed letter signed by author; TL, typed letter unsigned; ALS, autograph letter signed by author; AL, autograph letter unsigned; TL (cc), typed letter, carbon copy; WIRE, telegram. The numbers enumerating the total pages of the original letters refer to the pages designated by the author of the individual letter. Usually the number indicates one side of one leaf of stationery, but occasionally it refers to one side of a leaf of stationery when both recto and verso are used. Less frequently it refers to one-half of a side of a leaf of stationery, when the author numbered two pages of an individual letter on one side of a leaf of stationery. Stationery headings that appear on the originals have been transcribed in upper- and lower-case type regardless of the appearance of the original and have been printed under the description of physical form.

The position of headings has been standardized to appear flush to the left or right margin. Where the date or part of the date does not appear in the original, it has been supplied in square brackets, which have been reserved for editorial insertions. Superfluous terminal punctuation in dates, closings, and signatures has been omitted. The position of closings and signatures has been standardized as well.

O'Neill's habitual spelling and punctuation errors and misspellings of personal names have been retained. Obviously inadvertent misspellings and typographical errors have been silently corrected. The position of quotation marks with punctuation has been regularized. The length of dashes in O'Neill's letters has been standardized to one em, although his practice in typing was to use one hyphen for a dash. No attempt has been made to reproduce the unique holograph dashes of Carlotta Monterey O'Neill; all of them, regardless of length, have been printed here as one-em dashes. The abbreviation of ordinal numbers, which are used frequently throughout the correspondence, has been regularized to "1st," "2nd," "3rd," etc. However, the holograph practice of both O'Neill and Carlotta Monterey O'Neill was to raise and underline the letters. The letters "P.S." that precede most of O'Neill's postscripts have been regularized to appear on the same line as the text of the manuscript. His general practice was to put the "P.S." on a separate line.

Only meaningful deletions made by O'Neill have been retained, printed in footnotes. Insignificant deletions and obliterations have not been restored in the text. Interlineal insertions and marginal material have been printed as part of the letter or placed at the end of the letter. Angle brackets have been used to indicate substantial missing or obliterated text.

Acknowledgments

The editors wish to acknowledge their gratitude to Dr. Donald Gallup, former Curator of the Collection of American Literature at the Beinecke Rare Book and Manuscript Library of Yale University. This book was his conception, and he has been a faithful collaborator at every step. The Library graciously gave permission to publish the manuscript materials. We are grateful as well to Kenneth Macgowan's daughter, Mrs. Robert Faxon, for her interest and her assistance in providing details of her father's career. We owe a considerable debt to Louis Sheaffer, author of the two-volume biography of O'Neill, *O'Neill: Son and Playwright* and *O'Neill: Son and Artist.* He and his books have helped us immeasurably with information and photographs; and his reading of this edition in manuscript form was invaluable. Thalia Brewer, librarian of the Eugene O'Neill Foundation / Tao House in Danville, California, has supplied valuable information concerning the O'Neills' life at Tao House.

The job of preparing an accurate edited text of the letters could not have been accomplished without the skills of Mary Pat Bierle, who prepared the typescript of the letters. We are also indebted to Dr. Robert Corrigan, former Provost of the Division of Arts and Humanities of the University of Maryland, who provided a grant to defray the costs of the typing; to the General Research Board of the University of Maryland and the Committee on Research of the University of California, Berkeley; and to our able research assistants, Andrew Cohn and Katherine Stewart, in California, and Ruth M. Alvarez, in Maryland, who prepared the index for the volume, as well as performing other important tasks.

We are also grateful for a variety of kindnesses cheerfully performed by Mrs. Saxe Commins; Miss Florence Eldridge; Professor William Melnitz; Professor Horst Frenz; Anna E. Crouse; Clara A. Weiss; James Schevill; Dorothy L. Swerdlove and the staff of the Theatre Collection of the New York Public Library at Lincoln Center; Brooks Whiting, Curator of Rare Books in the Department of Special Collections of the University Research Library of the University of California at Los Angeles; Fred W. Hall, Jr., executor of the estate of Elizabeth Jones; and Carolyn S. Coles.

1: Peaked Hill Bar

In the first letter of what was to become a lifetime's correspondence, Eugene O'Neill wrote to Kenneth Macgowan that they had been "fated" to become friends. Whether it was an act of destiny or not, a meeting between the two men was inevitable, and, given Macgowan's eagerness to be useful to those with creative abilities and his capacity for easy friendliness, it would have been strange had friendship not followed first associations. The encounter that took place as the Macgowans visited the O'Neills at their home at Peaked Hill Bar on Cape Cod was vital to them both.

Both men came late to a mature definition of their professional aims. In the summer of 1921, they did not wholly know what they wanted. Working in association toward a common goal helped them both to achieve clearer self-definition, and mutual interests made each more certain of the direction he would take along the bewildering paths of the young century. O'Neill's ambitions were to lead him to attempt the highest ranges of the playwright's art, but to comprehend the scope of his ambition, he needed a mentor and a caretaker, roles that Macgowan for a time willingly assumed. Macgowan's varied interests in theatre aesthetics, in anthropology, in masks and in psychiatry were to help shape the course of O'Neill's playwriting for the next fifteen years. In his turn, Macgowan had yet to discover about himself what O'Neill's ambitions were to clarify: that his true profession lay not in critical writing or magazine editing as he had at first believed, but in the role of theatrical producer, a character he first assumed in O'Neill's service and continued in later years in two of Hollywood's major studios.

Before their meeting, Macgowan had led an errant and somewhat unfocused professional life. He was a journalist, and he wrote much about the theatre, but the decade between 1911, when he graduated from Harvard, and 1921, when he came to know O'Neill, is marked by an ambitious, but sometimes listless shifting of jobs that suggests boredom bred of ill-defined objectives.

Macgowan was born in Winthrop, Massachusetts, on November 11, 1888. He was a month younger than O'Neill, who had been born in New York City on October 16. A Massachusetts boy in comfortable circumstances had an almost inevitable destination, and Macgowan duly entered Harvard University in 1907 as a member of the class of 1911. In school, he blended study with the extracurricular activities of most literate youngsters. He wrote for the student literary magazine, the *Harvard Monthly*, and he functioned as business and stage manager for the Harvard Dramatic Club.

Being a facile writer, attracted to the theatre, Macgowan was able to persuade the redoubtable critic of the Boston *Evening Transcript*, H. T. Parker, to take him on as a second-string reviewer. He had earlier written a few reviews and "Sunday pieces" for the New York *Call*, but his apprenticeship was served under Parker's eye. Until 1914, he wrote reviews, and, in a column called "Plays and Players," he explored general theatrical subjects. Occasionally, too, he wrote pieces for *Collier's* and *Century* magazines.[1]

For a young, intelligent man at the beginning of a new century, who in a few years was to become an important champion of the New Theatre aesthetics, Macgowan's taste was surprisingly conservative, even dutiful. Voices concerned with new ideas in the theatre were to be heard in Cambridge in those years. One of the pioneer little theatres in America, the Boston Toy Theatre, under the direction of Livingston Platt, began its short life in 1911 with the participation of Amy Lowell and others of the local literati. Samuel Hume, freshly returned from study with Gordon Craig, mounted an exhibition of the new stagecraft that introduced young American designers, directors, and playwrights to exciting developments of the European *mise-en-scène*. Even in his domestic arrangements, Macgowan was in a position to learn, for his roommate was Hiram Moderwell, an enthusiast of the new theatre, who in 1914 was to publish the first important American documentation of the new European theatre movement in a book entitled *The Theatre of Today*.[2] Macgowan, however, wrote like a junior Parker, and formed his critical judgment around the canons of the conventional, well-made drama, dear to the heart of his mentor, Professor George Pierce Baker, in whose famous playwriting course, "The 47 Workshop," Macgowan enrolled. Like both his employer and his teacher, he championed the realistic prob-

1. A convenient compendium and analysis of Macgowan's critical writing can be found in an unpublished thesis submitted for the degree of Master of Arts by Earle Jones, "An Analysis of the Critical Writings of Kenneth Macgowan as Published in Newspaper and Magazine Articles," Department of Theatre Arts, University of California at Los Angeles, 1954. Macgowan read and corrected the thesis. Macgowan's own clipping books are in the Macgowan Collection, Department of Special Collections, Research Library, University of California at Los Angeles.

2. Hiram Moderwell, *The Theatre of Today* (New York: John Lane, 1914).

lem play that concerned itself seriously with life "as it is." He approved dramas that reflected "contemporary character in racy vivid speech," and he applauded those that appeared to give their audiences the "stimulus of thought." He praised Strindberg because he "sees life clearly and presents it to us sincerely," but was not struck by the Swedish dramatist's expressionistic works. Indeed, he inveighed against "mannerism in staging," the kind of stagecraft that less than a decade later he was to extol. A door was about to open onto a stage of beauty and excitement, but the young Macgowan was not yet of a size to reach the latch.

In the fall of 1914, the year O'Neill entered Harvard to study playwriting with Baker, Macgowan left Boston to take a post as critic for the Philadelphia *Evening Ledger*, where, in addition to his reviews, he wrote a column called "Playhouse and Players," modeled after his Boston forum. Within the year, he also undertook the editorship of both the literary and the "photoplay" reviews.

The Philadelphia commentaries, like those written in Boston, are noteworthy only for their conservatism. For the most part, the reviews are formulaic—the play's story is retold and specific comments on players follow. The comments are tasteful and responsive to the efforts of the actors, and they avoid the semi-satiric wit affected by many reviewers of the time. Like the Boston reviews, they are unchallenged by the theatre arts ideology that by 1914 was beginning to shape theatrical destiny. Platt's Toy Theatre had proved a great influence on Maurice Browne in Chicago; in turn, Browne's Little Theatre was to influence George Cram Cook in the founding of the Provincetown Players and Lawrence Langner in the development of the Washington Square Players, the parent organization of the Theatre Guild. Moderwell's *The Theatre of Today*, which its author intended "as a description and explanation of the new forces which have entered theatrical production in the last ten years, judged in the light of their probable historical importance as well as of their growing contemporary influence,"[3] was before him. The book is extensively illustrated with good photographs of the designs of Appia, Reinhardt, Josef Urban, Craig, Golovine, Livingston Platt and, prophetically, Robert Edmond Jones. It contains as well lengthy discussions of the work of the most interesting and advanced contemporary playwrights and designers arranged by country, including

3. Ibid., p. 9.

America. In the same year, Sheldon Cheney published *The New Movement in Theatre*, the first of his works defining the direction and purposes of the new theatre. To Macgowan, the books were closed, the influential enterprises little noted.

"The American stage," Macgowan insisted, "needs a mass of original and daring thought to match the progress it has made in freedom of technique,"—a strange adherence to intellectual drama from a man who shortly was to champion advanced scenic artistry almost above all. He praised Shaw, because Shaw thought and argued, and he praised naturalistic acting for its truth. He suggested that the new little theatre movement might become sufficiently powerful to break the monopoly of the theatrical syndicates and develop civic theatres of quality like those to be found in European cities. He displayed a continuing concern for the theatre's economics, and he inveighed against high ticket prices that choked off an "eager if yet undiscriminating public." In his columns, his range of subject matter was broad (at times one senses in his choices a desperation born of imminent deadlines and blank sheets of paper), including commentaries on child acting, actors' contracts, curtain times, censorship, and the like. He was a crusader for an obvious kind of sanity and social purpose in theatre, but the excitement that was growing in other theatrical circles was not to be felt in Macgowan's columns.

In 1917, he moved from Philadelphia to try a different career in New York City. For a short time, he served as publicity director for the designer Josef Urban, then producing plays on Broadway. Whatever he saw in his first real encounter with the new stagecraft had no immediate effect on his thinking or his career, for he shortly turned to managing the east coast public relations unit of the Goldwyn Picture Corporation. He left this work when he was hired as a feature writer and editorial writer for the New York *Tribune*. A muckraking attack on William Randolph Hearst and a series of articles on the city of Seattle were the principal products of this employment, which took him far from the theatre. As if to keep his hand in, he wrote occasional pieces on theatre for the paper and for such magazines as *The Dial*.

In 1919, aided by the designer Norman Bel Geddes, he transferred allegiance to the New York *Globe* as drama editor. The position was important in New York's critical hierarchy, and he shored up his throne with free-lance articles for *Vogue, Theatre Arts, The Dial, Collier's,* and the *Bulletin* of the New York Drama League, a society of which in 1920 he became executive director. In such work, he did well, and his rapid rise to situations of importance suggests that he was at last becoming fully a professional. He was now earning about $10,000 a year; in 1913 he had married Edna Behre; and his standing, as his apprenticeship came to an end, was firm.

There was also a new professional association. In New York, Macgowan became closely associated with Sheldon Cheney, the mercurial prophet of the new order of theatre in America. Cheney, with the aid of the designer-actor-director Samuel Hume, had begun publication of *Theatre Arts Magazine,* a quarterly publicizing and analyzing recent developments in theatre. Starting in Detroit, where Hume was director of an arts center, Cheney soon moved the offices to New York City, and the magazine began to appear on a monthly basis. It was the kind of outlet that would attract Macgowan, and he became a regular contributor. Under the blaze of Cheney's enthusiasm, it is not surprising to find Macgowan's Philadelphia conservatism melting away. Now he, who had championed a naturalistic theatre of ideas, wrote, "The stage is a place for honest make-believe. Realism, even romantic illusion, is stupid or stultifying. What we want . . . is a show. . . . We are in a playhouse; then let us play."[4] The conversion was quick and—a market being a market—even opportunistic, as he cried down his old loyalties, "well bred and uninspired culture. . . . [Theatre] must avoid both enemies of true theatricalism—the literary and the realistic."

In short order, Macgowan became entrenched as a New Theatre aesthete, a role which was made official when in January 1919 he was named a contributing editor to *Theatre Arts.* By the next issue in April, "contributing" had been dropped, and he was listed as one of four coeditors, along with Cheney, Edith J. R. Isaacs, and Marion Tucker. By 1922, Cheney's name was gone from the masthead and Macgowan, Isaacs, and Stark Young were listed as coeditors. In 1924, Isaacs assumed the general editorship, and Macgowan and Young became associate editors. His last appearance on the masthead was in December 1927, the year when his working association with O'Neill came to an end, and he embarked on a career as a fully professional producer.

Macgowan's work on the magazine—his regular contributions, reviewing the Broadway season and writing articles praising prominent

4. Quoted in Earle Jones, "Analysis," p. 86.

theatre artists—placed him where he became an arbiter of national theatrical taste. He was never so august as George Jean Nathan, nor such an aesthete as Stark Young, nor a promoter of favorites such as Alexander Woollcott, but in his way he exerted an equal influence. Information came through him. While other, more stylish writers were read by provincials in order to learn what attitudes to take, Macgowan in an orderly way described what was going on. He sometimes assumed a priestly role, but more often he served an important utilitarian function as a caster of theatre news, reviewing the professional theatre season in efficient, clear, neutral strokes. Macgowan was a useful man as he was to prove to be to O'Neill when at last they met.

O'Neill's journey to the point of encounter was more roundabout than Macgowan's somewhat orthodox career. By the time of their meeting, O'Neill had lived through depressing adventures, at sea, on the beach in South America, in Honduran jungles, in New York flophouses, in a tuberculosis sanitarium, and around the uninhibited courses of Greenwich Village Bohemia. O'Neill continually rejected what Macgowan accepted unthinkingly, the patrician humanism of a university education. After a four-year enrollment in a preparatory school, Betts Academy in Stamford, Connecticut, O'Neill entered Princeton in 1906. By the end of the academic year, he had become bored, was suspended, and withdrew. In 1914, at Harvard to learn playwriting from Baker, he soon struck the same pose of iconoclastic sophistication as he had at Princeton, and left after a semester of instruction in the formulas of orthodox popular dramaturgy. The edges of O'Neill's education were honed by the authors he discovered for himself, Nietzsche, Conrad, Shaw, Schopenhauer, Strindberg, the British *fin-de-siècle* poets, and the political writers whose thought added ballast to discussion in Village lofts and barrooms. As his plays to come would prove, he read them well, for he fed on them almost like an animal at the kill and used them throughout his life as a kind of energy source for his own creativity.

He had come late to writing. Some minor journalism, verse feebly imitative of a number of popular poets, and a collection of lackluster one-act plays, privately printed in 1914 as *Thirst and Other One-Act Plays,*[5] were the trivial sum of his tyro efforts at authorship. His meeting in 1916 with the dedicated amateurs who were to form the

5. *Thirst and Other One-Act Plays* (Boston: Gorham Press, 1914).

Provincetown Players brought him out of the isolation and the itinerant disaffection that had characterized his earlier existence. Suddenly he had associates in an endeavor—playwriting—that was to focus and ultimately to consume his life. After the production of *Bound East for Cardiff* on the Provincetown wharf stage, O'Neill moved forward, and it was not long before his work, staged in the Provincetown Players' playhouse in Greenwich Village and published in the pages of avant-garde magazines, garnered respectful attention.

For the amateur of theatre it was the best of times. In the professional theatres, the commercial syndicates had locked creativity into cheap and wearisome routines from which exceptional performers might occasionally escape to establish love affairs with their publics. The central profession, however, still labored under nineteenth-century rule—*Sherlock Holmes, Blossom Time, The Return of Peter Grimm.* Yet around the country different drums were distantly heard. In Chicago, in Berkeley, in Seattle, in Detroit, even in Boston, new possibilities were sensed and new theatrical gambits shaped to check old practices. The models at first were European, but quickly the "New Stagecraft," as it came to be called, found congenial American expression. Whereas Moderwell and, after him, Macgowan were preoccupied with transmitting European conceptions, largely of a technical nature, others, notably Sheldon Cheney, were concerned with the aesthetic possibilities of the new American theatre. Cheney's two works, *The New Movement in Theatre* (1914) and *The Art Theatre* (1916), were important to O'Neill's developing dramaturgy, as well as to Macgowan's thinking.

The realistic social drama that the young Macgowan had found so valuable had little interest for Cheney when it was compared to other foreseeable modes of theatre. He called such drama "psychologic," and praised its writers—chiefly Galsworthy—as being sincere and passionate, natural but not "slavishly photographic." The work of such dramatists, Cheney wrote, "is *social* drama in its best sense. It is concerned with inner, spiritual forces, rather than with melodramatic happenings, and it is humanitarian because it reflects contemporary life in a time when the spirit of the age is humanitarian."[6]

Similar views of the value of social drama had been heard in the United States at least since 1890, when Hamlin Garland and James A. Herne attempted to found a theatre in Boston modeled on An-

6. Sheldon Cheney, *The New Movement in Theatre* (New York: Kennerley, 1914), p. 16.

toine's *Théâtre Libre* and the *Freie Bühne* of Otto Brahm. The ideal of a theatre committed to social analysis underlay the sincerity and the photographic realism of Edward Sheldon's *Salvation Nell* and other American attempts to write of life as it is. Thus, by the early 1920s, Macgowan's admired social realism was nothing new, but other modes were and Cheney's description of these, like Moderwell's, took fire.

Cheney classified the alternative modes in two categories, the "aesthetic," by which he meant a drama removed from the emotional and intellectual elements of "psychologic" theatre so that it tended to become purely sensuous; and "re-theatralized" drama, the form of theatre that attempted to weld all the arts of the stage into a whole, giving music, painting and lighting equal importance with writing and action.[7] Such a theatre brought new technology to the service of art and created in the person of the *über-regisseur* a new kind of theatrical genius. In the early issues of *Theatre Arts*, Cheney was loud in his praise of such men as Reinhardt and Craig and of their American followers, Maurice Browne, Livingston Platt, Samuel Hume, and the first American designers, Robert Edmond Jones, C. Raymond Johnson, Herman Rosse, and A. A. Andries.

To beginners, even such thirty-two-year-old tyros as Macgowan and O'Neill, these were heady concepts. Macgowan was quick to follow Cheney's lead, assuming editorial responsibility for *Theatre Arts* and writing a book on European stagecraft, *The Theatre of Tomorrow*,[8] which called—in terms not unlike Cheney's—for a theatrical revolution that would develop along the lines of the new aesthetic. O'Neill, on the other hand, while he was aware of the new ideas, moved more slowly in the new theatrical currents. Setting aside the *Thirst* volume, which contained two plays in what can loosely be called the Expressionist mode, O'Neill, throughout his study with

---

7. Ibid.
8. Kenneth Macgowan, *The Theatre of Tomorrow* (New York: Boni and Liveright, 1921). By the time he wrote, Macgowan had studied Moderwell's *The Theatre of Today* with care. The organization of his book is closely parallel to that of his former roommate, stresses the same points of technical and literary interests, and uses several of the same illustrations. Macgowan's work as an explorer of new theatrical possibilities was to continue in a collaboration with Robert Edmond Jones, *Continental Stagecraft* (New York: Harcourt, Brace, 1922), and in a book that first announced his interest in folk culture, *Masks and Demons*, a collaboration with Herman Rosse (New York: Harcourt, Brace, 1923). An example of his reportorial skills is to be seen in his account of the little theatre movement, *Footlights Across America* (New York: Harcourt, Brace, 1929).

Baker and for several years thereafter, clung to a conservative, realistic manner of writing, more reminiscent of the Irish School than of the European continental theatre. However, in judging his response to the new movement, the plays yet in plan that sprang to his mind in great profusion must be remembered—plays about apes and blacks and Spanish explorers, all of them following the guidelines for the "aesthetic theatre" Cheney had laid down. For the moment, however, he remained a realistic writer, and his work in that vein brought him to the end of his apprenticeship. The realistic tragedy of rural life, *Beyond the Horizon*, written in 1918 and produced in 1920, won for him his first Pulitzer Prize and gave him major critical recognition.

Among those praising the play was Macgowan, who reviewed it for the New York *Globe* on February 7, 1920. Predictably it was much to his taste:

> The theme and its working out are inevitably slow and drab through the first half of the play. Then comes the power of the tragic denouement. It is real power. It wrings the emotions as no American play has done in a very long while. Eugene O'Neil [*sic*] sees life straight and strong. He writes superb natural dialogue. He builds for power, resolutely avoiding scenes that hold melodrama, physical action, surface strength, and always getting down to the big emotional root of things. A man like that will write big plays. He will not stop with a "Paid in Full" or an "Easiest Way." His is a genius that seems incorruptible.

However reminiscent of Cheney's definition of "psychologic drama," these are gratifying phrases, and, although Macgowan was to rethink some of his praise in a second review for *Theatre Arts* in April 1920, where he found fault with the acting and with a too leisurely narrative tempo, the review singles out O'Neill in terms that could not help but be pleasing. The "fated" friendship was not far in the future.

It was then, on February 17, two weeks after the first performance of *Beyond the Horizon,* that Macgowan communicated for the first time with O'Neill. Now spelling his name correctly, he invited the playwright to a meeting of the New York Drama League. The date of the invitation makes it clear that it resulted from the success of

Beyond the Horizon. O'Neill, so far as is known, did not attend. He had been ill; *Chris Christopherson,* the first version of *"Anna Christie,"* was in rehearsal for an opening in early March in Atlantic City; and O'Neill's liking for public functions was limited. A phrase at the end of Letter 2—"It is a great pleasure to have finally gotten to know you"—indicates that the first meeting of the two was deferred for the better part of a year. The meeting was eagerly anticipated, however, as the salutation suggests—not "Dear Mr. Macgowan," but "Dear Kenneth MacGowan," a salutation that seeks to do away with formality. This was quickly replaced with "Dear Mac," and finally, sedately and for a lifetime, with "Dear Kenneth."

Important to the future of both men was the hope O'Neill expressed that Robert Edmond Jones (then and thereafter "Bobby") could be with them. His presence at the point of intersection was not an accident, and he had come there by a more direct route than had either of his confreres. A year older than they, he had graduated from Harvard in 1910 and stayed on as a graduate student in fine arts. His musical ability led him to perform as a violinist in the college orchestra. When the orchestra was recruited for show business, he found himself in the theatre's orchestra pit playing second violin for a production of Percy Mackaye's *The Scarecrow,* for which Macgowan was stage manager. As a side activity, Jones helped actors with their make-up, and within a year, he was designing costumes for the Harvard Dramatic Club.

In 1925, Macgowan was to write of him, "His compass has always had a pretty definite notion of the whereabouts of the North Star, and from the moment he left college his ship swept along in the main currents of the modern theatre."[9] By 1912, his designs and his sketches of well-known performers began to earn him a professional reputation. Macgowan, now working on the *Evening Transcript,* showed Jones's designs to the European impresario, Morris Gest, who engaged him. He gravitated to New York and to Greenwich Village, where John Reed brought him into the circle of Mabel Dodge. It was soon urgently apparent to all of his patrons that Jones must go abroad to study with the master, Gordon Craig. Jones, however, was penniless. To accomplish their end, Reed, with Macgowan and other Harvard alumni, organized "The Robert Edmond Jones Transportation and Development Company," and Jones went

9. Kenneth Macgowan, "Robert Edmond Jones." *Theatre Arts* 9 (November 1925): 723.

abroad. Craig, for mysterious reasons, not only refused to accept Jones as a student but refused to grant him audience. The REJTDC promptly transferred him to Max Reinhardt in Berlin.

When he returned to America, he quickly became a leader in his field. His sketches for *The Merchant of Venice* were exhibited in the first showing of the new stagecraft, the display organized by Samuel Hume in Cambridge in 1914. The next year, his work came to the attention of Harley Granville-Barker, who commissioned him to do the sets for Anatole France's *The Man Who Married a Dumb Wife*. In 1916, he designed *Til Eulenspiegel* as a ballet for Nijinsky at the Metropolitan Opera House, and shortly thereafter for the producer Arthur Hopkins began work on the settings which were to establish him as America's most important designer—Tolstoy's *Redemption* and *The Jest* (1919), *Richard III* (1920) and *Hamlet* (1922), all with John Barrymore, and the controversial *Macbeth* (1921) with Lionel Barrymore.[10]

Jones's career reveals nothing comparable to the divagating course that led O'Neill from a rebellion against his father's kind of theatre back to the stage, or to the steady circling in on his career that Macgowan followed. Nevertheless, the three came together at the same time, of an age, with comparable reputations and a clearly defined future. Could "Bobby" and "Mac" come to Provincetown in May? O'Neill wondered, and he added, prophetically, "We might combine."

Letters 1–28, written between February 17, 1920, and October 12, 1924, detail the process of the "combining" that was to result in the formation of the so-called Triumvirate, a partnership of O'Neill, Macgowan, and Jones to run the Experimental Theatre at the Provincetown Playhouse. The letters trace both O'Neill's growing professionalism and his reliance on Macgowan's guidance. His trust sometimes verged on excess. For example, in Letter 9 he wrote that he "felt from the first that Eddie {Mrs. Edna Macgowan} and you were old friends—and, rarer than that, pals. . . . All of which is great stuff! So come again! Come often, stay late! You will always be as welcome as the waves."

That one thirty-three-year-old man should use such an adolescent vocabulary to express his admiration of another perhaps defies clarification, but if explanation is available, it is to be found in the earlier

10. Eugene Robert Black, "Robert Edmond Jones: Poetic Artist of the New Stagecraft" (Ph. D. diss., University of Wisconsin, 1955).

sections of the same letter, where O'Neill asserted that Macgowan's enthusiastic understanding of his work provided the necessary incentive for him to "hew to the line." Evidently, Macgowan's first visit to the O'Neills at Peaked Hill Bar and his readiness to provide background materials and to discuss at length the stylistic problems of *The Fountain* buoyed O'Neill: "I never felt so tremendously keyed up and eager to work."

O'Neill's willingness to babble like an eager teenager must have resulted from Macgowan's praise and from the flattery of his admiring interest. Macgowan, after all, was educated in a way O'Neill was not. He was a critic of substantial position and a magazine editor of stature. Furthermore he could talk the new line and was possessed of much of the information about the European scene that O'Neill needed to know. In Letter 6, O'Neill wrote of the failure of *Gold*: "Knowing the play was 'spotty,' I realized its only chance would be a highly imaginative artistic production that would hold the play up where I fell down." Macgowan, by means of his *Theatre Arts* forum, had become one of the country's chief propagandists of "highly imaginative artistic production," and, although O'Neill's view of the new stagecraft as a prop for failed dramaturgy is not to be countenanced, the sentence does suggest a reliance on Macgowan's theories. Macgowan's charm and his abilities made O'Neill more open to him than to any other theatre person. Leaving reticence behind, O'Neill hoped that he and Macgowan could be fellow workers "for the best that we can fight for in the theatre in all directions. Both members of the same club, that's what I mean." And they will "stick together" by "sincere mutual criticism" (Letter 3).

The same letter reveals the rapidity with which Macgowan moved to a point where he became a literary adviser, as he suggested that the work of Dunsany or Synge might provide models for the dialogue style of *The Fountain*. Later (Letter 13) O'Neill called for Macgowan's aid in a personal matter: "Be a counsellor to us!" By the summer of 1923 (Letter 15) O'Neill referred to Macgowan as his "manager" in a context that is not solely concerned with business affairs.

Quickly and enthusiastically, O'Neill accepted Macgowan as a mentor and began devising experiments in productions such as *The Fountain* and *Marco Millions* that would be "unique or nothing" (Letter 18) and that would provide opportunity for the pyrotechnics of designer and director. One of the most revealing sentences in the early correspondence is to be found in Letter 22, where O'Neill inveighed against the play choices Macgowan had suggested: "Some of our choices don't seem to me very imaginative or original—as *our* selection, mind!—or to offer very imaginative opportunities for Bobby." To provide such "opportunities for Bobby," to be in the vanguard of the new and exciting and imaginative, was clearly what O'Neill set himself to accomplish. The plays from *The Fountain* forward all give Bobby opportunities and demonstrate aspects of the new stagecraft which Macgowan championed.[11] O'Neill's only important experimental work written before his meeting with Macgowan was *The Emperor Jones* (1920). Of this play, Macgowan wrote in the *Globe* on November 4, 1920, that O'Neill had "done more with the eye than any playwright had attempted on our stage. By so much he is feeling his way toward the new drama that is going to match the new stagecraft." Had O'Neill needed urging in the new direction, Macgowan evidently was prepared to play goad.

Because the bulk of Macgowan's side of the correspondence is missing, the extent of his influence can only be inferred from O'Neill's responsiveness to the plans for their new theatrical enterprise, the Experimental Theatre. To the point of their meeting, O'Neill had worked with a variety of producers. John D. Williams had staged *Beyond the Horizon* and was soon to present *Gold.* George Tyler had given *Chris Christopherson* an out-of-town tryout and later, in 1921, was to stage *The Straw.* Arthur Hopkins in 1921 directed *"Anna Christie"* which brought O'Neill his second Pulitzer Prize, and in 1922 Augustin Duncan produced *The First Man* at the Neighborhood Playhouse. Although O'Neill fretted over the delays attendant on any professional production, he had demonstrated that he could command the attention of the more reputable "show-shop" managers. The problem was the backlog. Plays spilled out of him and piled up waiting their chance before an audience. He wrote rapidly and continually and, as with *Gold* and *The First Man,* often lost interest in the work before it appeared. "After all," he wrote when the play failed, " 'Gold' is no great matter—except financially" (Letter 6).

What O'Neill needed, what he searched throughout his life to find

11. The plays are *Welded, The Ancient Mariner, All God's Chillun Got Wings, Desire Under the Elms, The Great God Brown, Marco Millions, Strange Interlude, Lazarus Laughed,* and *Dynamo.* Several more theatrically orthodox plays mentioned in the letters—*Diff'rent, Gold, The Straw, The First Man,* and *"Anna Christie"*—were completed before the meeting with Macgowan.

in one person or another, was a caretaker. In a woman, performance of the functions of wife, mother, mistress, and chatelaine were sought; in a man, a combination of editorial solicitude, listening ability, financial acumen, and a producer's willingness to serve the demands of the artist were essential. At the time he met Macgowan, he was served less by his wife, Agnes, than by the director of the Provincetown Players, the idealistic enthusiast, George Cram Cook. Agnes, so far as her position can be judged from a distance in time, maintained a sturdy independence. She bore his children, received his guests, but insisted on her own career as a writer, and refused to be consumed by theatrical matters. Cook, on the other hand, found in O'Neill the talent that permitted him to fulfill a dream. At least for a short time.

Theatre to Cook was a kind of game. It was not a professional oc-cupation, but a "Dionysian Dance" in which a group of worshipful amateurs participated to create an "oasis of living beauty" in the soulless modern world. O'Neill had met Cook and the other enthu-siasts in Provincetown in the summer of 1916. Their amateur pro-duction of *Bound East for Cardiff* met with such gratifying success that they remained together and started a theatre that fall in Green-wich Village. O'Neill suggested that the group call itself the "Play-wrights' Theatre," a name which they readily accepted, as they pre-pared to present O'Neill and other young American playwrights to the world. They served O'Neill well. To the time of his meeting with Macgowan, the Provincetown Players had staged thirteen of his one-act plays and two full-length plays. In his turn, he had made the Provincetown Players the most famous small group in the country. The huge success of *The Emperor Jones* saw to that. But, as O'Neill matured and became increasingly a professional artist, the dedicated amateurism of Cook and his supporters came into mortal conflict with the demands of O'Neill's genius. Cook had taken care of that genius, had fostered it, and often had risked everything so that O'Neill might go forward. After all, O'Neill was becoming what Cook was seeking, a great American playwright. It is inevitable, however, that the disciplines of the maturing artist will in time re-ject the amateur's games. Conflicts arose, and Cook wearied of the service he once eagerly undertook. In 1922, he declared a "holiday" for the Provincetown Players and sailed for Greece, from whence he wrote a moving letter disbanding the players because they had failed to hold to their ideals:

Our individual gifts and talents have sought their private perfection. We have not, as we hoped, created the beloved community of life-givers. Our richest, like our poorest, have desired most not to give life, but to have it given to them. . . . The Provincetown Players end their story here.[12]

Only they did not do so, for waiting in the wings was the new caretaker. Kenneth Macgowan was no impractical idealist but a conservative professional critic, ready to define his own *métier* as a producer, or, as O'Neill phrased it, as "permanent First Consul" (Letter 15) of a new theatre to be built upon the base the Provincetown Players had laid down.

12. Quoted in Susan Glaspell, *The Road to the Temple* (New York: Frederick A. Stokes, 1927), p. 309.

1 • TO O'NEILL FROM MACGOWAN. TLS 1 p. (On stationery headed: New York Drama League Inc. / 7 East 42nd Street / New York City)

February 17, 1920

Mr. Eugene O'Neill,
Provincetown,
Mass.

Dear Mr. O'Neill:

The Board of Directors of the New York Drama League instructs me to ask you if you will not be a guest of the League at its second annual dinner at the Hotel McAlpin, Sunday evening, February 29th, at 7:30. The speakers are to be Granville Barker,[1] Maurice Browne,[2] Walter Lippmann,[3] Josephine Preston Peabody,[4] and Arthur Hopkins,[5] and the League is inviting as guests of honor a limited number of men and women of the theatrical world who have contributed notably to this season's work.

Sincerely yours,
Kenneth Macgowan,
Executive Director

---

2 • TO MACGOWAN FROM O'NEILL. TLS 2 pp.

Provincetown, Mass.
March 18, 1921

Dear Kenneth MacGowan:

I have finished the first draft of my new long play, "The First Man,"[1] and am now going to set it aside to smoulder for a while in the subconscious and perhaps gather to itself a little more flame

---

1. Harley Granville-Barker (1877–1946), English author, actor, and producer, who, in partnership with J. E. Vedrenne, presented many Shaw plays and the first London stagings of several Ibsen works.
2. English-born dramatist, manager, and actor (1881–1955), most famous as the founder and director of the Chicago Little Theatre, which is generally credited with starting the Little Theatre movement in the United States in 1912.
3. American essayist, political journalist, and editor (1889–1974).
4. American poet and playwright (1874–1922).
5. American producer and director (1878–1950), later to play an important part in O'Neill's career.

1. Eventually presented on March 4, 1922, by the Neighborhood Playhouse. It ran for twenty-seven performances.

therefrom. It looks so good now, I'm afraid of it. At this stage of developement, they all look fine, I've found.

But to my muttons. I want to ask a favor of you. I intend to start right in now with the preliminary work for the Fountain of Youth play[2] and stick right to it until I get at least a tentative first draft of it done. Could you suggest any books to read that might be of help in the way of atmosphere, mood, method or myth? If you can, it will be a great favor. I am thinking a reading of Frazers Golden Bough[3] might be the best background spiritually that I could get. I have always wanted to read it anyway.

I have asked Bobby Jones[4] also to suggest reading for me. I am hoping that he will be able to come up here either before or after his trip abroad. By that time my idea of the whole play ought to have more form and substance—and he could tell me just how the thing appeared to him from his angle—and we might combine. It would be an intensely interesting experiment, I believe, to work this thing out in harmony from our respective lines in the theatre—one not done before, as far as I know. For my part, a clearer understanding of what he is striving for would be of inestimable value.

You are not to forget that you have promised to visit us this spring, summer, or fall—and to bring Mrs. MacGowan and your heirs with you. We will have plenty of room, once we have migrated to our ocean shore home, which will be about May 1st. Perhaps you could fix it so that you folks and Bobby could make it at the same time. That would be fine if you could. I want all your suggestions on this "The Fountain" opus that you can give, you know.

I never got to writing the letter on Macbeth you spoke about.[5] Just after our return home here, our heir, Shane Rudraighe,[6] accomplished an attack of the measles with resulting upset to the household. Then whenever I thought of the letter, I discovered that some-

2. *The Fountain,* completed in September 1922 but not produced until December 10, 1925.

3. *The Golden Bough* by James George Frazer, first published in 1890.

4. Robert Edmond Jones (1887–1954), scenic designer and later associate director of the Provincetown Playhouse during the "Triumvirate" years of Macgowan, O'Neill, and Jones.

5. Macgowan had apparently asked O'Neill to write a public letter in defense of the controversial production of *Macbeth,* starring Lionel Barrymore and Julia Arthur, for which Jones had designed expressionistic abstract sets. The production opened on February 17, 1921 at New York's Apollo Theatre and ran for twenty-eight performances.

6. Shane O'Neill, Eugene O'Neill's second son and first child by Agnes Boulton, born October 30, 1919.

one else had already spoke my piece for me. Then again, my principal reaction to the production was a rage at Barrymore that wasn't fit to print. He got between the production and me, darn him. It was only when he was off the stage that I could become aware of anything else. That is my main trouble in theatre-going, by the way, and the real reason why I avoid the show-shops. I can't help seeing with the relentless eyes of heredity, upbringing, and personal experience every little trick they pull as actors. Thus the actor is ever present to me and the character is lost. Thus in the most tense moment of the play I am struck—with amusement or disgust as the case may be—by the sly, insidious intent—plain to me—of a gesture, a fillip, a change in tempo, a body wriggle. The actor stands revealed, triumphant in his egotistic childishness, his brazen—to me—disharmony,—and the drama goes skidding down the Golden Mountain. "The dead cling to Rosmersholm"—that's my tragedy as an audience member.

Well, all the above is beside the mark enough, Gawd knows, and I wonder that I bore you with it. Where is Dave Carb[7] these days? I wrote to him at the Harvard Club over a week ago but have received no reply. I know he was planning to go away somewhere and surmise that my letter hasn't been forwarded.

I want you to read "Diff'rent" when it comes out in the book.[8] I honestly believe you'll find something in it you haven't before when you do. To me its dialogue from curtain to curtain is the very completest I have achieved—and has its rounded rhythm.

Well, adios. All my best to you. It is a great pleasure to have finally gotten to know you. I feel, somehow, as if I'd known you for a long time and that we were fated for a real friendship.

Sincerely,
Eugene O'Neill

---

7. Member of the original Provincetown Players who had assembled on Cape Cod in the summer of 1915. He played the Captain in the first production of O'Neill's *Bound East for Cardiff* in the summer of 1916.

8. *Diff'rent* was presented by the Provincetown Players at the Playwrights' Theatre in Greenwich Village, opening on December 27, 1920. It was later transferred uptown, where it did very poorly. It was first published with *The Emperor Jones* and *The Straw* by Boni and Liveright in April 1921.

Provincetown, Mass.
March 29, 1921

Dear Mac:

Much gratitude for your long letter. I think I can quite understand the distrust you speak of at the beginning. Usually, I have no doubt,—knowing theatrical folk as well as I do—you have just grounds for suspicion. But with me you ain't got—even if you did have in spite of yourself. Because I don't think of you as a critic but as a fellow-worker for the best that we can fight for in the theatre in all directions. Both members of that same club, that's what I mean. Most critics are too tired to be that. Most playwrights, too. The rest of us ought to stick together—not by the usual mutual back-patting of "little groups of serious thinkers"—but by sincere mutual criticism. In that way we'll all be helped, and the theatre in the bargain.

But I'm diddering off the track. And what I've written above doesn't express my thought at all coherently—but I'll leave it at that, knowing you'll get what I really mean.

I've been reading John Fiske's "Discovery of America" and have found it very helpful. He seems to catch the spirit of the Spanish conquerors in quite wonderful fashion. I've also read lots of other books—most of them uselessly facty. I've mapped out a tentative scenario of the play—Prologue, Granada, 1491—Acts 1 and 2, Porto Rico, 20 years later, Ponce being then governor of that island—Act Three, Florida, in five scenes that sort of merge one into the other—Act Four, Cuba, a Dominican monastery. Of course, I'll have to combine and relate a lot of scattered facts and thus give history a slight rumpling up but it will be necessary to do that to bring out the full truth, the spirit of it, and behind the mere dates, etc. It's in a way lucky that so little real information has come down to us about Juan Ponce. One can recreate him.

I'm going to write to Professor Shepherd,[1] as you suggest. Also, I'll read the Golden Bough for background. If you should happen to go to the library, will you see if there is anything about Moorish minstrels and minstrelsy during their occupation of Spain? That is a

1. Possibly Odell Shepard of Harvard University.

point I am stuck at. If you find they have anything, let me know so that I can go there and get some info. on my next trip to N.Y. In the meantime, I'll also write to the Hispanic Museum.

I'll await Pompey the Great[2] with interest. Have never read it. I'm sure I know what you mean about the style and I think I can get it. At least I'll try damn hard. I've read all of the Dunsany[3] and Synge[4] things—know them very well. The idea of this Fountain play is so fundamental and deep in the roots of things that the proper expression ought to fall right out of it.

Be sure and fix it so you can make Provincetown someway or other. You'll like my old life saving station, I know. And you'll feel so far away from your job out there that it'll be like rebirth.

Have you seen Bobby Jones lately? I am hoping he'll be able to get up too sometime or other. Wrote him about it but haven't heard from him.

They are to put on my "The Moon Of The Caribbees" on the last review bill at the P.P., I hear.[5] If so, it is quite probable that I will come down for the dress rehearsal and will hope to see you then. Will let you know definitely later on.

All best to you and many thanks for the suggestions in your letter and all the trouble you have gone to in my behalf.

Be sure and put down Provincetown in indelible ink in the old date book as an inexorable engagement.

Eugene O'Neill

2. Possibly John Masefield's play, *The Tragedy of Pompey the Great*, published in the United States by Macmillan in 1916.

3. Edward John Moreton Drax Plunkett, Lord Dunsany (1875–1957), English playwright, poet, and short-story writer who was associated with the Irish literary renaissance. His short plays, which often deal with imaginary countries, unhistoric periods, and fantastic religions, were very popular in the United States, and Dunsany himself was greeted as an international literary celebrity on his first American lecture tour in 1919–20.

4. John Millington Synge (1871–1909), Irish dramatist associated with the Irish literary renaissance and known for his lyrical and poetical tragic dramas and comedies, especially *Riders to the Sea* (1904) and *The Playboy of the Western World* (1907).

5. *The Moon of the Caribbees* was revived by the Provincetown Players on April 25, 1921.

Provincetown, Mass.
April 8, 1921

Dear Mac:

Much gratitude for all that valuable information you gathered at the library—but I feel a bit guilty for having taken up so much of your time. I had already heard of the Ober-Harper book[1] and have been trying to locate a copy via Brentano's but with no success up to date. Think I will write to Harpers direct. However the more I ponder over this play, the more I feel that the less I know of the real Juan Ponce, the better. I want him to be my Spanish noble none other—not even his historical self. I want him a fine mixture of Columbus, Cortez, Las Casas, De Soto—in brief, *the* Spanish explorer of that epoch. And I am afraid too many facts might obstruct what vision I have and narrow me into an historical play of spotless integrity but no spiritual significance. Facts are facts, but the truth is beyond and outside them. And, moreover, judging from the many books I have read so far, the facts in this case seem to vary with the book. Only certain ones remain fixed and uncontroverted. So what the hell.

As for act or scene divisions, I have no rule either one way or the other. I always let the subject matter mould itself into its own particular form and I find it does this without my ever wasting thought upon it. I start out with the idea that there are no rules or precedent in the game except what the play chooses to make for itself—but not forgetting that it is to be played in a theatre—("theatre" meaning my notion of what a modern theatre should be capable of instead of merely what it is). I usually feel instinctively a sort of rhythm of acts or scenes and obey it hit or miss.[2]

Regarding Provincetown and its possibilities as a summer residence for you, I'm going to be down in New York a week from Sunday for a few days and can then give you all the dope in complete form. I'm coming down for dress rehearsal of "The Moon of the Caribbees" which the P.P. are to do on their last bill—also to attend to many other matters. I suggest that Mrs. Macgowan and you come up to stay with us just as soon as we're firmly settled in our ocean

---

1. *Juan Ponce de Leon* by Frederick A. Ober, published by Harper in 1908.
2. At this point in the letter O'Neill deleted "The prologue, instead of prologue, might be better called The Romance of Youth, the first act."

home and look around and see how P'town suits you. I'd ask you to come up flying right away now but we're so darn unsettled at this time, what with my having to go away, and the vast amount of moving to be done between now and May 1st, etc., etc., that it's pretty hard to plan on anything for the next weeks. I don't think you'd have any trouble nailing what you wanted here early in May. The real estate men tell me it promises to be a dull renting year—so many of the artists are going to Europe, etc. But I'll tell you all about this when I see you in a week or so. How about having lunch with me at the Club[3] at one on Monday, April 18th? I'll date this up, provided I don't hear from you to the contrary in the meantime. But keep the fact that I am to be in New York at that time under your hat, will you? For this reason, that someone from the Club wrote me in the name of the 47 Workshop asking me to serve on a committee for their performances in New York.[4] I can't do this because my main reason for going to New York is to see my mother for a day or so before she leaves for Europe. I haven't seen her hardly at all during the past year—she has been in New London—and will want to be with her all the time I can the few days I will be able to be there. So I really could not pledge myself to anything. I didn't want to enter into lengthy explanations to the 47 man who wrote me, so simply wrote I wouldn't be able to get to New York. In fact, when I wrote him, I didn't know whether I could or not.

Mrs. O'Neill and I are both tickled to death that your wife and you are really coming to stay with us—for as long as you can, mind! We'll sure be glad to have you.

See you soon.
Eugene O'Neill

P.S. But I'm forgetting. Perhaps you will be all tied up with this 47 Workshop reception, etc. on the Monday I mention. As I remember it, they will play in town that Monday and Tuesday. If so, let me know where and when to reach or see you on Monday, Tuesday, or Wednesday of that week when you'll have a few moments free.

Then again, if this Workshop business wouldn't tie me down—especially at nights which I'll have to spend with my mother—I might be able to join in. I'd love to see Professor Baker again. Do you know anything about this matter?

3. The Harvard Club in New York.

4. English 47, George Pierce Baker's Harvard course in playwriting, which O'Neill took in the academic year 1914–15. Apparently some works by the current members of the class were being presented.

5 • TO MACGOWAN FROM O'NEILL. ALS 1 p. (On stationery headed: Eugene O'Neill / Provincetown, Mass.)

April 12, 1921

Dear Mac:

Gawd, your two line note has me skeered! As Doctor Johnson should have said to Boswell: "Dammit, sir, you are too damned hard to live up to!" But I think Sayler's plan is confined to a "money" biography-article for Shadowland, garnished with a photo, which he or his wife intended to do.[1] I know they came to see me in New York to get some authentic dope to that effect.

By the way, they are to be here in our midst this summer—have rented a cottage—on the town side of the Cape, of course. Out where we are there is nothing but our villa and a wrecked coal barge.

Thanks for sending me the article.[2] I was the more anxious to see it because The Freeman turned it down as being too lavish. The P.P. inform me that the same thing has happened to Wilson's article on "Diff'rent" for the New Republic.[3] Darn these liberals, anyway! They don't seem to believe in freedom of the press for their critics.

See you soon.

Sincerely,
Eugene O'Neill

---

6 • TO MACGOWAN FROM O'NEILL. ALS 1 p.

Provincetown, Mass.
June 8, 1921

Dear Mac:

I'm glad Mrs. O'Neill was able to get in touch with you and explain my rather precipitate departure from N.Y. Mack[1] and the general stupid ensemble proved more than I could swallow. I had to get

---

1. Oliver M. Sayler's interview-essay on O'Neill, "The Artist of the Theatre," appeared in the April 1922 issue of *Shadowland*. "The Real Eugene O'Neill," which Sayler published in *Century* in January 1922, also included an interview with O'Neill.

2. Probably O'Neill's defense of *Diff'rent*, published in the February 13, 1921, New York *Tribune* as "Eugene O'Neill's Credo and His Reasons for His Faith."

3. Probably Edmund Wilson. This piece was never published.

1. Willard Mack, who played the lead role of Capt. Isaiah Bartlett in the premiere production of O'Neill's *Gold*, which opened June 1, 1921, at New York's Frazee Theatre and closed after ten days.

back where there was a little sanity and awareness of life. Knowing the play was "spotty," I realized its only chance would be a highly imaginative artistic production that would hold the play up where I fell down. One glance at rehearsals showed me this was not to be hoped for. The reverse was due to transpire. And then to have Mack spoil the best thing in the play—the rhythm of his dialogue—by extemporizing every damn speech, and repeating the lines he liked best whenever he forgot—Oh boy! There was nothing for me to do but a Pontius Pilate water cure.[2]

But enough of post-mortems. After all, "Gold" is no great matter—except financially. Requiscat. I'm full of future hopes. Hopkins has, I think, taken my "The Ole Davil"[3]—(which you must read when you come up). It gives me a tremendous urge that more than compensates for ten "Gold" fiascos to know I am at last with H.

Of "The Fountain," not one line yet. As you can imagine, have been in no mood. But am now, and expect to start at once.

Mrs. O'Neill says Mrs. Macgowan and you will be up in July. Fine! You'll like it out here, I know, and the w.k.[4] ocean will be in bathing shape by then.

All best to you. Drop me a line if the spirit moves you.

Gene O'Neill

---

7 • TO MACGOWAN FROM O'NEILL. ALS 1 p. (On stationery headed: Eugene O'Neill / Provincetown, Mass.)

July 1, 1921

Dear Mac:

Yes, I think you are quite right about the middle part of "Gold." Certainly I would do it quite differently if I were writing it now. To be candid, I had to wait so long for the production, and there were so many disagreeable incidents connected with that wait, that by the time rehearsals started I was "fed up" and rather apathetic about its fate. Its failure hardly even peeved me. It just didn't seem to matter much one way or the other, the thing was already such a failure in my own mind.

We'll expect you-alls about the 16th. Write and give us the exact

2. O'Neill means he got drunk.
3. A working title for *"Anna Christie,"* which, produced by Arthur Hopkins, opened at New York's Vanderbilt Theatre on November 2, 1921.
4. Well-known.

data in advance and we'll meet you. All the way by boat is my advice. The P'town boat doesn't leave Boston until 9 or 9.30 and you've plenty of time for breakfast in peace and make the connection.

Dave[1] tells me you recently received some wonderful illustrated pamphlets on the German theatre. (He says tell you the ones he saw and you'll get me) Can you be persuaded to bring them along? I'd love to see them.

Here's hoping your book[2] is coming along according to highest hope. As for me, I've finished first draft, prologue, "The Fountain." It's great joy doing and seems to be behaving as I would wish.

All best to Mrs. Macgowan & you from Mrs. O'Neill & her husband. See you soon, we hope.

Gene

---

8 • TO AGNES O'NEILL FROM EDNA MACGOWAN. ALS 2 pp. (On stationery headed: Kenneth Macgowan / One Fifty Five Spruce Lane / Pelham Manor, N. Y.)

Tuesday
[July 1921]

Dear Agnes—

The home-coming was great, the adjustment to normal affairs comparatively easy and the recollection of our lovely visit to you so very satisfactory! You cannot know what our two weeks with you meant to us. And for fear of appearing verbose and gushy—all I can do is to thank you both.

You heard me say so often how happy I was in your charming surroundings and in your presence. And now that I am more disinterested, as it were, I feel as tho' my friendship for you were something quite unique, something I have never felt before—and something which I consider a privilege to be allowed to feel. Does this sound sentimental to you? I do hope not—for I mean it so deeply. I hope you may feel as happy with me someday—or rather, I dread lest this charm I have experienced may be broken on closer contact!

But still—I want you to come to me—you and Barbara[1]—when

---

1. Probably David Carb.
2. *The Theatre of Tomorrow* (1921).

1. Barbara Burton, Agnes's daughter by her first marriage.

you find it convenient. And don't forget the apartment in town—and to tell me your plans when you have them.

A bit of business—do tell Mrs. Clark[2] that the blue linen doilies are cut and will be sent in a day or two—ready for her fingers to finish. My warmest thanks to her for all her business. I am constantly comparing Peter[3] with Shane, who was such a little dear.

My heart is really full of gratitude to you both.

Ever
Edna Macgowan

P.S. Bobbie has his suit case O.K.—and our trip was agreeable—tho' we found ourselves very impatient towards the end!

---

9 • TO MACGOWAN FROM O'NEILL. ALS 1 p. (On stationery headed: Eugene O'Neill / Provincetown, Mass.)

Aug. 9, 1921

Dear Mac:

Much gratitude to you for your fine letter. You cannot know how much it means to me to stand so highly in your regard and have you so enthusiastic and understanding about the work I am trying to do. It is a big incentive to go on and "hew to the line," I can tell you!

As for "Edward's"[1] and your visit up here, I'm damned certain you couldn't have liked it one-half as much as we enjoyed having you. It was a real tonic for us. I never felt so tremendously keyed up and eager to work—which probably made me a rather remiss host, locked up in my fastness upstairs most of the time. But I knew the conventional idea of my duties wouldn't be yours for a second. That's the corking part of it. I felt from the first that Eddie and you were old friends—and, rarer than that, pals—and that I was free to do as I liked with every confidence that you would do the same and enjoy yourselves doing it. All of which is great stuff! So come again! Come often, stay late! You will always be as welcome as the waves.

Am now about to tackle the vision scene of Act III.[2] It will take some doing but—well, we'll see. So far this act has developed very

2. Fifine Clark, the O'Neills' housekeeper-nurse.
3. The Macgowans' son.

1. Edna Macgowan, called "Eddie" by her friends.
2. Of *The Fountain*.

well, I believe, with many added touches creeping in since I discussed it with you.

You must come for longer next summer. Perhaps—if all goes well—we can have the studio-barn fixed up as we have always planned, in which case we'd have a home all to yourselves to offer you—or we might convert it into a children's house with Mrs. C.[3] as overseer and you could bring up the heirs with you. At any rate, anyhow, remember you're hereby dated up.

You'll see Agnes soon and me before so very long, I expect. Agnes left here yesterday for Litchfield.[4]

All best to you both.
Gene

---

10 • TO MACGOWAN FROM O'NEILL. ALS 2 pp.

Peaked Hill Bar,
Sunday
[After August 15, 1921]

Dear Mac:

I'm writing this in bed where I am held in durance by one of those damned summer colds in the head which you get no sympathy for but which make you feel as rotten as if you had leprosy in the 3rd stage. So I am in a position to be truly sympathetic toward your hay fever. And I know you will understand this pencilled script, I'm too low for the energy of ink.

Frankly, I don't think I am the right choice to do a review of your book.[1] For many reasons. First and foremost, I don't know how. It's an honest-to-Gawd fact that I've never written a review or article of any kind in my life. I've attempted to on more than one occasion but the result has been worthlessly unprintable. My mind can't seem to concentrate along those lines and I invariably find—after a painful blood-sweating that is all out of proportion to the product—that I've made a tremendous fool of myself, expressed myself awkwardly and misrepresented everything I really stand for. Then again, the greater part of your book deals with developements in the theatre about which I cannot have any critical opinion since I know them only by

3. Fifine Clark.
4. Agnes Boulton O'Neill's family lived in Litchfield, Connecticut.

1. *The Theatre of Tomorrow*.

hearsay. My remarks on the larger section of the volume would, therefore, be absolutely of no value to you—or anyone else. Bobby Jones would seem to me the one who could best do a comprehensive analysis. Why don't you get him to do it?

The jist of the matter is this: I have a devil of a disturbing conscience which plays hell with me whenever there is a question of my undertaking something for which an inner hunch warns me that I am unfit. In this case the pangs would be doubly keen for I would be tortured by the thought that I was not only running the risk of doing an injustice to myself but also, what is more important, of misrepresenting the meaning of your book. Perhaps this will appear to you a rather exagerated seriousness with which to regard a Times review[2]—and I suppose it is. But, darn it, that is the way I am constituted—to my endless irritation. That is the main reason why I have refused all the many offers for reviews, articles, lectures, etc. heretofore—and why I am even now thinking up an excuse whereby I must dodge Oliver Sayler's scheme for a public presentation in the New Republic of some views anent the theatre, suggested by a script of his, which I misexpressed in a letter to him this summer.

No, to write a review of your book which would leave me without a feeling of guilt toward anyone concerned, I'd need a couple of months concentration on that alone and more intensive labor in learning how than would be required by a whole long play. And it is my firm conviction—and a part of my religion—that, things being as they be, here is one playwright who will best serve the interests of all by preserving a dense silence outside of his work.

Which is about enough for a sick man for one day. I know you'll understand what I have told you. The spirit is only too willing but the spirit made flesh—the written word—would be too damnably weak.

All best to Edna and you from Aggie, Shane & self. All about "Expeditions"—won't use that title—"The First Man," "The Oldest Man" perhaps[3]—when I see you. In meantime, keep it mum. Tell Oliver[4] likewise. No play of mine is nearly finished, sabe?—all still very much in flux stage. This necessary because W. is dangerous. As

---

2. Macgowan had suggested that O'Neill offer to do a review of *The Theatre of Tomorrow* for the *New York Times*.

3. "The Oldest Man" was an early title for *The First Man*.

4. Oliver M. Sayler served as Arthur Hopkins's press agent.

for his letter to Vogue, sounds to me as if the hootch he is consuming is getting ranker & ranker.[5]

I give you greeting of a sneeze of fellow-misery.

Gene

---

11 • TO MACGOWAN FROM O'NEILL. TLS 1 p.

Provincetown, Mass.
Dec. 24, 1921

Dear Kenneth:

I have been sorely tempted to cheat by unveiling your Christmas gift before the due time—for I know that it is your book and I am darned eager to see how it is gotten out and to be able to read it as a whole. However, so far I have resisted the impulse to play the little girl on the tag, and the enjoyment should be all the greater for my impatient patience. I, too, had planned a present for you—my complete and unabridged works with the autograph of sincere friendship attached—thinking you and Edna might care to add the same to your library; but at the last moment I found I had no copy of the "Jones" volume, and a wire to B. and L.[1] for it brought the reply that they were all out, pending a new printing or something. So it will have to be a New Years gift or Washington's Birthday—depending on B. and L's celerity—which is not much to depend on, as you know.

Well, the Hairy Ape—first draft—was finished yesterday.[2] I have been taken with a terrific splurge of intensive labor on it and was able to get it done in a little less than three weeks. It was one of those times when the numbers seemed to come. I was so full of it it just oozed out of every pore. And the result, I think, is at least astonishing, whether for good or evil. It has changed and developed immensely in the doing and you will find it much different from the bare outline as I sketched it out to you. I don't think the play as a whole can be fitted into any of the current "isms." It seems to run the whole gamut from extreme naturalism to extreme expressionism—with more of the latter than the former. I have tried to dig

---

5. This reference to W. and his letter to *Vogue* could not be identified.

1. Boni and Liveright, O'Neill's publishers.
2. *The Hairy Ape* was produced by the Provincetown Players on March 9, 1922.

deep in it, to probe in the shadows of the soul of man bewildered by the disharmony of his primitive pride and individualism at war with the mechanistic developement of society. And the man in the case is not an Irishman, as I at first intended, but, more fittingly, an American—a New York tough of the toughs, a product of the waterfront turned stoker—a type of mind, if you could call it that, which I know extremely well.

But you will know all about it when you read the script—which I sure want you to do as soon as I get it typed and revised. Suffice it for me to add, the treatment of all the sets should be expressionistic, I think. The play will run full evening, I think—eight scenes.

All the Merriest of the Tomorrow to Edna, the heirs,[3] and yourself. Why don't you two try—or one of you if both can't come—to come up for a visit? Couldn't you make it for a week-end? After your worry about the book, a change would buck you up.

Write us.

Gene

---

12 • TO MACGOWAN FROM O'NEILL. TLS 1 p.

Provincetown, Mass.
Jan. 22, 1922

Dear Kenneth:

I have just finished reading your book. Now that I have "got" it as a whole for the first time, I have the same feeling I had after I read Wells "Outline"[1]—that of having seen a thing in its entire significance which before was scattered about and had meaning only in its episodes. I think you have done a remarkable and inspiring thing for the future of the theatre. Speaking as a playwright, I feel your book cannot help but encourage and sustain anyone worth his or her salt in our craft to shoot at new stars.

But more of this when I see you. This letter is really only to tell you that I expect to be in town by the end of this week or the first part of next. "The Hairy Ape" is finished and typed and rehearsals will start as soon as a cast can be gathered. Hopkins has offered to help in the directing gratis although he has not seen the play—prov-

3. The Macgowans' two children, Joan and Peter.

1. *The Outline of History* by H. G. Wells (1920).

ing him a sport.[2] I am quite satisfied with my "Ape." He seems to me to have realized more in the doing than any other of my plays. He is new, American, and a bit astounding, I think. He will be either a riot—or a complete fizzle—when produced. He is no middle course animal.

But you will see the script as soon as I arrive and have a look at him yourself.

And—whisper for it is still a secret (I think)—there is a very great probability that the Duncan forces will do "The First Man" (changed from "Oldest") at the Belmont, rehearsals to start immediately.[3] So it is on the cards that I will again have the ghastly joy of attending two sets of rehearsals at the same time. If the two plays open as close to each other as "Anna" and "Straw,"[4] they will certainly offer about as wide a diversity in mood, treatment, etc. as could well be found.

But I'll see you soon—so no more chatter for this nonce. All our best to all of you.

Gene

---

13 • TO MACGOWAN FROM O'NEILL. ALS 2 pp. (On stationery headed: Peaked Hill Bar / Provincetown, Mass.)

Sept. 23, 1922

Dear Kenneth:

I know I should have written long 'ere this to thank you for sending up the books. My conscience has peeved me about it but, until the last ten days, I've been in such a fit of the psychological "willies" that writing even a letter has been a hair-raising ordeal. The aftermath of my battle with Ponce, I guess. Added to which, long forgotten progeny[1] and other relatives, each with their own problem,

---

2. Arthur Hopkins collaborated with James Light in directing *The Hairy Ape* for the Provincetown Players.

3. Augustin Duncan, Isadora's brother, produced, starred in, and directed the premiere production of *The First Man*.

4. *"Anna Christie"* opened at New York's Vanderbilt Theatre on November 2, 1921, *The Straw* at the Greenwich Village Theatre on November 10, 1921.

1. O'Neill's oldest son, Eugene Jr., by his first marriage, to Kathleen Jenkins, had spent two weeks on Cape Cod earlier in the summer. Aside from brief meetings in the springs of 1911 and 1921, it was the first time they had ever met. Eugene, Jr., was born on May 5, 1910.

made a congregation out here which rather scrambled the mental eggs—at any rate, deferred any hatching. But why speak of the past? Am now "in the pink" again.

When does the book come out? Have received letters from several feeble-minded lecturers who are to "do" my work on the circuit this winter asking my views on the future of drama—to which have replied it was all in the latter part of your book and, being as I refused to resay what you had said so well, they better read the volume and recommend same to their hearers. Whether this will bear fruit or not, don't know. At any rate, it is refreshing to have you to fall back on in my laziness.

Our plans for the winter remain chaotic. We will probably, in a fit of desperation, wind up in China. I'd like that, too, while Europe somehow means nothing to me. Either the South Seas or China, say I. I'm willing to omit the sophisticated stage. Aggie, however, I grieve to relate, has different notions on this subject—and it is likely her will will be done. But until "The Fountain" is definite, all plans are useless. The Barrymore fiasco[2] threw that out of gear and I know nothing certain about it.

Be a counsellor to us! Who can you think of for that part? That's the problem now.

Do you ever see Dave?[3] If so, ask him if he is sore at me that he never answered my letter of last spring.

Is there a good play in town so far?

All best to you alls from we alls
Gene

(over)

P.S. Am working on the preliminaries to "Welded"[4] now. Think it demands evolving into some new form of its own if I am to say what I want to. My conception of it as Strindberg "Dance of Death" formula[5] seems hard to fit on. But have no inkling yet of the "belonging" method. Little subconscious mind, say I each night, bring home the bacon!

2. Arthur Hopkins had tried unsuccessfully to get John Barrymore to play the lead in *The Fountain*.

3. David Carb.

4. The play on which O'Neill worked through 1923. It opened on March 17, 1924, at the Thirty-Ninth Street Theatre in New York.

5. *The Dance of Death* [*Dodsdansen*] (1900), by Swedish novelist, poet, and dramatist August Strindberg (1849–1912), dealt, as did *Welded*, with the love-hate nature of a marriage.

Peaked Hill Bar
P'town, Mass.
[Spring 1923]

Dear Kenneth:

Excuse this delay in answering yours. I've been all tied up moving in—with the usual bloody bother of water pump on the bum and pipes busted, imploring the plumbers to deign to come out, etc. As a householder you can sympathize—but Peaked Hill with its intervening dunes makes the householder's lot even more poignantly plumber-smitten.

However, it's worth it once you're planted here. The sea is the same old sea. Enough said.

Your scheme for the P.P. sounds fine to me.[1] You can rely on my being all for it and cooperating as actively as possible in every way. It seems to me the only way to save the P.P. theatre & stimulus—(its real contribution, a thing well worth saving.)

Many thanks for the five hundred. Sure, it's all right about the rest whenever you feel it won't "cramp" you. No rush, you know. I'm not worrying.

Are you going to try & get up to see us later on—Edna & you? Why don't you Ford up?

Agnes joins in all best. Write us. (This is brief because am off for Town via the C. Guards)[2]

Gene

Peaked Hill Bar
Friday
[Summer 1923]

Dear Kenneth:

Many thanks. Only too tickled to have been in a position where I could. But what is the extra ten about? Do you really owe me that

1. Macgowan had suggested that the Provincetown be run by a triumvirate of himself, O'Neill, and Jones, with disputes to be settled by Macgowan. He had also proposed a program of plays for the 1923–24 season that included productions of *The Brothers Karamazov*, *The Taming of the Shrew*, a play by Sidney Howard (a recent graduate of Professor Baker's 47 Workshop), and an adaptation by O'Neill.

2. The Coast Guard helped transport mail and visitors from Provincetown to Peaked Hill Bar.

for something or other I've forgotten—or is it simply a grand gesture to prove to an author that *that's* the kind of manager *you're* going to be? Well, in either case, I am impressed—and grateful.

Your ideas of how I can help on the P.P. sound reasonable. As I wrote before, I'd like to take as active an interest as my work—(meaning actual writing time)—permits. This would mean a good deal more active interest than I ever showed in the old P.P. except during their first year—and even then my participation was alcoholically erratic. Physically and every other way, I feel up to more in a cooperative sense than I believe I ever have before—constructively speaking. Also, barring the chance of a trip to Europe, I'll be in Ridgefield[1] where I can come in any time—or anyone come out.

As for actual writing, there is the "Homo Sapiens" Express. effort[2] which I have felt at times very much like doing and which I may do if I ever feel that way again. Not very definite that, but with a mind full of "Polo"[3] I'm sort of "off" everything else original at the moment.

There's "The Ancient Mariner" adaption[4] might be worked out as a novel form of recitative, pantomime, Express. set drama—and one of the Norse sagas (of Eric the Red, for example), if I remember their quality aright. These in addition to what you mention as possibilities for experiments in new treatment.

I'd be very much interested, I feel sure, in "The Gilded Age" thing.[5] Dig up the play along with the book and bring them when you come. We could go over them together.

The other (Solagub)[6] doesn't hit me from the bare idea as you've told it to me.

My greatest interest in this venture, as I guess you know from

1. With funds partly derived from Eugene's mother's estate (Ellen Quinlan O'Neill had died on February 28, 1922), the O'Neills had bought a house on thirty acres in Ridgefield, Connecticut, in the fall of 1922.

2. O'Neill's notebooks contain a list of characters and a description of the locations of twelve scenes for a play titled "Homo Sapiens" and dated 1922. Lines are inked across the page and the word "discarded" is written, apparently in O'Neill's hand. "Express." refers to the Expressionistic mode in which the projected play was to be styled.

3. *Marco Millions*, which O'Neill began writing in the summer of 1923.

4. O'Neill's dramatic version of Coleridge's poem was produced on April 16, 1924 by the Provincetown Playhouse.

5. Possibly the dramatic adaptation that Mark Twain wrote, using an outline by Gilbert S. Densmore, from the novel Twain had written in collaboration with Charles Dudley Warner.

6. Sologub was the pen-name of Russian poet, novelist, and playwright Fyodor Kuzmich Teternikov (1863–1927).

what I've said, would be as a person with ideas about the how & what of production[7] rather than original writing—I mean there are so many things outside of my own stuff that I have a creative theatre hunch about as being possibilities for experiment, development, growth for all concerned in working them out. Perhaps I'm mistaken about myself in this capacity. At any rate, I'm willing to work these out with whoever is interested & pass them on to whoever is interested—to work as one part of an imaginative producing scheme, if you "get" me from this jumble. You see, all these ideas of mine are being incorporated into my own plays bit by bit as they fit in but I can't write plays fast enough to keep up with the production-imagination section of my "bean." It would be suicidal to attempt it particularly at this time when I am reaching toward the artistic wisdom that in order to keep moving I've got to treat each play with more & more concentration of mind & effort over a longer period of time. In other words, if I wish to grow steadily more comprehensive & deeper in quality, I've got to give it more & more of my possible sum-total.

"M. Polo" is proving grand pleasure. I have tentative plans drawn—floor plans—for all of it about. Am reading & taking millions of notes, etc. A lot of what the actual writing must be is now clear—and a lot isn't but will, God willing! I'll soon start a lengthy scenario of the whole to find out just how & where I stand—then get right after the writing, I hope. There's a lot of reading still to be done. I feel satisfied with the developement—elated, even! The child will be either a surpassing satiric Beauty—or a most Gawdawful monster. Beauty, I fondly opine. Satiric or not remains to be seen—but Beauty must be the word!

You speak of "directors" for your theatre. I don't just "get" you. "Director" in what sense—theatre or organization? Here's a hunch for your Senate of this theatre—(you to be permanent First Consul,—Pichel[8] other—not bad idea, Roman Republicanism, for theatre perhaps)—Two actors, Roland Young (comedian) & Ben-Ami (tragedian) (if he has learned to think in American (best sense) yet)—one actress, Clare Eames (?)[9] (Don't know her or work. Take her on

---

7. "& acting" deleted by O'Neill after "production."

8. Actor Irving Pichel later created the title role in the premiere production of *Lazarus Laughed* at the Pasadena (Calif.) Community Playhouse on April 9, 1928.

9. Roland Young, Jacob Ben-Ami, and Clare Eames were successful stars of the Broadway stage who eventually agreed to be guest-players at the Provincetown.

what I've heard—woman with brains & imagination)—Two play-wrights, your humble & (?) devil take me if I know! You want a playwright who loves the theatre outside of his own plays, who is interested in the theatre as theatre—a writer of comedies & lover of them preferably. Who is?[10] You will know, if anyone. I think it is harder to find an intelligent selfishness here, imaginative enough to realize how unselfish love loves itself, than in any other of the capac-ities named. With the others its simpler & more direct returns. But to continue, last but not least Bobby & Norman[11] who stand for such equally fine but totally distinct aspiration plus accomplishment. You to preside over this august body—eight in all—plus Pichel, of course, nine—function of this body being to discuss what to do, how & who to do it along general plan for each production as whole—powers limited to this government of general scheme embodying ideal of this theatre.

But enough. This is merely a suggestion which may prove non-sense. At any rate, what I think you need is an imaginative body back of you & Pichel who will cooperate where they can and be out of the way when they can't. But you ought to be absolute head with an absolute veto. To hell with democracy! As Director—with a cap. D!—you'll need to use all you can extract of theatre blood from our eager frames but never let anyone think his blood is what keeps the theatre going. Each one of the old P.P. got to think that. When each became sure of it the theatre up and died of aenemia—which insulted each so each blamed everyone else!

Tuesday

The above has lingered on my desk since Friday. I'll wind it up right here & now and save the airing of any further of my views until I see you—otherwise the letter'll never get off!

This about Djuna B's play.[12] Read it by all means! I think its one of the finest pieces of work by an American in any line of writing. A real deep original play! Its too wordy maybe and marred by her old fault of the consciously bizarre & ultra-sophisticated in a few

10. "Susan would" deleted by O'Neill. Susan Glaspell (1882–1948) was an American playwright and novelist, and co-founder, with her husband George Cram Cook and others, of the Provincetown Players.

11. Robert Edmond Jones and Norman Bel Geddes, set designers who agreed to design shows for the new Provincetown.

12. Possibly *The Dove,* by Djuna Barnes (1892–), published in *A Book* (1923). During their 1919–20 season, the Provincetown Players had produced three of Barnes's one-act plays, *Three from the Earth, Kurzy of the Sea,* and *Irish Triangle.*

spots but as a whole its corking stuff—and it's practically certain it will probably never get a chance except through a theatre such as you plan. (The Guild[13] wanted to rewrite it for her!)

Late August will be fine—or any time a'most you-alls can arrange it. Only give us warning.

All best to "Masks & Demons"![14] I'm looking forward to reading it.

Love to Eddy & you from us.
Gene

---

16 • TO MACGOWAN FROM AGNES O'NEILL. TLS 1 p.

Peaked Hill Bar
Provincetown Mass.
[August 18, 1923]

Dear Kenneth:

Gene has asked me to write to you, as he is in the midst of work, and yet wants you to get an immediate reply to your letter of the 14th.

About Harry Weinberger:[1] Gene thinks he is a very useful person in a legal way, as he knows all about theatre law, etc, and is a good lawyer, and has been of great assistance in the past to the P.P. in that way, and probably could be in the future. He does not think however he should have anything to do with dictating the policy of the theatre.

Now about your letter from Vienna. It is all a great mystery. There is no young american girl, no question of any play of his being translated by Trebisch (?) or any other Austrian, and certainly, as would follow, no contract signed or to be signed.[2] Evidently some minx has been putting it over for her own reasons! Or perhaps your friend is mistaken. She seems very sure of it, however.

The plays that are being or have been, translated into German,

13. The Theatre Guild.
14. *Masks and Demons* by Macgowan and Herman Rosse (1923).

1. O'Neill's personal lawyer and legal advisor for the Provincetown Playhouse.
2. Macgowan apparently had written O'Neill that he'd heard from someone in Vienna that one of O'Neill's plays was being translated in Austria. The reference may be to Siegfried Trebitsch (1869–1956), who is known as the major German translator of Shaw. Trebitsch never translated an O'Neill play. For what may be another reference to this matter, see Letter 21 below.

carry a clause for Austrian productions I believe. But Trebisch is not doing them.

Grace Potter[3]—do you know her?—wrote to Gene about this same man Trebisch translating his plays, saying he was good, and suggesting that Gene *pay* him to do them. This was a long time ago and Gene did not answer her letter, mislaid it or something. It could hardly be that, could it? Grace is fifty, and has been abroad for a couple of years. It doesn't sound like the same thing at all. And beside, she had no permission, not even an answer.

If Trebisch is translating anything of Gene's it is entirely without Gene's knowledge. Naturally he is not going to sign any contract.

Now I know why I have not been able to buy Shadowland here. Well, I'm sorry. It was amusing, and I'm sorry about your job, too.[4]

Now, are you and Eddie coming duneward or no? We are looking forward to having you very much. Do let me know when, Gene is anxious to talk to you about the new theatre, and I imagine can talk better here, than when he gets back among New York distractions. Tell Eddie I will pose for her with nothing on but a bath mat.[5]

Have you seen anything of Bobby. Is he back? He must be, if he sailed the first. I hope he lets us know when he is coming up. Do you know? Also, do you hear any news about the Fountain?

Our best to you all. How do you like brewster[6] in the summer?

Ever yours,
Agnes

3. One of the original Provincetown Playhouse group, she had gone to Europe and, with O'Neill's permission, was trying to get some of his plays translated and produced there.

4. *Shadowland* magazine, to which Macgowan had been a regular contributor and for which he had served as a reviewer, was to cease publication in October 1923. Macgowan's last piece appeared in the February 1923 issue.

5. Edna Macgowan was a serious amateur painter.

6. The Macgowans had a home in Brewster, New York.

September 24, 1923

Mr. Eugene O'Neill
Peaked Hill Bar
Provincetown, Mass.

My dear Gene:

I send you herewith papers promised re the estate.[1]

Macgowan said he wrote you a long letter and is expecting a reply back re the Provincetown. In case you have not written him, I wish you would immediately send me your opinion on the proposition. As I see it, the Provincetown Players are going on. Mr. Macgowan is to have absolute power as a director just the same as if we had hired Mr. Stanislavsky[2] or Mr. Reinhardt,[3] to be assisted by all the great dramatists of the world including Eugene O'Neill. I think that this is the proper way to do it and certainly as far as Mr. Macgowan is concerned and his doing effective work, there should be no hitch. But let us assume that Mr. Macgowan got a million dollars or ran away with somebody else's wife or died. Would that mean that the Provincetown Players would not be able to go on? It seems clear to me that inasmuch as we determined that the Provincetown Players should go on, we should go on, giving due credit and due publicity to the proposition that Mr. Macgowan, Mr. Jones and Mr. O'Neill will be in active control and cooperation.

For instance, on the question of the first statement to go out. The statement itself is perfectly alright, but both Edna[4] and I contend that the outside cover of the statement should state "Season of Provincetown Players for 1923–1924" and not "Macgowan, Jones and O'Neill with Provincetown Players Announce." Edna, Throck,[5] Macgowan and myself are to meet at five o'clock Tuesday evening at the theatre and we will thresh it out. I am awfully sorry that this is holding it up and I wish you were here. As I said to Macgowan to-

1. Material relating to the estate of O'Neill's mother.

2. Konstantin Stanislavsky (1863–1938), Russian actor, director, producer, and founder of the Moscow Art Theatre.

3. Max Reinhardt (1873–1943), director of Berlin's Deutsches Theatre and founder and director of the annual Salzburg Festival.

4. Edna Kenton, one of the original Provincetown Players.

5. Cleon Throckmorton, who created the set designs for O'Neill's *The Emperor Jones* in 1920 and became the first permanent technical director of the Provincetown Playhouse under the triumvirate.

The Triumvirate: Robert Edmond Jones (*left*), Kenneth Macgowan, Eugene O'Neill

day, it seemed to me like straining at a gnat and swallowing a camel. It is the Provincetown Players that are going on. It is the Provincetown Players that took the theatre. It is the Provincetown group that is going to be just as active as before. Some of us more active than before but on the production end Mr. Macgowan is to be absolute Mussolini. But of course if Mr. Pritchel[6] had come on he would have been Mussolini with Macgowan.

I also told Mr. Macgowan that until he had a regular meeting so that we could pass regular resolutions, inasmuch as he knows what you and Fitzie[7] want, that Throck, Edna and I would sign a statement giving him full power to go ahead as a director. But I certainly do not expect that the Provincetown Players would step aside and practically hand over their name to Macgowan or anyone else. There is no reason why Macgowan with absolute power cannot go on and "play." Let us assume that at the end of one production or even before the end, Mr. Macgowan should determine to step out which he would have the power to do. If we have it in this manner, we would be nowhere. The other way, we would, like any other organization which has been crippled by the loss of a member, still carry on.

Sincerely yours
[Harry Weinberger]

---

18 • TO MACGOWAN FROM O'NEILL. ALS 4 pp.

Peaked Hill,
Sunday
[late September 1923]

Dear Kenneth:

Frankly, things are happening a bit as I had dreaded, and I already see a wild-eyed Jig Cook[1] returning hot-foot from Greece to denounce the kidnapping of his child. But if you insist upon having the name, you'll have to accept a bit of the old game—no help for it.

This is my very emphatic advice, Kenneth! I've never really favored continuing the P.P., even though in name only. I by no means

6. Irving Pichel.

7. Mary Eleanor Fitzgerald, who first joined the Players on a part-time basis in 1918 to do bookkeeping and handle the box office. Eventually she became the company's business manager and was officially listed as "Manager" under the triumvirate.

1. George Cram Cook, who had gone to Greece in 1922 with his wife, Susan Glaspell.

share in the belief about the commercial value of "P.P." They were absolutely dead financially when the "Ape" came[2]—and noone knew that better than the subscribers. I believe the name will be a hindrance rather than an asset. Personally, the mere idea of being *actively* associated where any of the old bickering has a legal right to operate kills all my interest instanter. I won't be mixed up in any organization which has to straddle the old and new.

Make it entirely a fresh effort! To hell with the old name! Any name will do if you've got the stuff. For example, did "Sun-Up"[3] need P.P. affixed to it? Or "God of Vengeance"?[4] There's really no reason, except a doubtful financial one, for wanting the name—yet the name will share in all credit for your success and be absolved of all blame for a failure! (de mortuis nihil nisi bonum!). I think you ought simply to lease the Provincetown theatre and then take into your new group what little of value there was left in old P.P. but under an entirely new understanding.

In short: Either start off entirely and absolutely on your own feet—or postpone the opening of the new organization until you can. After all, when it comes down to it, I feel this new thing has no right to the P.P. name. It's a false pretense. The new group stands for an entirely oppossed policy to the old—or so I have understood it—and the freer it is from all the old connotations which will inevitably arise in people's minds at the mere sight of the name, the greater your opportunity for achievement.

I hope this doesn't sound like a belated howl for I argued—with Fitzie and, I think, also with you—along these same lines last spring. What persuaded me otherwise was the idiotic notion that the financial help of the name could be inherited as a free gift—a blessing upon your undertaking—from the dying P.P. But there's nothing so unreliable as a corpse that doesn't believe in death—or so unbenevolent!

As for your manifesto, I don't like some of it, to be frank. First, I agree with Edna that if you're to be the P.P., then your cover is presumptious for the accent ought always to be on the organization

2. The Provincetown Players' production of *The Hairy Ape,* which opened on March 9, 1922, was a great artistic and financial success and had enabled the Players to pay the debts accumulated during an otherwise disastrous season.

3. Play by American playwright Lula Vollmer (1898–1955), which opened as an "outside" production at the Provincetown Playhouse on May 24, 1923.

4. Play by Polish-born Yiddish playwright Sholem Asch (1880–1957), which opened as an "outside" production at the Provincetown Playhouse on December 20, 1922.

where it is an established thing. I think people would be quick to criticize this cover—and justly so. If you decide on "canning" P.P., I still think the names ought to come at the end. I may be wrong but the publicity of this front page is won at the expense of dignity, in my opinion. Everyone in the B'way theatre is following Hopkins now and getting out personal "announcements"—Gest,[5] etc. Then I think another name ought to be added—that of an actress, preferably, to represent what is intended to be an actors' theatre also. Then again it is *your* announcement, Kenneth—not Bobby's and mine. We are to figure, as I understand it, as active aids in consultation with you as are Bel-Geddes, etc. but this is to be *your* theatre where your final word is to govern absolutely. I want to help, to contribute all I can of the best I can, but I don't want the responsibility of an authority implied by that first page. It would weigh down and obstruct the work I can do. I haven't the ability of that sort or the time. I think I outlined all I felt I could do in my long letter of early summer. I'm looking for a director of new—or old-new—things in the theatre but I only wish to be a worker therein myself, a consultating engineer, as it were.

All this above deals only with your first page—the thing implied by it as I see it. The rest of your announcement is O.K. except "American play" by me. Cut out the "American." What that signifies is an original "all-my-own" play and, as you know, that isn't my idea—at least, I mean, I can't promise it. Again, I don't think it is good policy—or publicity—to announce any definite plays as "3 Amer. plays" "Karamazoff,"[6] etc. Just give them a promise that something mysterious, new, daring, beautiful and amusing is going to be done by actors, authors, designers—that the purpose of this theatre is to give imagination and talent a new chance for such developement—ask them to subscribe because you promise them things which they *can't* see anywhere else—and then keep your promise to them! It seems to me this is the one and only reason for this theatre, Kenneth—and unless they can be promised that, it has no excuse much. I think this kind of announcement, backed up by all the names you can really depend on to contribute, is a sure way to arouse genuine interest, publicity, and subscriptions. Your manifesto is too

5. Producer Morris Gest, who, early in 1924, was to present the first American production of Max Reinhardt's *The Miracle*.

6. Macgowan had suggested producing an adaptation of *The Brothers Karamazov* for the 1923–24 Provincetown season.

meekly explicit, the plays you list too much what might be found on the repertoire of a dramatic club. I think you ought to inject a lot of the Kamerny[7] spirit into your statement with the emphasis on imaginative new interpretation, experimentation in production. Thats what that theatre ought to mean in New York today, Kenneth! That's what N.Y. lacks right now! That's the gap we ought to fill. And that idea is the idea we've been interested in, it seems to me. But where is it in your manifesto? Nowhere! And do you know why? Because that old man of the sea, P.P. is on your neck. You're trying to collect subscriptions in the name of a dead issue, in the spirit of a straddling compromise.

Don't get sore at the above. I'm raving because this isn't developing as you, Bobby & I dream—as Bel-Geddes & others dream—and unless it's going to be that dream, or at least, approximate it in spirit, then what's the use? If this is going to be just another repertory Guild on a smaller scale, what's the use? If it's going to be anything of anything that is or has been in N.Y., again what's the use? The opportunity is for the unique or nothing.

This is the way I feel—that your plea for subscriptions ought to rest on a pledge of originality, of daring experimentation, of imaginative reconception, of a unique theatre—as unique as the P.P. group was at its inception. And I'm also absolutely convinced that such an idea can succeed down there again—as it did then—both financially & artistically, but I doubt if any other idea can—or ought to.

Here's some ideas for plays: "Menschen" or "Jenzeits" of Hasenclever[8] as example of essence of Expressionism in acting, scenic, everything. I think Philip Goodman[9] would give us rights to these easily. "The Black Maskers" by Andreyev for wonderful use masks, etc. also very fine play—or "King Hunger" by the same author.[10] "Erdgeist" by Wedekind[11] done entirely with masks as by a lot of

7. The Kamerny Theatre in Moscow, founded by Alexander Taïrov in revolt against the naturalism of Stanislavski's Moscow Art Theatre.

8. Die Menschen [Humanity] (1920) and Janseits [Beyond] (1920), by German expressionist poet and dramatist Walter Hasenclever (1890–1940). Beyond was presented at the Provincetown, opening January 26, 1925.

9. The New York producer who held the American rights to Hasenclever's plays.

10. Black Masks [Chyornye maski] (1908) and Tsar Hunger [Tsar golod] (1906), by Russian short-story writer, novelist, and dramatist Leonid Nikolayevich Andreyev (1871–1919).

11. Der Erdgeist [Earth Spirit] (1893), by German dramatist Frank Wedekind (1864–1918).

mannequins! Strindberg's "Spook Sonata"[12] with masks—or his "Dance of Death," the two plays joined together with each act cut and intensified into a scene—one play of eight scenes (there are four acts in each play of 2 parts as I remember) etc., etc.—there are lots and lots of plays that would lend themselves to imaginative new treatment besides what we've already talked about together.

I'll write Harry at once and tell him to see Edna. I'll tell him just what I've told you in regard to the P.P. name—that my dope is for you to go ahead without it. Otherwise, my honest opinion is that, especially with Fitzie away, you'll be in for a lot of interference, well-meaning but hard to take. But if you insist on P.P. I'll tell him my vote is that if the committee—or whatever the hell it is—approves of your program then there must be no strings attached to the presentation of the custody of the name.

I thought last spring there were only the five on the old Executive Committee to be considered—of which Edna, Fitzie & I were three—but it seems that's "out" and there's now seven on some other board or other of incorporation, three of whom are in Europe. Well, it's great stuff but I must confess I don't quite "get" it. I've a letter from Harry today, too, but it only suggests waiting for a meeting when I get down in a week or ten days. Well, I'm agreeable. Then we can thrash it all out. As I see it, noone seems to understand just exactly what the other is getting at.

All best to Eddy & the heirs from all of us! Don't mind if this letter is a bit carping in spots. I'd like to see this a real Big Thing, Kenneth, for you as much as for myself, for the Theatre more than for either of us, and I hate to think that any mistake now might ruin the Main Chance—for which we can afford to wait, if necessary.

All best! Yours with writer's cramp.

Gene

---

19 • TO HARRY WEINBERGER FROM O'NEILL. ALS 2 pp.

Provincetown,
Sunday
[September 1923]

Dear Harry:

I won't be back in town for about ten days. In the meantime, my

12. *The Spook Sonata* [*Spöksonaten*] (1908).

position is this—(and I have so understood the situation all along since Fitzie & I first took it up last spring)—that the Provincetown Players, being about to expire as a working organization, having cabled Jig and being advised by him to let the theatre go, seeing no way favorable to their continuance and not wishing to continue anyway along the lines which made them the old P.P., hereby acknowledge death and will their name, as a sign of their goodwill to the Theatre in general, to Kenneth Macgowan & others, some of whom are old P.P.ites, as a help to his establishing in their old theatre and with their blessing, a new organization whose *emphasis* shall be upon *experiment in production,* utilizing any play ancient or modern, foreign or native, to that end. (besides the necessary virtue that it be also a good play) When I say "production" above I mean experiment in acting, directing, scenery—everything. It is to be a directors' theatre, as it had been a playwrights. Therefore, an absolute dictatorship! Therefore, if we're going to turn the name—purely for its financial help—over to Macgowan let's turn it over with no strings of the old bickering democracy attached. That's my dope on one hand.

On the other hand, I'm writing Kenneth that I believe he ought to go ahead without the name—as a wholly new idea. I've never been much in favor of continuing the name—only of leasing the theatre. I think the new scheme can, and ought to, stand on its own feet. Its policy isn't P.P. and the old title is really a misnomer.

In this connection, I understand Edna's objection to the lead-off of Kenneth's manifesto and share it. If he wishes to be known as P.P., then P.P. is the important thing. Neither do I approve of our three names—(Jones, Mac. & self)—"announcing" on the front page. I have written this to Kenneth. In fact, I am not very favorably inclined to his announcement as a whole and I've Told him so. It is not what I expected.

So there you have all my dope. Talk it over with Mac, Edna & Throck.

How about my little old estate? Keep after 'em for Gawd's sake! If you don't get some action—and money!—out of that pretty soon I'll begin to suspect your rep. as a "go-getter." Honest!

All best!
Gene

20 • TO MACGOWAN FROM O'NEILL. WIRE 2 pp. (PROVINCETOWN MASS 1230P OCT 3 1923 / at foot of wire 315P)

KENNETH MACGOWAN
HARVARD CLUB NEW YORK NY

I AM WIRING HARRY STRONGLY EMPHASISEING MY STAND PERIOD DO NOT DIVULGE MY LETTER MIGHT CREATE MORE ILL FEELING WITHOUT GAIN I WILL BE DOWN IN ABOUT A WEEK EXPECTED IT TO BE SOONER BUT AM MADLY RIDING NEW PLAY[1] ALONG LINES JONES APE TEN HOURS A DAY TO FINISH FIRST DRAFT BEFORE DEPARTURE HAVE REFINISHED ALL WAS GOING TO DO ON POLO BEFORE RIDGEFIELD WHEN THIS FIT CAME MANY THANKS FOR YOUR LONG LETTER IT LISTENS FINE I THINK THE MATTER OF PROVINCETOWN THEATRE WILL ADJUST ITSELF FAVORABLY AS LEASE PROPOSITION AS I HAVE URGED HARRY ALL REGARDS

GENE

---

21 • TO MACGOWAN FROM O'NEILL. ALS 4 pp.

Peaked Hill,
Sunday
[April–July 1924]

Dear Kenneth:

Thanks for your news—and for the Vienna program which I opine is about all in the way of a return on "Anna C" I shall ever get from that burg.[1] But I hope "Anna" redeemed herself there for her Berlin flop.[2]

Let's pray the "Horse Thief" will be a dead one. Marion[3] would be a fine asset to get with us. I'm glad "Desire"[4] pleased him. What d'yuh mean, the things he says about me? If they were good you

1. *All God's Chillun Got Wings*, which O'Neill had undertaken in response to critic and editor George Jean Nathan's invitation to contribute to the inaugural issue of the *American Mercury*, due to appear in January 1924. The text was published in the February 1924 issue and the play opened at the Provincetown Playhouse on May 15, 1924.

1. This may be another reference to the unauthorized Austrian translation and production of O'Neill's work referred to in Agnes's earlier letter (see Letter 16 above).
2. *"Anna Christie"* had failed in its Berlin production, in which O'Neill's script had been altered by having Anna commit suicide. See Rudolf Kommer, "O'Neill in Europe," New York *Times*, November 9, 1924, sec. 8, p. 2.
3. George Marion, who had played Chris Christopherson in the original production of *"Anna Christie"* and was currently playing in a Chicago production of *The Horse-Thief* by Lewis B. Ely and Sam Forrest.
4. *Desire Under the Elms*, which O'Neill had recently completed.

shouldn't—them aside like that. I like hearing the boosters now and agin. But perhaps it wasn't that, after all.

⟨Lower half of first page of this letter is missing⟩
ought to go on at the G.V.[5] and not at the P. When you think of it, there's nothing experimental in any way about it. It's quality of beauty in the "Cherry Orchard" meaning can't be called experimental any longer. I honestly believe this will be commented on with accompanying loud razzes and that the play itself & all concerned would fare better at the G.V. What say you?

Please read Strindberg's "There Are Crimes And Crimes" as a P'town possibility. We surely ought to place one Strindberg there. That's experiment in this country. Noone else dares to do him—and yet we all laud him justly as one of the two or three modern "great ones."

Copyright on Desire?[6] I don't know whether Madden[7] got a script from Fitzie or not. If so, he has probably sent it in. If not, Fitzie ought to do so at once. Will you ask her?

I've never heard of the MacMahon[8] so will have to take your word for it. Mary B.[9] ought to reopen in "Chillun," if she wants to. When does she start rehearsing in Bunny's?[10] It would only pay to put someone else in part if Mary had to be replaced in couple of weeks, and you could get some name with publicity value. How about Kelly girl for replacing Mary whenever necessary—one who wanted to alternate[11] in Erdgeist,[12] you know. I think it is good idea to put off opening until Sept. 1st.

Did Mary Morris[13] give you anything in talking over play and part

5. The Greenwich Village Theatre, where some of the Triumvirate's productions were presented and where *Desire Under the Elms* opened on November 11, 1924.

6. *Desire Under the Elms* was copyrighted on August 29, 1924.

7. Richard Madden, O'Neill's literary agent.

8. Probably Aline MacMahon, who later appeared in a 1926 revival of O'Neill's *Beyond the Horizon*.

9. Mary Blair, who had created the role of Ella Downey in *All God's Chillun Got Wings*. The production had played at the Provincetown Playhouse during May and June. It was scheduled to reopen on August 18th at the Greenwich Village Theatre.

10. *The Crime in the Whistler Room* by Edmund Wilson (1895–1972), known to his friends as "Bunny," was the first play scheduled for the Provincetown's 1924–25 season. It opened on October 9, 1924, with Mary Blair (Wilson's first wife) as Bill.

11. The text of the holograph letter is unclear; the reading is conjectural.

12. Probably Margot Kelly, who starred as Lulu in *The Loves of Lulu*, a translation of Wedekind's *Lulu* (1905), which opened at the Forty-Ninth Street Theatre in New York on May 11, 1925.

13. Actress who created the role of Abbie Putnam in *Desire Under the Elms*.

that gives you any line on her understanding of work cut out for her? I mean, did she seem to "get" it & be gotten by it?

It's great stuff about "Fashion."[14] Here's hoping it holds and builds.

I heard some word of Fitzie having some royalty money for me. If so, let her shoot by all means. We are pretty nigh cash bust. Your Straight-secretary gal[15] didn't say nothing in her note about any further thousand. Are you sure she understood that? I'm trying to get some cash out of estate administrator but he says it can't be done for a large while to come. Nothing is selling and this years taxes are coming due down there, eating up all he has. So!

Peaked Hill is grander than in years. Water wonderful. I'm perfecting a new trudgeon-crawl, 8 beat stroke and have a quarter mile course staked out along the beach which I swim daily at full tilt. I've cut out smoking again and honestly feel fitter and with better wind & speed than I had way back at 17 and 18 when I was rated as some shark. Have only been to town once since arrival. Am working hard as hell on Marco. It is coming along in great shape and I'm tickled silly with it. It's going to be humorous as the devil if the way it makes me guffaw as I write is any criterion—and not bitter humor either although its all satirical. I actually grow to love my American pillars of society, Polo Brothers & Son. It's going to be very long in first draft, I imagine, but I'm letting the sky be the limit and putting every fancy in. I imagine its pretty nearly ½ done now but it's hard to estimate. One thing is sure, it's going quicker & is much more full of fun than I had conceived it at first.

Come up & hear it! When are you coming? Also when is Bobby coming? How is he? When will he let us know? We're rather expecting him any time now.

Madden, allegedly familiar with the ways & means of boob-tickling plays, flatly contradicts your estimate of "The Guilty One"[16] He thinks it "there"—only lack being a comedy character for relief. Well, I hope he's right.

14. The Provincetown's highly successful production of Anna Cora Mowatt Ritchie's nineteenth-century American comedy of manners moved uptown, to Broadway's Cort Theatre, on July 14, 1924.

15. Secretary to Mrs. Willard Straight, one of the Provincetown's leading financial backers.

16. Play written by Agnes Boulton O'Neill under the pen-name Eleanor Rand and based on a scenario written by O'Neill about 1918 and entitled "The Reckoning."

It will be O.K. for Mary Morris to stay out here. We lack bed clothes but lets hope it will be hot—or bring your own. We're running the joint more like a camp this summer—for various pertinent reasons—and I'm glad because it's better fun and better for work.

Embraces & other tokens of affection to you-alls from our gang.

Gene

P.S. I'm writing in answer to a note of Oliver Sayler's about his book[17] and sort of suggesting at the possibility of getting Reinhardt interested in doing Polo over here and collaborating with us to the extent of letting us have some say in the directing and producing. What do you think?

---

22 • TO MACGOWAN FROM O'NEILL. ALS 4 pp. (On stationery headed: Peaked Hill Bar / Provincetown, Massachusetts)

Aug. 19, '24

Dear Kenneth:

I'm sorry you didn't get up here. There is a lot I wanted to talk over—principally financial. Are you sure the Straight Secy. dame understood about the other thousand? I had a note from her the other day in which she signally failed to mention it. I don't want to bother you again about this—or her—but I need to know where I stand— and prepare. Next month is a bad one—with the income tax installment, my son, Eugene's, quota for schooling as per contract with my former frau,[1] and the summer's bills, and—but why go on? Her thou. would just about cover the first two items. Meanwhile, this firm is rapidly drifting toward insolvency. There has been nothing coming in of any account now in over a year and my back is beginning to creak under the strain. "Welded," the biggest asset, didn't bring enough to pay the income tax on the last years prosperity. Fact! I know of nothing more irritating—and astonishing!—than an income tax which is way beyond one's incoming means. The O'Neill estate continues quiescently in probate. An endeavor to auction off a choice bit of New London real estate[2] to pay off the lawyers & ad-

17. *Max Reinhardt and His Theatre,* edited by Oliver M. Sayler, published by Brentano's in 1924. The book was a collection of materials by and about Reinhardt.

1. Kathleen Jenkins O'Neill, married to O'Neill from October 9, 1909 until October 12, 1912.

2. O'Neill still owned property inherited from his parents in New London, Connecticut, where he had lived as a boy and young man.

ministrators failed lamentably. A large crowd gathered, they say, but they evidently thought it was a philanthropical outing for the highest bid was thousands below real value and the estate bid it in. Noone profited but the auctioneer, and the estate is more balled up as to any definite end of its present uselessness than ever.

All of which moves me to the heartless inquiry as to a possible advance on "Desire," provided your backing for the G.V. enterprize is now available. Needs must when the devil drives! And that theatre really ought to advance to its playwrights anyway.

I must overcome my reluctance, I guess, and pay a visit to Otto the Magnificent, the Great Kahn,[3] when I get to town and see if he won't help me in this estate matter—on good security—or at least advise me what to do. There must be a way out, if one had the tired B.M.'s[4]—and not the weary author's—instinct to see it.

Seeing the "Glencairn" cycle of one-act plays—(which, by the way, were well done (considering) and which proved very popular.[5] They go together in great shape and would make a good paying bet for the G.V. sometime, I'm convinced!)—makes me homesick for homelessness and irresponsibility and I believe—philosophically, at any rate—that I was a sucker ever to go in for playwriting, mating and begetting sons, houses and lots, and all similar snares of the "property game" for securing spots in the sun which become spots on the sun. Property, to improve upon Proudhon,[6] is theft of the moon from oneself.

However, I'm not so "glumy" as this sounds. Though landsick, we do work, swim, eat, and other perquisites, with hearty appetite for more. "Mister Mark Millions" moves apace and I hope to have a first draft around Sept. 1st Also I have new ideas—one for a play to be called "Dynamo," queer and intriguing.[7] So all is well enough.

I've been going over, with the English translations of the separate plays as a trot, the combination made by Wedekind himself of "Erdgeist" & "Pandora's Box" which he called "Lulu."[8] Margot

3. Otto Kahn, New York financier and philanthropist and one of the earliest supporters of the Provincetown Players.

4. Business Man's.

5. O'Neill's four one-act *S.S. Glencairn* sea plays—*The Moon of the Caribbees*, *The Long Voyage Home*, *Bound East for Cardiff*, and *In the Zone*—had been presented for the first time as a unit by Frank Shay's Barnstormer's Barn in Provincetown on August 14, 1924.

6. Pierre Proudhon, a French anarchist.

7. O'Neill did not actually begin writing *Dynamo* until 1928.

8. *Lulu*, a fusion of Wedekind's *Der Erdgeist* [*Earth Spirit*] (1893) and *Pandora's Box* [*Die*

Kelly dug a copy of it up in Library of Congress. It looks good. I'm strong for it, provided we can get a good translator. I'll even promise to help on the dialogue. This Erd-Pandora work of Wedekind's ought to be done somehow. It's the best thing of its kind ever written and we ought to do it at the P.P. My sole objection to our program for this year is that it ought to be much more adventurous. Some of our choices don't seem to me very imaginative or original—as *our* selection, mind!—or to offer very imaginative opportunities for Bobby—etc.—but perhaps here I am wrong. But the shameless fact remains that there isn't a play on either of our lists to represent any of the "Big Men" we recognize as the Masters of Modern Drama, whatever the reason may be. And whatever the reason is, bum translation or whatever, we ought to find some method of dealing with it. Two plays by Stark[9] and two by Wilson and two by me[10] and none by Strindberg, none by Wedekind, none by Hauptmann,[11] none by Ibsen,[12] none by Andreyev, etc. doesn't seem right to me. However, I don't mean to kick. This is mostly self-reproach.

A wire from Jimmy[13] says "God's Chillun" opened to a full house & much enthusiasm. Good enough! But it wants more than anything a lot of shrewd press-agenting to let people know about it. Why not bring that suit against the Mayor and the Gerry Society, what?—on the grounds that now it's in a public house, their refusal constitutes a direct injury to receipts.[14] After all, it is true. Who is doing the

Buchse der Pandora] (1904), was first produced at Nuremberg's Intimes Theatre on April 18, 1905.

9. American critic and playwright Stark Young (1881–1963), whose play *The Saint* opened at the Greenwich Village Theatre on October 11, 1924.

10. During the 1924–25 season, the Triumvirate produced four O'Neill plays: new productions of *S.S. Glencairn* (opened November 3, 1924, at the Provincetown Playhouse) and *Desire Under the Elms* (opened November 11, 1924, at the Greenwich Village Theatre), and revivals of *The Emperor Jones* (opened December 15, 1924, at the Provincetown Playhouse) and *Diff'rent* (opened February 10, 1925, at the Provincetown Playhouse).

11. Gerhart Hauptmann (1862–1946), German novelist, poet, and dramatist.

12. Henrik Ibsen (1828–1906), Norwegian dramatist.

13. James Light, director of *All God's Chillun Got Wings,* which, after successful runs at the Provincetown Playhouse in May and June, had reopened at the Greenwich Village Theatre on August 18, 1924.

14. After months of pre-production controversy in the press over the play's depiction of an interracial marriage, New York mayor John F. Hylan tried to prevent *All God's Chillun Got Wings* from opening by refusing to grant what was normally a routine request to permit children to act on stage. In this action, the mayor's office was assisted by the New York Society for the Prevention of Cruelty to Children and its president, Elbridge Gerry. Throughout the play's initial run at the Provincetown, director Light read the first scene—

press work now? Louis Kantor[15] might be a good bet here. A reopening simply must have a foxey press-agent to get it any attention, as you know.

Arthur[16] wired me some time ago asking if I would revise my father's "Monte Cristo"[17] for Bill Farnum.[18] As I need the jack, I wired back for details which haven't come. The idea of it rather tickled my sense of irony. It might be amusing to play with. It was a grand old romantic melodrammer, and might make a pile with Farnum, I think, as it would hit his Movie public just right. But alas, poor Arthur! But it's a million times more interesting (as it is even) than "Virginius"[19] ever was—so Arthur's taste is showing slight improvement.

You should have come here for the "Glencairn" cycle. You'd have been surprised, as I was, how the plays were held together and given a continuity by the characters persisting from one to another. Also the whole effect was of a single complete play about sailors. It really gave a feeling of a new sort of thing. An artist in town did exceptionally well with the sets considering the frightful handicaps he worked under. In fact, the whole affair pleased me very much, although I went under protest expecting to be bored stiff.

The water's fine. So are we. Try & come up.

Our love to all of you.
Gene

P.S. I'm glad to hear about Mary Morris being so good. Tell Jimmy L. & Bobby I'll write soon—and thank Bobby for sending drawing.

If you see Lee,[20] or any Guild folk, from now on ask about "Fountain," will you?[21] Is Teresa Helburn[22] back yet?

---

in which the children were supposed to appear—to the audience and then the rest of the script was performed as written.

15. Pen-name of Louis Kalonyme, reporter and critic for the New York *Tribune,* who had often visited O'Neill in Provincetown.

16. Arthur Hopkins.

17. *The Count of Monte Cristo,* the play in which O'Neill's father, James, had starred and toured for many years.

18. Movie actor William Farnum, who at one time had been considered for a role in *"Anna Christie."*

19. Play by Sheridan Knowles, also once a star vehicle for James O'Neill, Sr.

20. Set designer Lee Simonson, a member of the Board of the Theatre Guild.

21. O'Neill was trying to get the Theatre Guild to do a production of *The Fountain.*

22. Member of the Theatre Guild's Board of Directors.

23 • TO MACGOWAN FROM O'NEILL. AL 2 pp. (On stationery headed: Peaked Hill Bar / Provincetown, Massachusetts)

August '24

Dear Kenneth:

No "Makropolous Secret"[1] has come from Eames[2] yet. Better open at the G.V. with an American play if it's humanly possible, say I. That would do more to shunt off any Guild connotations than anything else we could do, I think. When do you expect to open at the G.V. anyway? And for what date is "Desire" set? This last, because my plans for leaving up here, etc. depend on it.

Yes, be sure and send Bunny's play.[3] No, I haven't read "Right You Are."[4] As for Harrington,[5] I never heard of his being a bad study. Is Marion[6] hopeless? Perhaps he can get out of "Thoroughbreds"[7] in time. Sure hope so.

Susan is in bad shape physically, from what I hear, and still plunged in grief.[8] I don't want to bother her. Her letter to me last spring was explicit enough. Provided we said Experimental—*at* the P. Playhouse she made no objection. By the way, if we're going to do anything about the memorial plaque to Jig in theatre, we ought to have it there by our opening. Why not appoint someone to get on that job and have it done? We ought to. It would be a fine thing for her, I think, to have it noticed there and commented upon at the opening. And it's just common decency justice, too. The theatre wouldn't be there if it hadn't been for him.

I've only seen Susan once—Agnes a couple of times. She's in Truro[9] a good deal. We expect her to visit us later out here.

1. Play by Czech novelist, essayist, journalist, and dramatist Karel Capek (1890–1938), published in 1922 and first produced in Prague in November 1922. It was eventually produced on Broadway on January 21, 1926, at the Charles Hopkins Theatre.

2. Probably Clare Eames, actress-director and wife of playwright Sidney Howard. She had leading roles in the Provincetown productions of *The Spook Sonata* and *Fashion*.

3. *The Crime in the Whistler Room.*

4. *Right You Are—If You Think You Are [Cosi e (se vi pare)]*, 1917 play by Luigi Pirandello (1867–1935), Italian short-story writer, novelist, and dramatist.

5. Possibly actor John Harrington.

6. Actor George Marion. He was probably being considered for the role of Ephraim Cabot in *Desire Under the Elms.*

7. Play be Lewis B. Ely and Sam Forrest, which opened on September 8, 1924, at New York's Vanderbilt Theatre, starring George Marion.

8. Susan Glaspell had returned from Greece shortly after George Cram Cook had died there on January 14, 1924.

9. Town on Cape Cod, approximately ten miles from Provincetown.

Marco is coming along fine. Have just finished what might be approximately the third fourth of it with ¼ more to go. I've felt lazy the past two weeks and haven't worked so hard. Also there have been quite a few unexpected—and unavoidable—interruptions. But, in spite of these, haven't missed doing a bit every day.

Kay Laurell[10] came up to town on pilgrimage last week for a day or so. Over here. Quite different from the "Wild One," I imagined. Very reformed and seriously ambitious, she seems. I told her to see you on return. She wants a favor which I promised you would grant. So don't fail me! If you had seen her in a one piece bathing suit as I have, there isn't anything in the world you wouldn't do for her! But don't quote me. Joking aside, she's a good egg, convinced me she is serious, and if she is, with her rep. she has a harder handicap to starting right in the legit. than any beginner. The favor is, she's playing a lead in the dramatization of Swinnerton's "Nocturne,"[11] an invitation performance of which is to be given at the Cherry Lane in two weeks or so. She wants us to look her over and, if she has the stuff, give her a chance for a decent part with us sometime, preferably in one of mine. This is fair enough—and "Nocturne" might be worth seeing anyway. So will you arrange to go? You'd

⟨the bottom of this page was torn off⟩

---

24 • TO MACGOWAN FROM O'NEILL. ALS 3 pp. (On stationery headed: Peaked Hill Bar / Provincetown, Massachusetts)

Sept. 4, '24

Dear Kenneth:

The enclosed is a letter I wrote you last week and then in the haste of getting off to Nantucket forgot to mail. I'm sending it on for what it's worth.

Yes, we've been to Nantucket on a week's visit to Wilbur Steele's[1]—had a grand time there—I was beginning to get stale here and now I feel refreshed by new scenes and people and ready to tackle

10. Actress who had recently appeared in a New York production of *L'Agent 666* (1923).

11. Henry Stillman's adaptation of Swinnerton's novel, which opened at New York's Punch and Judy Theatre on February 16, 1925, with Kay Laurell playing the lead role.

1. American novelist, dramatist, and short-story writer Wilbur Daniel Steele (1886–1970), who had contributed plays to the Provincetown Players' first two seasons, 1915 and 1916.

"Marco" again. It was a ginless visit for me, however, although there was lots of it around but I did dissipate with a little smoking.

My financial worries begin to get my goat—it being now the bad month of income tax, school tuition to wife, etc. So if you can get the advance on "Desire" to me at the earliest possible, it will help. As for the Straight secretary I suspect she couldn't have got your letter in spring as her note to me was blandly unaware. A little action from her would also help. As for Kahn, it would be perfectly O.K. for you to sound him on the estate matter—and a great boon. You can mention the assets as being property in New London with an estimated equity above mortgages of close on to ninety thousand—Columbus Ave. in N.Y. property with an equity of about twenty-five thou—eleven thousand due to estate on long term lot sale of Los Angeles property—and sundry other small assets. The estate, outside of N.Y. property, does not pay for itself but can be made so to do if we can sell the stuff which costs money to hold. My idea is to retain only 2 pieces of the twenty or more properties in New London, which, with the N.Y. property, would give me an income of nearly five thousand clear. The expenses to get this estate out of probate will be (as near as I can make out. I can't get anything out of the lawyers definitely) around fifteen thousand dollars. As things are in dead New London this will never be raised (by sale of property) until God knows when. In the meantime the administrators fees, etc. keep right on accumulating. Unless I get help I can see no end to the mess except a gradual taking over of the whole thing by the lawyers, etc. In five years they'll automatically own it all!

That's that. If Kahn knew any way to use his power or coin to force this issue on the above security it would be more magnificent than Lorenzo, say I. Even his advice, if that's all he sees in it, would be valuable.

As for giving me the salary you speak of, I am grateful but I can't accept. I know myself, Kenneth, and it wouldn't work out. In spite of reason, I would feel a compulsion and a peculiar small obligation about such an arrangement that would cramp my style and hurt me and make me in every way less valuable to all concerned. Besides, it's really too ridiculous to burden other people who shouldn't be burdened when there's such good security behind me for a bona fide loan. The devilishness of it is that it will have to come from some plutocrat with a friendly interest for, technically, nothing is *my* property yet and I can't go out to banks for it on any regular line.

What I need is capital to set me on my own inherited legs but where, when, how, what to do about it, I don't "get."

Here's a hunch bet for a revival at the G.V. sometime which would grab some "jack" for us all I'm sure. Pauline Lord[2] in "The Straw" & "Diff'rent." She'd be crazy to play them. What think you? Not to mention "Anna Christie." It would be a fine thing for her, too. I'd like to see "Straw" come into its own. Reading them over, I'm again convinced it has some of the best writing in it I've ever done, and with the right woman, it would find its public. It's ten times the play "Gold" is, I think. No, I know!

I don't think much of Margot Kelly in "Chillun" (if I "got" you right on this). Between us, she was not good in the "Glencairn" cycle.[3] In fact, she was one of its weakest spots. She was very much "ham." And again between us and not for quotation, she is the Dumb-dumb Dora of our Western Hemisphere. She is so thick in spots, it hurts you. Not that I wish an intelligence test for actorines. (None of them would get a job then.) Or that I don't like the lady. I do. She is a nice girl—the kind your own mother would approve of you "keeping," so to speak—but in spite of my affection for genuine red hair, I found her work in "The Long Voyage Home" pretty crude. Kay Laurell, about whom I rave more or less in the previous enclosed edition, has a good deal more real possibilities in her acting, I'll bet. However, Margot should make good publicity for "Chillun" and maybe she was just miscast in "Long Voyage."

Do come up as soon as you can. All our best to you all!

Gene

---

25 • TO MACGOWAN FROM O'NEILL. ALS 1 p. (On stationery headed: Peaked Hill Bar / Provincetown, Massachusetts)

Sept. 6 [1924]

Dear Kenneth:

The news about Kahn is fine. However, I wouldn't care to make any small loans from him. Either he's there for the big help or he isn't. A couple of thou. would only put me that much more in debt

2. Actress who created the title role in *"Anna Christie."*
3. Margot Kelly had appeared in the Frank Shay production of O'Neill's four sea plays in Provincetown in August. Macgowan had apparently suggested her as a replacement for Mary Blair in *All God's Chillun Got Wings,* which was still running at the Greenwich Village Theatre.

without getting me any nearer a solution. It would also spoil him as a possibility. Neither can his lawyer help me, I think—or at least I don't see how, beyond looking up matters to prove my claims to assets aren't lies and that my security is valid. The case is simple enough. The estate has no debts but lawyers and administrator fees. All else is clear. But it has no cash wherewith to pay said fees and so must remain in probate no-mans land accumulating more administrator fees to pay. A simple ruinous circle! Under present conditions in N.L.[1] they can't sell property without giving it away—except the two pieces I want to keep! That's all there is to it.

Mary Morris was up. We talked "Desire" but I didn't have her read the part. I'm willing to take Bobbie & Jimmy's word for her ability. She wasn't in much of a mood for reading, I expect, as she & Jimmy M.[2] were to be married in the town this evening. It would have been too unfair a test to ask her to read it out here with nothing to help. The important thing is her whole attitude and conception and there she's O.K. I'll be at rehearsals from the first gun, anyway.

I hope "Chillun" has picked up. This weather should help. As for a substitute for Margot in Mary's[3] part, I can't think. Mary herself might suggest someone. Kay Laurell? There's publicity! But I imagine the lady is color-proud.[4] I really can't think of anyone.

All best & much gratitude for your endeavors in my financial behalf. Have Fitzie send that advance quick.

Gene

---

26 • TO MACGOWAN FROM O'NEILL. ALS 2 pp. (On stationery headed: Peaked Hill Bar / Provincetown, Massachusetts)

Sept. 21, '24

Dear Kenneth:

This is just a note to cover some pressing points in your letter. In the first place, I don't know as I shall accept the 500 from Bogue.[1] Her notes sound pretty snotty and I am debating with myself

---

1. New London.
2. James Meighan, who appeared in the Provincetown Playhouse presentations of *The Ancient Mariner* (1924) and *S.S. Glencairn* (1924), as well as in several other productions.
3. Mary Blair.
4. "Would Mary Morris" deleted.

1. Secretary or treasurer who distributed funds from philanthropist Mrs. Willard Straight to the Provincetown and other causes.

whether I shall not send the check back to her with—politely expressed—intimations that I am no beggar of Mrs. Straight's "curtailed giving" and that she, Bogue, can take the check and shove it up her secretarial jazbo with my best wishes for resulting piles. She sounds like a mighty poor squirt and my letter would be on its way now if I didn't feel that Mrs. S's spirit is not represented by Bogue. Still I'm much tempted to refund the coin. There is such a thing as some money being too hard to take, no matter how much you need it.

I'm glad about "Chillun."[2] It certainly helps. As for Margot Kelly she told Agnes she had waited in her room every day for 3 days waiting for a promised phone from Jimmy as to "Gods C." Then she got sore and closed with Hoppy.[3] However, no matter. She wouldn't have been good, I don't believe.

The news about Marion is too bad. I suppose he's broke and, I believe, he has heavy responsibilities. Why not get Hume[4] to read play and demonstrate to Bobby? Where is Bobby now? And I don't understand what you mean by "if Saint goes on successfully, then Bobby can do second bill at P.P." Won't he be doing "Desire" then? Isn't "Desire" slated to open up the first week in Nov.? Certainly "D" is enough for one man to direct at one time and even more certainly it ought to go on as soon after Nov. 1st as the four weeks repertoire time at the G.V. of "Saint" will permit. If "Saint" is a success it can be moved uptown, no?—as per the scheme we discussed in spring? One thing I think you've got to make up your mind to is that no play in the regular season be allowed to run more than four weeks. Otherwise, how will you get in your schedule? I'd like very much to know what definite date "Desire" is to open. In fact, I must know approximately I've been counting on its going on four weeks after "Saint" and making plans accordingly—iron bound plans this time. So your failure to mention "Desire" worries me. I won't be in Ridgefield where I can get to town anytime—not after the middle of Nov.[5]

---

2. The Provincetown production of *All God's Chillun Got Wings* was still prospering at the Greenwich Village Theatre, where it ran until October 10, 1924, closing to make room for the first production of the new season.

3. Arthur Hopkins signed Margot Kelly to appear in his production of Arthur Wing Pinero's *The Second Mrs. Tanqueray*, which opened at the Cort Theatre on October 27, 1924.

4. Actor-director and producer Samuel Hume.

5. O'Neill was planning to spend the winter in Bermuda.

I'll see what Susan has to say for the stuff for the plaque. I can't think of just what would be right.

So long for this one. Come up if you do get a chance.

Gene

P.S. How about "Lulu" for second P.P. bill if you could get trans. made in time?

---

27 • TO MACGOWAN FROM O'NEILL. ALS 2pp. (On stationery headed: Peaked Hill Bar / Provincetown, Massachusetts)

Sept. 21, '24

Dear Kenneth:

A few things I forgot last night: Don't think there is anything to be done about Kahn's lawyer until I get to town. I expect to stop off in New London on way down and see the administrator and go over things. Then I'll have more dope for Kahn's man to work on.

Before I forget, I see Basil Dean[1] is in town now. Why not try to arrange to let Robeson[2] give a special mat. for his benefit of "Jones"? I'm sure a London "Jones" with Paul would mean money for us all.

I'm returning the Vienna article.[3] It sounds horrible but what can one do?

No, I haven't a thought for the program. What thoughts I have, save those which are still going into "Marco" as I go over it, are too pessimistic for publication and my only message to the w.k. world is that it can go f—— itself! "Marco," however, is a joy. I fear it may be two plays long but it is worth it, I believe. I'm writing a new first scene for it and using my former first scene—the only one I had written last winter & which you read—as one of the last scenes. I feel "M" is *real* satire—and a lot else besides.

I'm very anxious to see you and talk over my winter's plans. I've made a discovery about myself in analyzing the work done, etc. in the past six winters which has led me to a resolve about what I must do in the future. But it's too long to write about.

I can't think of much for Jig Cook's Tablet except something of

---

1. British producer.

2. Paul Robeson had starred in the May 1924 Provincetown Playhouse revival of *The Emperor Jones*.

3. Probably a reference to an article about the unsuccessful Vienna production of *"Anna Christie"* (see above, Letter 21).

the usual banal sort: To the memory of George Cram ("Jig") Cook, poet of life, priest of the ideal, lovable human being, to whose imagination and unselfish devotion this Playhouse owes its original inspiration and developement as a home for free creative expression.

That's a stab. But I understood from some P'towner that Susan was sending you some quote from Jig's poetry to use.

I'm sorry to hear about the Edmund-Jimmy racket.[4] Well, it's his first play and I guess he's inexperiencedly sensitive to the difference there must be always between the author's idea as he sees what he writes and the horrible puppet-show the actors transform it into, willy-nilly, good or bad.

Well day-day for this time & again much gratitude for your activity in my financial affairs. Get up if you possibly can. I think the trip by water to Boston or F. River[5] & a day or so on the dunes would do you "a world of good."

Gene

---

28 • TO MACGOWAN FROM O'NEILL. ALS 2 pp. (On stationery headed: Peaked Hill Bar / Provincetown, Massachusetts)

Oct. 12, 1924

Dear Kenneth:

I've owed you a letter for some time but this isn't it. This is just a line to cover a few matters.

I hope the openings "went big." Haven't seen any notices of Bunny's play. Can't get N.Y. papers in town this late in season. Hope Bunny, Stark, etc. got our wires. We are on outs with Coast Guard captain just for the nonce owing to "Finn"[1] having killed a few chickens—so communication with world is uncertain.

The first draft "Marco" play is now finished. It has been an interesting job but a long one. I should say the play is two good long plays of 2½ hours each—at least! So you see it's really two plays I've done. Luckily, without premeditation, the piece falls into two very distinct—and exactly equal in length—halves. Which may prove a

4. Apparently a dispute had arisen between Edmund Wilson, author of *The Crime in the Whistler Room* (scheduled to open the Provincetown season), and James Light, stage manager of the theatre.

5. Fall River, Massachusetts.

1. Finn MacCool, the O'Neills' Irish wolfhound, who was named for the famous ruler-warrior of ancient Ireland.

la Peer Gynt that "God is a Father to me after all even if He isn't economical."

I don't like "Crew of the Glencairn." Doesn't sound like anything. "Blow The Men Down" is a good title or some other chanty phrase. "S.S. Glencairn" isn't so awfully wrong. "The Sea Tramp" is another suggestion.[2]

When I wrote about the four week G.V. runs I was thinking we had six bills to go on there.

Haven't received the play you said you were sending. Sounds interesting.

I'm reading proof on my "collected works,"[3] God stiffen them! It's a hell of a job but it does serve to acquaint me with stuff that is so forgotten, it's new.

We expect to be down in about ten days, I guess. I am going to stop off in New London couple of days on way.

When is "Desire" due to start rehearsals? Is "Glencairn" on the fire now? Is there no old man in sight for "Desire" yet?[4]

All best!
Gene

2. Macgowan had apparently asked O'Neill to suggest titles for the fusion of his four sea plays, which the Provincetown was planning for its second bill in November.

3. *The Complete Works of Eugene O'Neill*, published in two volumes by Boni and Liveright in January 1925, contained twenty plays.

4. No actor had as yet been found to play Ephraim Cabot in *Desire Under the Elms*.

2: Spithead

By comparison with its predecessor, the Experimental Theatre at the Provincetown Playhouse was of limited importance. For all his idiosyncrasies, George Cram Cook was a man with the courage of his vision, and since the vision, however romantic, had at its center a core of truth born of his understanding of the theatre's need, his courage was a source of energy to those he gathered around him. When his animating presence was gone, acrimony set in, chiefly in the opposition to Macgowan led by Edna Kenton, a charter member of the Provincetown Players, who bitterly opposed any development of the organization that did not adhere to Cook's idealistic principles. Something of the acrimony can be felt in the tortured, amateur legal agreement drafted to consummate the negotiations on November 8, 1923:

> We agree that Kenneth Macgowan be appointed director of the production season 1923–1924, at the Provincetown Theatre, and that he be given full and final power both in production and business management. It being understood that when Kenneth Macgowan takes production out of the Provincetown Theatre, the Provincetown Players Inc. shall not be responsible financially. The Provincetown Players shall not interfere in anyway with the removal of such plays from the Provincetown Theatre, but shall receive 2½ per cent of gross receipts until the two year's rent beginning with Oct. 1st, 1923 and ending Oct. 1, 1925 is secure, said percentage to be mutually decreased if financial condition of the play necessitates. We agree that Robert E. Jones and Kenneth Macgowan be added to the member list of The Provincetown Players, Inc.
>
>
>
> The Provincetown Players, Inc.
> Cleon Throckmorton
> Edna Kenton
> Harry Weinberger
> M. Eleanor Fitzgerald[1]
>
>

1. A copy of the agreement is to be found in the Macgowan Collection in the Department of Special Collections of the Research Library, University of California at Los Angeles. The fullest account of the history of the Provincetown theatre under each of its managements is that by William Vilhauer, "A History and Evaluation of the Provincetown Players," (Ph.D. diss., University of Iowa, 1965).

Kenton's was a losing fight, and Macgowan took over. By all accounts, Macgowan was a sweet, modest, and gentle man. His demeanor bred affection and confidence. Perhaps something in his Scots manner suggested that he was more experienced, more professional, and more daring at the job of making theatre than he was in actuality. *The Theatre of Tomorrow* and *Continental Stagecraft* had been warmly received. In the latter work, Jones's on-the-spot sketches of European stage production excited readers, and Macgowan's prose turned inspirational: "We are seeking an intense inner vision of spiritual reality which will push the selective process so far that to call the result realism will be an absurdity." There was no reason for anyone to note that Macgowan's sentence, phrased in the standard jargon of the theatre aesthete, said very little that was new or even sufficiently specific to be readily translated into stage practice. Nor did anyone see that the former champion of a conventional theatrical realism had changed direction.

Macgowan had at last absorbed the message of his first associates, Moderwell, Cheney, and Hume, and, no doubt, he was now listening to Robert Edmond Jones and to the excited O'Neill with increasing interest. He was literate, quick, and a ready propagandist, and he saw with greater alacrity than many critics that "expressionism" was the name of the new game, because it was a style of presentation that used the new stagecraft to discover and project the "inner vision of spiritual reality." To achieve new forms, he argued that collaboration between the playwright and the painter was essential. Indeed, their collaboration might make other elements of theatrical practice unnecessary—elaborate stage machinery, for example, and perhaps even stage directors. One cannot train a director to be a great painter, he reasoned, but perhaps the artist could "acquire the faculty of understanding and drawing forth emotion in the actor." Thinking probably of Jones's ambitions to turn stage director, he analyzed the difference in temperament between artist and director:

> The director is ordinarily a man sensitive enough to understand
> human emotion deeply and to be able to recognize it and sum-
> mon it and guide it in actors. But he must also be callous
> enough to meet the contacts of directing—often very difficult
> contacts—and to organize not only the performance of the play-
> ers, but also a great deal of bothersome detail involving men
> and women who must be managed and cajoled, commanded and

worn down and generally treated as no artist cares to treat himself in the process of treating others. The director must be an executive and this implies a cold ability to dominate other human beings which the artist does not ordinarily have.[2]

The problem of making an "artist" practical was a dilemma, he felt. Perhaps a talented stage manager could oversee the routines of "action and business," following the guidelines of the artist's overall design. Perhaps a metamorphosis in acting styles would evolve, so that the actor would no longer be a purely "representational" integer, "retreative" and "feminine," but would arrive at a presentational "open, assertive—may I say masculine—manner as objects of art and emotion."

In such discussion, Macgowan was dallying with a separation of church and state, the high aesthetic line of the new theatre advocate and the business details required by any "show shop." What he was developing in theory is the definition of the position he would ultimately come to hold, both in the Triumvirate as it formed and in Hollywood later—that of producer.

Whatever its merits, the suggestion of a working alliance between the artist-director and the functionary who would take over the "difficult contacts" formed the basis of operation of the Experimental Theatre, once the consular organization proved unrealizable. Jones was installed as artist and stage-director-in-chief, to work in close collaboration with O'Neill, who, as playwright, was taking care to provide Jones with "imaginative opportunities" and writing work in each of the categories laid down by the art theatre promoters.[3] Macgowan cast himself in the role of the callous, cold-eyed commander, the comptroller, and—although the term was not yet in vogue—the producer.[4]

2. Kenneth Macgowan, "Enter the Artist—as Director," *Theatre Magazine* 36 (November 1922): 292.

3. Intensified "psychologic" realism was apparent in *Welded, Desire Under the Elms,* and *Strange Interlude.* The expressionist mode was manifest in *The Hairy Ape* and *The Great God Brown,* while *The Fountain, Marco Millions,* and *Lazarus Laughed* were in the vein of "retheatralized," poetic, total theatre. Not all of these plays were produced by the Experimental Theatre, but the influence of the new theatre aesthetic is to be found throughout the plays written between 1920 and 1930. For a fuller discussion of O'Neill's concern with theories of the new theatrical art, see Travis Bogard, *Contour in Time, The Plays of Eugene O'Neill* (New York: Oxford Univ. Press, 1972), ch. 6 and 7.

4. O'Neill uses the word "director" without differentiating between Jones's and Macgowan's functions.

There was no reason why the scheme should not have worked. Both Jones and O'Neill were men of genius, and Macgowan, although he was new at the game, had native ability as a producer. But the plan did not work. As a director, Jones was unskilled. Indeed, in the Triumvirate's first production, Strindberg's *The Spook Sonata,* he codirected with an old Provincetown hand, James Light, who perhaps supplied the "action and business," while Jones supplied the art. Later, when he assumed full directorial control as well as taking charge of the settings, costumes, and lighting, he left some actors baffled. It seems doubtful that an actor who needs to know whether to sit or stand will prove entirely responsive to directions about "overtones" or to being told to read a line "like a ship coming into a harbor."[5] Harold Clurman has recorded the conduct of an early rehearsal of Stark Young's *The Saint* at which the three members of the Triumvirate were present. Macgowan began with a series of semi-confidential interviews, at which each of the actors, all of whom were seeking work as extras, was asked how small a salary he could afford to accept on a scale ranging from five to fifteen dollars. This settled, Jones, who was to direct, addressed the company:

> Recently I heard the story of a blind child on whom a successful operation had been performed. When the bandages were finally removed from its eyes, the child looked around in ecstasy and murmured, "What is this thing called light?" To me, the theatre is like a light that blind people are made to see for the first time. The theatre is a dream that the audience comes to behold. The theatre is revelation. That is what I want to tell you.

Clurman recalled, "He walked up the aisle and disappeared. Macgowan asked Gene if he had anything to add. Gene indicated he didn't. There was a tense pause. That was all. The actors got up and left."[6]

However subjective, Jones's directorial work proved adequate to the staging of several critical and popular successes, among which were *Desire Under the Elms* and *The Great God Brown.* His designs, however, were his central contribution.

As for Macgowan, there is little beyond the implications of the

5. Quoted in Louis Sheaffer, *O'Neill: Son and Artist* (Boston, Toronto: Little, Brown, 1973), p. 192.

6. Quoted in Harold Clurman, *The Fervent Years* (New York: Knopf, 1945), pp. 6–7.

present correspondence to clarify the nature and quality of his work with the Triumvirate. It appears that he, with Jones, chose the final repertory from suggestions made by others, among them O'Neill. It is evident that he was responsible for the financial administration. The result of his work as a theatre manager is worth inspection.

The 1923–24 repertory was originally scheduled to open with O'Neill's new play, *All God's Chillun Got Wings,* but the play was not ready. The season opened, therefore, on January 4, 1924 with Strindberg's *The Spook Sonata* as a substitute.[7] Although O'Neill praised its author in a program note as "the precursor of all modernity in our present theatre," the play was not a success with critics or the public. Macgowan, feeling doubtful, perhaps, about such an unusual experiment as the Strindberg work, followed it with a play that was anything but experimental, Anna Cora Mowatt Ritchie's 1845 comedy, *Fashion.* In Jones's hands,[8] *Fashion* proved entirely captivating. Old-style drop scenery and charming costumes, together with performances that were enchantingly mannered, made the comedy a solid hit; it soon was necessary to move it from the Provincetown Playhouse to the somewhat larger Greenwich Village Theatre. Then, as its appeal grew, it was transferred to an uptown run. Thus, both failure and success left the Provincetown Playhouse dark. O'Neill's play was still not ready, so another makeshift bill, partly classical— with an eye to the success of *Fashion*—and partly experimental—with an eye to the theatre's expressed raison d'être—was presented. Molière's *George Dandin* was double-billed with one of O'Neill's lesser efforts, a hastily contrived adaptation of Coleridge's *The Ancient Mariner,* in which the playwright used a masked chorus. The offering closed quickly, and yet a third stopgap bill was offered. Since Paul Robeson had been hired to play the lead in *All God's Chillun Got Wings,* his talents were put to work in a short revival of *The Emperor Jones.* Finally, on May 14, 1924, directed by James Light and designed by Cleon Throckmorton, O'Neill's play about an interracial marriage opened. Before its première, the public outcries against the play were hysterical and vicious. In the event, they proved stupid. Once the play was seen, the critics found it singularly lifeless, but

7. It should be noted that Macgowan, Jones, and O'Neill joined forces with the Selwyns for a professional production of O'Neill's *Welded* at the 39th Street Theatre in March 1924. This fell a little outside their work with the Experimental Theatre.

8. Jones shared design credit with Reginald Marsh and Cleon Throckmorton and directorial credit with James Light.

the scandalous press caused it to play to good houses for the remainder of the season. Together with *Fashion*, it provided the audiences that enabled the young organization to survive.

The popularity of *Fashion* excited Macgowan, and he became convinced of the desirability of operating the second season in two houses, the Provincetown Playhouse and the Greenwich Village Theatre. In 1924–25, he offered a substantial season of unusual dramatic works. At the Playhouse, he presented Edmund Wilson's *The Crime in the Whistler Room*, followed by revivals of four of O'Neill's early sea plays, under the title *S.S. Glencairn*. Next came another revival of *The Emperor Jones*, and finally a production of Gilbert and Sullivan's *Patience*, which Jones and Throckmorton designed and which was evidently patterned in the glass of *Fashion. Patience* played for 104 performances and was followed by Walter Hasenclever's *Beyond*, which closed quickly. Then the Triumvirate offered a double bill of Sherwood Anderson's *The Triumph of the Egg* and a revival of O'Neill's portrait of a New England spinster, *Diff'rent*. This was succeeded by Charles Vildrac's *Michel Auclair*, and the season ended with thirty performances of Hatcher Hughes's folk drama, *Ruint*.

At the Greenwich Village Theatre, the season opened with Stark Young's *The Saint*, which, after seventeen performances, gave place to O'Neill's *Desire Under the Elms*, directed and designed by Jones. The tragedy held on for 208 performances, first in the Village and later uptown with the cooperation of two professional producers, A. L. Jones and Morris Green. The season ended with a fillip with Jones's production of Congreve's *Love for Love*, the choice suggested perhaps by the substantial success the Cherry Lane Players had had with *The Way of the World* earlier that year.

The two-theatre season was a reputable attempt. Jones and Macgowan worked to exhaustion to bring it off.[9] A company of ten actors

9. Other designers and directors worked with Jones, notably James Light and Cleon Throckmorton. In the Provincetown season, Jones directed only *Michel Auclair* and *Patience* and designed these two and *Beyond*. At the Greenwich Village Theatre, he directed and designed all three offerings, although he shared directorial credit on *The Saint* with Stark Young and Richard Boleslavsky, who was brought in as a troubleshooter when Jones and Young proved incompatible as colleagues. In the technical areas Jones was exceptionally efficient. Joseph Verner Reed, in his account of his collaboration with Macgowan in a later producing venture, describes Jones's "fine efficiency" during the technical rehearsals of Edwin Justin Mayer's *Children of Darkness* (Joseph Verner Reed, *The Curtain Falls* [New York: Harcourt, Brace, 1935], pp. 110–11); Macgowan, in an essay entitled "Jones as a Director and Film Designer" (in Ralph Pendleton, ed., *The Theatre of Robert Edmond Jones* [Middletown, Conn.: Wesleyan Univ. Press, 1958], pp. 139–43), speaks more of his technical efficiency than of his directorial prowess.

played the central roles, working at both theatres as need arose. Around them, a group of cheerful extras filled in. From *Patience* they borrowed a theme song:

> We're Robert E. Jones young men,
> We're Kenneth Macgowan young men,
> We're greenery yallery, don't get much salary
> Working for art young men.[10]

Working for art it was, for fun and experiment did not produce visible profit. To stage eight productions in a house seating 200, as Macgowan tried to do at the Provincetown, was managerial madness. Most of the offerings there lasted less than a month, and the Provincetown season ended $35,000 over budget. Only O'Neill's tragedy and Jones's elegant staging of *Patience* and *Love for Love* enabled the group to hold together.

In June 1925, Macgowan and Jones visited O'Neill in Bermuda, where O'Neill had first moved in the winter of 1924, to take stock of their enterprise. Sensibly, they determined to stop producing in the Provincetown Playhouse. Although they retained nominal control, they gave full artistic direction of the theatre into the hands of James Light. At the Greenwich Village Theatre, the following season, they presented Maxwell Anderson's *Outside Looking In.* Anderson's success with *What Price Glory,* produced in the fall of 1924, gave impetus to his new play, and it ran for 113 performances. It was followed by Rostand's *The Last Night of Don Juan,* translated by Sidney Howard, and in December by O'Neill's *The Fountain.* Neither play lasted a month. Early in January the theatre was leased for a short run to Oliver Morosco, and then, on January 23, *The Great God Brown* opened to good reviews and audiences. Its success was sufficient to permit Macgowan to move it to a larger theatre, but nothing was available to replace it. In March, therefore, Light's group took over the Greenwich Village Theatre with a burlesque production of *East Lynne.* When this closed, the theatre was rented to Alice Brady.

The three seasons of the Experimental Theatre were, on the whole, worthy of approbation, but the work was hard and success spasmodic. O'Neill, as the letters reveal, was frustrated by weak or deferred productions; Jones bowed out of the group in 1926; and although Macgowan did his best to keep the theatre moving, the

10. Quoted in Helen Deutsch and Stella Hannau, *The Provincetown* (New York: Farrar and Rinehart, 1931), p. 130.

necessities of commerce increasingly dictated the policies of art. O'Neill, whose belief in Macgowan's potential as an artist of the theatre was unwavering, wrote him, "You are—and have been, except a little that 1st P. P. year—not getting any chance to give what you have to give toward a new theatre, you are not getting any chance to work creatively with me in the art of the theatre, to dream and plan the executing of dreams, you are not becoming what I urged you. . . . You are being forced into the job of manager instead of a European director" (Letter 59).

That Macgowan could ever have become an artist-director in the European tradition is doubtful, but certainly, as his later career was to demonstrate, he had the capabilities to become a successful commercial producer.

The special character of a theatrical producer is difficult to define with exactitude. In one view, not infrequently his own, the producer is something of a Renaissance man—a playwright, a director, a creative collaborator of designers, musicians, and choreographers, the Prospero of the stage's fantasy world. In the eyes of others, he is a nuisance, an inhibitor of the creative process, a miser, a compromiser, a late upstart on the theatrical scene, and an excrescent adjunct to vital theatrical activity. The idea of the producer is relatively recent in theatrical history. (The word is not defined in its current usage in the *Oxford English Dictionary*.[11]) The modern concept of his controlling presence most probably arose from the idea, which many theorists and stage practitioners evolved in the late nineteenth and early twentieth centuries, that the theatre should be under the direction of a single, supreme artist. Such organization had been suggested by many earlier precedents—the stage under the guidance of the great actor-managers of earlier times, Wagner at Bayreuth, the innovative theatres of Otto Brahm and Jacques Copeau, the theories and designs of Appia and Gordon Craig, and, nearest to the experience of O'Neill and Macgowan, the exciting example of Max Reinhardt, whose shaping hand created spectacles that were highly individual works of theatrical art.

The true *über-regisseur,* as the theorists called such a man as Reinhardt, is rare. Not only must he have talent equivalent to his vision, but the circumstances in which he works must be entirely

11. See, however, the discussion of the producer by Sheldon Cheney, "The Failure of the American Producer," in his *The New Movement in Theatre* (New York: Kennerley, 1914), pp. 151–73.

favorable to his domination. Money must be easily available, talent willing to be commanded must be plentiful and varied, and the social groups that he proposes to address must be responsive to his imperatorial conduct. A Reinhardt, a Henry Irving, a Chaplin, even a Belasco cannot readily be found today, but theatres have grown used to the idea of such overseers, and lesser persons, producers, have emerged to fulfill some of the functions, although without the artistry.

Whatever else he may be, a producer is not an artist. His is the nature that abhors the vacuum developed when love falls out among artists. The producer sees the artist as a source of energy to be tapped, channeled, developed. He expedites, urges, schemes, projects. A ready improvisor, in his world he is a universal collaborator. He can doctor scenes, even write them, but he is not a dramatist. He can discuss intelligently scenic metaphor and spatial arrangements, but they are the designs of another. He is no actor, although he knows the difference between professional and amateur. He may direct, but it is doubtful that he will ever shape a play with full creative freedom, risking everything on his vision of the action; the compromises that safeguard investments and spell box office are too much with him for that. He can assemble artists in daring combinations, and he can risk much on the auguries of public interest that his personal tastes, enthusiasms, and responsiveness provide. His overview of the full production permits him to retain control of it, but in the main he is a facilitator, whose needs are met by the truths of the artistry of others. In compensation, the producer sets himself to serve those who have what he has not, taking comfort and finding purpose in their talent, in the way that Macgowan tried to serve O'Neill.

The Experimental Theatre ended in a meaningless merger in the late spring of 1926 with a group called the Actors' Theatre, sponsored by Actors' Equity Association. Originally called the Equity Players, the organization had begun production in 1922. The merger came about as part of an Equity scheme to assist art theatres that were having financial and production problems. Macgowan assumed the directorship, taking over from the actor Dudley Digges. A managerial committee of some theatrical prominence remained in supervisory control.

The enterprise was ill-fated. Macgowan opened the season with a production of a fantasy by J. P. McEvoy titled *God Loves Us* and followed it with a revival of *Beyond the Horizon*. Although the O'Neill revival had some success, the losses during the latter half of 1926, the period of Macgowan's directorship, amounted to $61,175. Macgowan left the organization in the fall, giving ill health as the reason. He may well have been exhausted after the three seasons of the Triumvirate, but the New York *Evening Post*, on November 26, 1926, suggested other reasons: "From the outset, it is understood, Mr. Macgowan found opposition within the group directing the destinies of the Actors' Theatre. The failure of 'God Loves Us,' together with his insistence upon the revival of 'Beyond the Horizon' brought about a situation which Mr. Macgowan preferred to relieve." He was replaced by Guthrie McClintic.

As the letters show, Macgowan's role as one of O'Neill's caretakers was at an end. He struggled to find ways to produce the epic-scale *Lazarus Laughed* under the direction of Max Reinhardt or Nemirovitch-Danchenko, or, alternatively, with the Goodman Theatre in Chicago. The schemes failed, and in some financial need, he turned to other producing ventures and to activities in non-theatrical fields of interest, notably a collaboration with Dr. Gilbert V. Hamilton in the preparation of a popular version of Hamilton's study of the problems of modern marriage. The scientific results of Hamilton's pioneering study, along lines later to be followed by Alfred Kinsey, were issued under the title *A Research in Marriage*. A popular version called *What Is Wrong with Marriage*[12] was published in 1929. It credited Macgowan as a full collaborator. Judging from the style of the book, Macgowan was the writer, and it is probable that he suggested to Hamilton that publication of a less scientific version of the study would prove profitable.

In the same year, he reappeared as a theatrical producer in association with a wealthy naïf named Joseph Verner Reed. Reed, who was fourteen years Macgowan's junior, proposed a partnership, holding his checkbook at the ready. Macgowan was then, as Reed put it, "out of the theatre,"[13] but Reed employed him and persuaded him to assist in developing a producing organization. In Reed's account of the

---

12. Gilbert V. Hamilton, *A Research in Marriage* (New York: Albert & Charles Boni, 1929) and Gilbert V. Hamilton and Kenneth Macgowan, *What Is Wrong with Marriage* (New York: Albert & Charles Boni, 1929). Both O'Neill and Macgowan offered themselves as subjects for Dr. Hamilton. The experience for O'Neill had a formative influence on the writing of *Strange Interlude*.

13. Reed, p. 30.

partnership, Macgowan emerges as a man of great charm and enthusiasm, motivated by an indefatigable love of theatre to lavish expenditures of energy:

His energy astounded me. He kept no allotted hours for work; he worked all the time. He read plays voraciously; he talked about them keenly. Rather than wait for a tied-up telephone call with someone he wanted to talk to, he ran eight blocks to get a personal interview. He had time and courtesy for everybody.

There was nothing he liked better than a full, complicated day. He never approached a point simply and directly. He devised complications by putting three or four irons in the fire at once. Then, from a welter of schemes, he suddenly made a distant, far-reaching decision. All this was very exciting.[14]

Such energy impressed Reed, who frequently commented on his partner's capacity for surviving crises by lightning solutions to problems of temperament and finance. Smoking a pipe and making bad puns (Reed ill-advisedly recalls a joke about adding insult to insulin), Macgowan filled the office with a spiritual gaiety, never more apparent than when he had too much work to do. Reed likens his eagerness to that of "a young student wishing to hear about the stars from a professor, or about China from an explorer."[15]

As a producer, Macgowan advocated what he called the "Stagger System," a method of scheduling so that as one production neared its final rehearsals, the cast was put into rehearsal for another play. It was not a system that boded well for an untried producing group with a narrow financial base, especially in the wake of the 1929 market crash. The system worked against the polishing of either production to its final professional finish. For example, the pair produced *Twelfth Night* with Jane Cowl and Leon Quartermaine. In its Boston tryouts, the comedy was evidently in serious trouble, but the producers had committed themselves to opening a second play, *When Hell Froze* by Wilbur Daniel Steele and Norma Mitchell, three weeks after *Twelfth Night*. Art gave way to exhaustion. *When Hell Froze* finally appeared after only a single dress rehearsal and quickly closed. *Twelfth Night* tottered to other pre-Broadway tryouts, finally achiev-

14. Reed, p. 41.
15. Reed, p. 112.

ing a satisfactory form. It was never a popular success, and when it ran in tandem with the team's popular production of Benn W. Levy's comedy *Art and Mrs. Bottle,* it consumed all the profits and the staggered repertory ended in deficit. The expense and disappointment was appalling. As he had done earlier, when he committed the Triumvirate to production in two theatres, Macgowan overextended his production capabilities and ran well beyond his resources. The season of 1929–30 showed a deficit of $81,000.[16]

Nevertheless, the two producers—who later took in Richard Aldrich as a partner and business manager—mounted several plays of merit, including Edwin Justin Mayer's comedy *Children of Darkness,* with the British acting team of Basil Sydney and Mary Ellis. They also offered Leslie Banks in Ronald Jeans's *Lean Harvest* and Benn Levy's *Springtime for Henry.* The bills, all respectable commercial enterprises, were far from the avant-garde experimental theatre Macgowan had praised in his books and had tried to evolve with O'Neill and Jones; but economic depression was at hand and Macgowan's future was uncertain.

When the partnership with Reed came to its inevitable moment of dissolution, Macgowan's next move was predictable. With the assistance of the actor and director Irving Pichel, he was hired as a story editor at RKO Studios in Hollywood. Eight months later, in September 1932, he began his career as a motion-picture producer. At RKO he was put in charge of a varied series of films, both trivial and serious, including *Little Women* with Katharine Hepburn, who had played a small role in *Art and Mrs. Bottle* three years earlier. With John Hay Whitney, he pioneered the first "live action" three-color Technicolor film, a short subject called *La Cucaracha,* in 1934 and the next year, the first full-length feature in the Technicolor process, *Becky Sharp,* starring Miriam Hopkins. To design both, he brought Robert Edmond Jones to Hollywood.[17]

The pioneering Technicolor films were Macgowan's last working association with Jones or O'Neill. He moved in August 1935 to the newly formed Twentieth-Century-Fox Corporation and produced thirty films, many of no significance but some worth remembering: *Lloyds of London, In Old Chicago, Young Mr. Lincoln, Stanley and Livingston, Brigham Young, Manhunt, Life Boat,* and *Jane Eyre.* In an in-

16. Reed, p. 156.
17. An effort that never emerged on film was his attempt to develop a workable script to star John Barrymore in Shaw's *The Devil's Disciple.* Negotiations were affable until Shaw saw the "treatment" of his play. Then all smiles stopped together.

terview with a reporter for the Boston *Herald*, published May 1, 1938, Macgowan described his Hollywood work in a revealing image: "It is the same role that the supervisor of an automobile plant plays in the manufacture of cars. If anything is wrong with the finished product, it's the supervisor's fault. In my case, if you don't like a certain moving picture, I'm to blame. To sum up, a good synonym for the job of producer is responsibility." The reporter noted that as he said it, he smiled. Considering the aesthetic idealism of the 1920s, well he might.

Macgowan emerged from the studios in 1947 and accepted an offer to develop a department of Theatre Arts at the Los Angeles campus of the University of California. At the same time, he found a way of using his interest in ethnic art, which had first come to the surface in 1923 when he collaborated with Herman Rosse on *Masks and Demons*. That book, which undoubtedly stimulated O'Neill's interest in masks,[18] was now to bear further fruit as Macgowan worked to support developments in academic departments concerned with anthropological research and ethnic art and music.

Macgowan's professional association with O'Neill ended with the production of *The Great God Brown* in January 1926. By November 1927, O'Neill had left Bermuda for a new life and had found a new producer in Lawrence Langner and the Theatre Guild. What was left between the two men was a firm friendship and a few minor chores, such as delivering roses in secret to Carlotta Monterey.

As for Robert Edmond Jones, disaffection with the course of the Experimental Theatre is revealed in a number of undated letters to Macgowan: "If something different doesn't happen soon about something I'm going to split a gut. Do you realize that you and Gene and I have never once met together to discuss this thing? And that we haven't any plans beyond the first play?" And again, "How can you develop the American Drama better than by developing a designer who can keep pace with the dreams of your new dramatists? Said he patiently."[19]

18. Macgowan's definition of the book's purpose was to bridge the gap between primitive man and the Greek tragedies, "between the Duk-Duk dancer who regulates morals and acquires riches in New Guinea and some artist of the theatre who wishes to bring the mask back to the stage" (Macgowan and Herbert Rosse, *Masks and Demons* [New York: Harcourt, Brace, 1923], p. xiii).

19. The Jones letters are to be found among the Kenneth Macgowan papers in the Department of Special Collections of the Research Library, University of California, Los Angeles. They are reprinted by permission of the Library and the estate of Robert Edmond Jones.

A crisis of sorts developed in April 1925. A telegram dated May 2, 1925 from O'Neill to Jones reads,

DO NOT BE FINAL UNTIL WE HAVE ALL TALKED STOP IF YOU ARE OUT I AM OUT STOP THINK YOUR DECISION UNFAIR TO KENNETH STOP LOOKING FORWARD TO SEEING YOU

GENE

Jones's restlessness is easily explained. His designs, unlike the services of Macgowan or the plays of O'Neill, were in constant demand. For a designer of genius in a prosperous theatre climate, work is continually available. Jones's reputation was such that he could not afford to be locked into the stages of small off-Broadway theatres. It was also true that, while there was ample work in the offing, he was undergoing a psychological crisis, which would take him to Switzerland, to Karl Jung in Zurich, and into psychoanalysis. On November 26, 1926, he wrote from Zurich in reply to a letter of Macgowan's informing him of the merger of the Experimental Theatre with the Actors' Theatre:

Dear Kenneth,

Your letter with the account of the merger has just come. I think on the whole it is a good move, though not having Dudley Digges continue as director is a pity. You should keep reminding the Actors' Theatre that it is a theatre for actors and hold them to it. It is splendid for you and I have a strong hunch that you will make it go. But you must leave me entirely out of it. I mean it. I have been meaning to write you for weeks about this work here, but it is not easy. If you will take the trouble to read about the *Extraverted [sic] Intuitive Type* in Jung's *Psychological Types* you might get a better idea of it than I could ever give you. When I got here it was all very serious indeed. Well, to put it in the fewest words, it looks as if my career were shot. Anyhow I have money enough to stick around till spring and see what happens. And I can't get the real benefit out of the work [with Jung] unless I give my entire self to it. Presently I'll come back scraped and cleaned with a marvellous self-starter. But till then—no promises. Just say I'm taking a year off in Europe.

For O'Neill, the years with the Triumvirate were a period of crucial transition. As the letters attest, he was writing with ambitious fecundity, and the projects grew in scope and strove continually for the invention of astonishing theatrical devices—the masks in *The Great God Brown,* the massive choruses of *Lazarus Laughed,* the asides of *Strange Interlude.* O'Neill set himself to reach into areas where no American playwright—and few of any nation or time—had ventured. Whether the plays succeeded or failed as works of art is not to the present point. They were all works of extraordinary artistic courage—if, indeed, "courage" be the word to describe the energy of his libidinal imagination. It is almost as if no controlling ego existed to caution him as to social and physical limitations as he pressed to the existing boundaries of theatrical art. This is not to imply that O'Neill was unaware of the disciplines of art, once the theme and the mode had been envisioned. The lengthy scenarios evolving the plays in plan and the constant, sometimes total reworking of the scripts, together with the days spent cutting and rewriting in order to ready them for production or publication, testify to the artist's care. In other areas of his life he was irresponsible and excessive, particularly in his drinking, but to his writing he was totally committed. The social excesses that the letters occasionally reflect may be viewed as an outward aspect of the central drives that produced the massive creative yield. In one way, at least, they were profoundly linked, for in these years in Bermuda, his drinking threatened to destroy his writing.

He had drunk since he was an adolescent; and in flophouse and speakeasy, in Village garrets and the cellar of his first "stately mansion," Brook Farm in Ridgefield, Connecticut, he had gone on debilitating carouses. If such drinking indicates a desire to escape from a difficult present, O'Neill had ample excuse for his way of life. The slow, cancerous death of his father, between June and August 1920, was followed in 1922 by his mother's death, under circumstances of particular horror which he was later to recount in *A Moon for the Misbegotten.* A year later, his brother, Jamie, who had been confined to a sanitarium, succeeded in drinking himself to death. Beyond the family tragedies, and adding fuel to the personal sense of loss, was the stockpile of plays. O'Neill had had many successes, but there were an equal number of failures in his early professional years. Most difficult was the pile of unproduced work that continued to mount up with no sign that the Experimental Theatre could really measure up to his demands. *The Fountain* had waited for years. *Lazarus Laughed,* into which he had poured so much of himself, wanted a hearing, not to mention his satire *Marco Millions.* What was being done about *Brown*? Was it cast? Were the masks designed? These were not petulant questions.

There were marital and familial responsibilities. He was the father of three children, and he had finally come to some terms with the son born of his first, brief marriage to Kathleen Jenkins in 1909. Eugene O'Neill, Jr. was eleven in 1921 when he was at last introduced to his father, in a Manhattan apartment the O'Neills shared with Robert Edmond Jones.[20] Other children, including Shane, his second son, and Oona, his daughter, and Barbara, Agnes's daughter by her first marriage, brought new and distracting responsibilities, which he fulfilled only intermittently. He was making a reasonably good income, and at Brook Farm, a fifteen-room mansion on thirty acres, he undertook a substantially improved standard of living. But Brook Farm became a millstone when, having decided that he wrote better in warm climates than in cold, he determined to winter in Bermuda.[21] Financial and social obligations grew with the purchase and renovation of his Bermuda home, Spithead, and he could not surely count on Agnes to give him the protection he needed to write. Add to the bill of particulars the unsettled parental estates and related fees and taxes, and it is possible to see O'Neill as harried almost beyond patience. Then, to cap the list, there came a love affair with the actress Carlotta Monterey, who had replaced Mary Blair as Mildred Douglas in *The Hairy Ape* when the play moved from the Village to Broadway. In 1926, he met Carlotta again at Loon Lodge on the Belgrade Lakes in Maine and his life changed.

The cumulative effect of the pressures might well have led to alcoholic binges, but even before the weight of responsibilities O'Neill had drunk deep. The difference between the Homeric toping of his youth and the drinking during this period is that now he was close to chronic alcoholism and was reacting to pressure with a drive that, like Jamie's, was directed toward self-destruction. The choice was without shading: write, or drink and die. Although an occasional lapse was to follow, in 1926 he did in fact stop drinking. Louis Sheaffer quotes Macgowan's explanation of the phenomenon: "Gene quit when it came down to a choice between his writing and his drinking. He knew he couldn't go on indefinitely as he had—all that

20. Sheaffer, p. 66. Macgowan was on hand at the meeting to lend O'Neill moral support.

21. Sheaffer, p. 154. This was the "discovery" about himself to which he refers in Letter 27.

drinking in the previous year—and his writing meant everything to him."[22]

That writing meant "everything" led him to make demands that at times could not be met, and he reacted with impatience against the frustrating delays and what seemed to him to be the neglect of his associates. Letter 59 demonstrates this eloquently. Macgowan had written, "I'm getting tired, but I do see that from the abortive idealism of our first attempts at the P.P., we've worked slowly towards more rep., more money, and a chance in a year, I think, to have the opportunity of moving steadily into real repertory" (Letter 58).

O'Neill rejected such optimism as facile, replying:

If you are "getting tired" of conditions in the show-shop from your end as a director, I am certainly getting God damn tired of them—of eternally putting up with the inexcusable—in the sense of avoidable in a true theatre with more time and preparations—*approximations* to what I've written. . . . I'm sick and tired of old theatres under old conditions, of new theatres handcuffed by old conditions, of "art" theatres with fuzzy ideals and no money or efficiency—in fact of *the* American theatre as it exists. I've had exactly ten years of it as a playwright—considerably more than your three as a director—and my ambition to see my stuff performed on any stage I know . . . is beginning almost to cease, and this at a time I *know* I have most to give to a theatre. (Letter 59)

In March 1927, a visitor came to Spithead to discuss the possibility of his theatre's staging *Marco Millions.* Lawrence Langner from the Theatre Guild felt that O'Neill, like Shaw, was a playwright his organization was obligated to stage if it was to be a top-ranking company. Sneering at the Guild was easy. The members of the board of directors were widely known as difficult personalities, the Guild's financial status was uncertain, and nothing they had yet produced had achieved the prestige of, say, Arthur Hopkins's productions of *Richard III* and *Hamlet* with John Barrymore. Not without reason, the board had rejected *The Straw, The First Man, Welded,* and *The Fountain.* With less reason they had turned down *"Anna Christie."* As a result, O'Neill had found the organization unlovable. However, as

22. Sheaffer, p. 190. Sheaffer discusses the relation of the sessions with Dr. Hamilton to O'Neill's cure on pp. 188–91.

doors slammed, as David Belasco and Arthur Hopkins and the Experimental Theatre itself did not find a way to present O'Neill's new work, and as the playwright had to go begging, Langner became a welcome guest.

Langner had come to Bermuda to mend fences and cement alliances. He was interested in *Marco Millions,* and the possibility of its production was gratifying to the playwright. But more was to come. At Spithead, Langner was allowed to read the as-yet-unfinished script of *Strange Interlude.* He was staggered by its power and worked to seal an alliance between the Guild and the dramatist. The Guild produced both *Marco Millions* and *Strange Interlude* in January 1928, and with the latter play achieved one of the phenomenal successes of the American stage. Thereafter, O'Neill and the Guild worked together. O'Neill had finally found a theatre that would do for him as a fully professional playwright what the Provincetown Players had done for him as an amateur.

The Bermuda years can be seen as a period when O'Neill sought to bring the outer world to order so that in the inner world he would have the freedom to create. It was not a simple proposition; like Jones, he needed to be "scraped and cleaned."[23] Little by little the end was achieved. Theatrical urgencies were eased, drinking was put aside. Only in his domestic life did disorder remain.

Carlotta Monterey O'Neill said, "He came to me and asked me to serve him tea. 'Tea?' I thought, knowing all about his drinking, *'that* man wants tea?' But I served him tea and he drank it, and he came again and several more times, and one day he said to me, 'Carlotta, I need you,' and I thought, 'Oh, oh, here it comes.' But he said, 'I've been making some money and people know me, and I have to live respectably, and I don't know how. I need someone to plan the meals and put the guest towels in the bathroom, and . . .' "[24] Although she did not say so, he asked her to take charge of the outer courses of his life, to clothe him, make his home, and create the isolation he needed in order to work.

23. Jones's phrase "scraped and clean" is perhaps echoed in a speech of Charlie Marsden's at the end of *Strange Interlude:* "So let's you and me forget the whole distressing episode, regard it as an interlude, of trial and preparation, say, in which our souls have been scraped clean of impure flesh and made worthy to bleach in peace." Eugene O'Neill, *The Plays of Eugene O'Neill,* 3 vols. (New York: Random House, 1964) 1:199.

24. Carlotta Monterey O'Neill's words are reconstructed from notes taken by the author, following a meeting at the Carlton House in New York City in 1957.

To put work ahead of all other commitments and desires was not an easy act, especially as it involved leaving his present world. He reiterated his love for Agnes and the "heirs": "Nothing could ever take their place—but oh Christ, there are also other things—'on the other side of the hills' " (Letter 65).

Carlotta's beauty, her efficiency, and her dedication to him won out. When O'Neill left Spithead in November 1927, he did not return.

"Campsea"
South Shore, Paget W.,
Bermuda
Mar. 1, '25

Dear Kenneth:

It's a shame the way our letters have to cross. I'm always answering old news at the time when I'm expecting new news to arrive in a couple of hours on the new mail. But it can't be helped. I'm anxious to know if the jury came and what their decision was. Suppose I'll hear tomorrow night or Tuesday a.m.[1]

Your letter and the clippings were a treat! I certainly appreciate your shrewd activity in holding down the fort and I think you made a grand job of it! Also, it doesn't take much to imagine that the job was a rather trying one when you had to deal with bastards of the Banton variety. But alls well that ends in publicity only—if this finally has! "God bless Gene"? Well yes, if you're looking for excitement a play of mine is a good thing to have in your house, seems like. First "In the Zone" in England—then the "Ape" in N.Y.[2]—last year "God's Chillun" and now "Desire." But this is the first time any real money has resulted. We all deserve it after the all-mud-without-balm of "God's Chillun." I have thought of several wicked cables I could send to friend Banton which would make him feel like

1. *Desire Under the Elms,* after a successful run at the Greenwich Village Theatre, had moved uptown to Broadway's Earl Carroll Theatre on January 12, 1925. District Attorney Joab H. Banton, who had been frustrated in his attempt to force closing of *All God's Chillun Got Wings* the previous year, threatened to seek a grand jury indictment unless the play, which he called "too thoroughly bad to be purified by a blue pencil," was closed. Macgowan proposed inviting a "citizens play-jury" to a performance and agreed to abide by their decision. Amidst outcry from the press and the public, Banton dropped his case. On March 13, 1925, a jury selected from a panel of several hundred persons in the arts and professions acquitted O'Neill's play. The publicity generated by the controversy considerably increased the production's box-office receipts.

2. When *The Hairy Ape* was transferred to Broadway in April 1922, the police department had tried unsuccessfully to close it as "indecent, obscene and impure."

the cat's arse for a gangreened moment or two—but I guess not—
I'm too detached about this to get "my back up" really—it isn't so
much being out of touch as the fact that so chuck full of "Brown"[3]
that "Desire" seems out of my range of worry. It's fortunate for me.
The first half of "Brown"—first draft—is just about finished.
Well, there's nothing much else to say. Bye'bye for this time.

Gene

---

30 • TO MACGOWAN FROM O'NEILL. ALS 1 p.

"Campsea"
South Shore, Paget W.
Bermuda
Mar. 6, '25

Dear Kenneth:

Just a line to enclose the long promised snaps. They're pretty good
and might be usable with Finn for "human interest"—and one of
them is smiling over the sea at Banton!

This play jury thing seems to be hanging fire. Hope to get some
more dope on it by tomorrow's steamer.

There's no news on this end. Working hard. Hope the Vildrac
play[1] went over—or is it still to come?

Has Bobby done anything on "Fountain"?

Love & kisses to all.
Gene

P.S. In these snaps, if they could blot out the window in background it would look as if taken on the edge of the cliff which, as a
matter of fact, is only about 20 feet away.

---

3. *The Great God Brown*, the new play on which O'Neill was working.

1. *Michel Auclair* by Charles Vildrac opened at the Provincetown Playhouse on March
4, 1925.

"Campsea"
South Shore, Paget W.,
Bermuda,
March 14 [1925]

Dear Kenneth:

Your cable arrived yesterday with the glad news. It was a relief—not that I doubted the result but I did think one or two of the jury would be anti.

I read your letter with interest. Your dope for next season sounds reasonable—in fact, very good. Certainly we can't hope to go on this way. Your idea for the G.V. suits me in every way and I believe it can be worked—although the theatre is not the best place for the scheme unless we have built up a considerable audience there this year. And your plan for the P'town seems absolutely the right thing if actors can be got, etc. at the unlivable wage rate again, and if Dickinson[1] or someone with the proper poise & administrative clarity can be in with Jimmy & Fitzie. Jimmy ought, in his own interest, to be able to go to London next season to put on "Jones" & "Ape"—(not to add, my interest!). They have made him a good offer and I think it really opens up one of those "big chances" for him to establish himself solidly. Don't you?

I wish we had more definite proof—perhaps we have by this—that there *are* interesting experiments all written for the doing at the P.P. We had no reason to believe so up to the time I left. That's our main trouble, as it is everyone else's. Where's the stuff? And if there ain't none, what's the good of hanging on to the P.P.? I wish the G.V. had a studio loft that could be used—or a cellar—as a real experimental theatre. It would unify things immensely. Couldn't it be financed?—the construction, I mean? It would hardly take more, maybe, than the upkeep of a P.P. season.

Put down "Lulu" as a G.V. good bet for next—if you can get a whale of an actress for it.

The two women's parts in "Brown" will take some playing. Clare[2] would be wonderful for one if it turns out as difficult and important as so far—and she has nothing better to do—and Helen F.[3] might

1. Possibly playwright Thomas H. Dickinson, whose *Winter Bound* was done at the Provincetown in 1929.
2. Clare Eames.
3. Helen Freeman, who had played Freda in the Provincetown Playhouse production of *S.S. Glencairn.*

do the other well or Mary M.[4] But the man? The man?

Fitzie seems put out that we didn't grab "Processional."[5] It was never submitted to us for production, was it? Who's backing it now uptown? I know it can't really be the Guild. Speaking of them, they must decide soon on "Fountain." Their contract ceases April 1st.

Helen MacKellar[6] would be a good bet for "Lulu."

I'm going to read Gorki's new play.[7] Have you read it?

"Dynamo"[8] will probably turn out a G.V. thing. The P'town doesn't hit my mind's eye any more. Maybe it's the ventilation which I have detested for so many years that has finally got me. Imagine writing of the cosmic tides of Being when you're thinking of how nobody in the audience will be able to draw their own breath after Scene One! There is such a thing as knowing one's theatre too darn well!

I don't like "Love For Love"[9] as next G.V.—not this season—the Cherry Lane have taken our wind on that.[10]

I wish you & Bobby & Jimmy—all together or in divisions would come down. Pull some wires for reduced rates. It's a cinch. Bermuda courts every bit of publicity it can get, also its steamer lines. After Easter the Tourist rush is over and bookings easy. Try it. We'll have this camp bungalo to put at your disposal as we're moving to more of a house for Agnes' sake[11] on April 1st or near that but still have this on lease and will use it in daytime to bathe from, etc. but not for sleeping. Bring a blanket apiece at least. We're low on bedding. Middle of April would be grand here—weather & water wonderful—it would really repay you to spend 10 days—4 trip and back—six here—some of your meals at small hotel ¼ mile up beach—I'm sure

---

4. Mary Morris.

5. Expressionistic play by American dramatist John Howard Lawson (1894–1977), which, produced by the Theatre Guild, opened January 12, 1925 at New York's Garrick Theatre and aroused great interest and controversy.

6. Actress who created the role of Ruth Atkins in *Beyond the Horizon* (1920) and who reportedly refused to play the lead in *All God's Chillun Got Wings* because it meant playing opposite a Negro.

7. Probably *The Judge* by Russian dramatist Maxim Gorky (1868–1936), translated by Marie Zakrevsky and Barrett H. Clark, published in late 1924 by R. M. McBride.

8. O'Neill did not complete this play until 1928. It was produced by the Theatre Guild in 1929.

9. William Congreve's play opened at the Greenwich Village Theatre on March 31, 1925.

10. Congreve's *The Way of the World* had been produced at the Cherry Lane Playhouse, opening on November 17, 1924.

11. Agnes Boulton O'Neill was pregnant.

you'd never regret doing this if you can possibly afford it. This applies all 3 of you.

So come and let's talk. "Brown" ought to be done by then too.

All best!
Gene

---

32 • TO MACGOWAN FROM O'NEILL. ALS 1 p.

Bermuda—Mar. 18 [1925]

Dear Kenneth:

The middle of April would be fine. Even if Agnes' "party" were on then, you being here wouldn't disturb. As I explained in my last our "camp" will be vacant and at your disposal. Your meals you can get at the hotel about a quarter mile—(less)—off—perhaps arrange have woman come in and get your breakfasts. Bobby's expenses (via David) ought to finance the whole trip for you both, what?

Has Bobby got a new script of "Marco"? If so, you can see how much I did to it. Dave claims he intends to spend 75000 to 100000 bucks putting it on.[1]

No more news of Guild—"Fountain." Have you? I never got any copy from them of Bobby's new designs. They're hanging on without a decision as long as their contract holds, I imagine, now that they know I'm willing to renew. I'd "jump" them, only it wouldn't be exactly square.

I've just read Mike Gold's first long play[2] and like it *damn well!* It's a comedy of Mexico—character stuff with the plot negligible— and to me it was extremely fresh and amusing. A good one for the Greenwich V., say I! Fine chances for Bobby in it, too. This Gold, as I've told you before, has the stuff! He would be good to grab hold off. He's going to give up everything for playwriting from now on, he says. Just back from Russia. He's broke and has a mother to support. If you like his play, this is a time to be generous. Give him a

1. Producer David Belasco had decided to finance a lavish production of *Marco Millions* with Robert Edmond Jones as designer. Belasco later dropped this plan.
2. *La Fiesta* by American novelist, radical journalist, and dramatist Michael Gold (1896–1967). It was completed in 1925 but not produced until September 17, 1929, when the Provincetown Players presented it as *Fiesta* at the Garrick Theatre, with James Light as director. Gold had been a friend of O'Neill's since their days together in Greenwich Village in 1917–18.

decent advance and contract. And I feel sure both you & Bobby will like it. I'm writing Gold to see you at once.

Gross "D"[3] 12800 last week? Is it slumping off too fast to be healthy or what? Of course, it was bound to come down somehow.

Day-day! See you soon, remember! Don't let anything side track you!

Gene

---

33 • TO MACGOWAN FROM O'NEILL. ALS 1 p.

Bermuda
[ca. March 25, 1925]

Dear Kenneth:

Just a few words in a rush to answer the Wertheim[1] question. I consent to being a fellow chairman of Lamont's,[2] although thereby incurring the Wall Street-association taint which will prevent my ever being elected President! Anything for dear old Harvard?

Did you hear loud cheers today from the southward? It was your humble in the act of finishing "The Great God Brown." Yep! Will now go over and have typed, pending your & Bobby's arrival—and Jimmy's if & when he comes. I think it is grand stuff, much deeper & more poetical in a way than anything I've done before, and the masks will work in fine with it.

But—wait till you read it!

Ta-ta for this time!
Gene

P.S. If "Desire" business keeps dropping they ought to plan moving it to smaller theatre with better terms, don't you think? Then it ought to run through to June.

---

3. *Desire Under the Elms.*

1. New York stockbroker Maurice Wertheim, who was on the Board of the Theatre Guild.

2. Thomas W. Lamont was the senior partner of J. P. Morgan and Company, the most prestigious and influential private banking firm in the U.S. He was an alumnus and a major benefactor of Harvard; apparently O'Neill had been asked to serve with Lamont in a philanthropic venture in support of Harvard.

Southcote
South Shore, Paget West
Bermuda
May 1st [1925]

Dear Kenneth:

This isn't an answer to all your letters that I owe an answer to but is a note of introduction that I am anxious to get off by todays mail to explain another note of introduction that I have given a young Princeton grad., who has spent the winter down here, to give to you. This boy, who is a hell of a nice fellow—one of the few real ones we have met in this tourist infested isle!—is very anxious to break into the newspaper game as a prelim. to independent writing. I would not bother you with him unless I felt pretty certainly that he had the foundation stuff, you know that. Besides which, I am sure you will like to meet him.

Now here's the idea: Will you have a talk with him—he will phone you and make an appointment—and tell him what you know from experience is the best way to go about things to get a job, give him all the advice he wants, and—most important of all!—give him a few notes of introduction where they will do most good? Anything you can do for him will be aces with me. I thought of giving him a letter to Walter Lippmann[1]—then reflected that I hardly knew Walter and that it would be much better if it came from someone else nearer the throne.

Another thing about the subject of this letter—Jack Pierce—he has just gotten himself married down here—a real love match on spec. and no finances—and this was done partly on my advice![2] So you see I feel myself in the position of a marital God-father, and a responsible party. So again let me urge you to do all for Jack that you can. Besides wanting a job, he needs it to start the home fires burning.

I'm sorry we lost the Gold play—and so, I think, will he be before he gets through. From what I deduce from what he wrote me, that brother of Brock Pemberton's,[3] who saw Mike before he had received

1. Walter Lippmann was at this time chief editorial writer of the New York *Herald*.
2. Pierce had married Alice Cuthbert, an Englishwoman whom the O'Neills had met and befriended in Bermuda.
3. Brock Pemberton was a Broadway producer.

an answer from me, handed Bobby's direction in particular, and our whole organization in particular, such a vindictive panning that I guess Mike, in spite of his enthusiasm for me, never quite recovered from it and, even after you had made him as good an offer as he'll get elsewhere, still had his doubts. But after all, the play is no work of any immense account—only a damn good play—and I guess we can survive the shock. And he needs the uptown "jack," Broadway.

I haven't yet read the Anderson play[4]—in fact, the script got mislaid somehow in our moving and I'll be damned if I can find it. Bring another when you come.

Jack B.[5] for the "Great God Brown," say I! He might do that. Jimmy L. can tell you, hes about the only actor who could do "Brown" and I think it would tempt him. "The Fountain" never would. I don't want to do anything about "F" until you and Bobby arrive and I have read it over in the meanwhile. Maybe I'll decide to produce and publish it myself[6]—in a good hot stove!

But no more of this. Come soon and let's talk.[7] All best to Bobby. Our twin girls are expected any moment now—but then ladies always make you wait, don't they—but it's getting on my nerves while Agnes is as calm as calm—couvade,[8] is that what they call it?

Adios! I've relied on Jimmy to tell you a lot.

Gene

---

35 • TO THE O'NEILLS FROM THE MACGOWANS. WIRE 1 p. (Brewster N.Y., 14.5.25)

AGNES WHOOP[1]

–EDDIE KENNETH.–

4. *Outside Looking In* by Maxwell Anderson (1888–1959), which opened the season at the Greenwich Village Theatre on September 7, 1925.

5. John Barrymore, whom O'Neill wanted to play Dion Anthony. Barrymore, after reading the script, turned down the part.

6. The Theatre Guild had dropped its option on *The Fountain*.

7. Macgowan and Jones came to Bermuda for a week on June 6, 1925.

8. A primitive custom in which the expectant father took to his bed as if he were giving birth to the child.

1. Oona O'Neill was born on May 14, 1925.

36 • TO O'NEILL FROM MACGOWAN. WIRE 1 p. (New York, 16.5.25)

BOBBY POSTPONING EUROPE REACH BERMUDA TWENTY EIGHTH

KENNETH

---

37 • TO O'NEILL FROM MACGOWAN. WIRE 1 p. (New York, 17.6.25)

SEND DOG WITH INSTRUCTIONS DELIVERED TO RICHARDS.

KENNETH

---

38 • TO THE MACGOWANS FROM O'NEILL. TLS 1 p. (Envelope postmarked: Nantucket Mass Jul 31 7-PM 1925)

5 Mill Street

Nantucket, Mass

Dear Eddy and Kenneth:

I've meant to write you a long time before this to tell you both how very grateful I am for all you did for me out at your place. I must have been a pretty sorry sight to have about the house and by no means a welcome addition to any family retaining their sanity. You were as kind as you could be and I shall never forget it.[1]

Everything is all jake up here although we are more in the town than I would like but late comers can't be choosers. I'm very much on the old cart again and feel as well now as ever I did, what with swimming, boating and the rest of it.

Have been doing a bit more work on the "Fountain" but can't seem to get interested in the old thing—probably because I'm really anxious to get going on something new and yet my conscience makes me go over this.

I hear Kenneth is coming up here to speak. When? We'll look forward to seeing him and hearing the latest.

This is just a note dragged off on Wilbur Steele's reserve ancient Corona with much brow-wrinkling and is merely to say hello and thank you! Give my best to Buddy—and to Peter and Chief.[2] Our

---

1. The O'Neills had moved to Nantucket for the summer. O'Neill had spent time in New York attending to theatrical business in connection with his own plays as well as with the future of the Provincetown Players. Before returning to Nantucket, he had started to drink after a period of being "on the wagon" and had spent several days sobering up at the Macgowans' home in Brewster, New York.

2. The Macgowan children, Peter and Joan, and their pet.

own heirs are flourishing—but thank God we have no dog at present!

Let me know what I owe you for the car, beer, booze etc and I'll send you check pronto. Also I want to add something so that Eddy can get a present for Peter and Buddy from their old alcoholic pal, Yours truly (as the late John L.[3] (bot' members of dis club![4]) used to say)

Gene

---

39 • TO MACGOWAN FROM O'NEILL. WIRE (autograph version) 1 p. (Nantucket Mass / 8-1-1925 / RECEIVED, AT 9 30 AM 8 / 2 / 25 / at foot of WIRE Phoned to Mrs. MacGowan 10 15 AM)

TO KENNETH MACGOWAN. BREWSTER NY

HUSTON[1] WOULD NEED LONG INTENSIVE WORK WITH BOBBY AND CARRINGTON[2] AS YOU KNOW STOP IS THERE TIME FOR THIS UNLESS YOU POSTPONE FOUNTAIN STOP HAS BOBBY TIME TO GIVE ANYWAY STOP AS MATTERS STAND WITH DESIRE COMPLICATION ATWEELL[3] PERHAPS NECESSARY ALTHOUGH DOES NOT BELONG OUR THEATRE STOP DEPENDS LARGELY HOW BOBBY FEELS DIRECTING HIM STOP ONLY ALTERNATIVE SEEMS POSTPONE FOUNTAIN OR OPEN ATWELL FORTY EIGHTH STREET SEPARATE VENTURE AND FIND SUBSTITUTE FOR GREENWICH STOP THIS IS THE BEST I CAN DO AT DECIDING ALL BEST

GENE

---

40 • TO MACGOWAN FROM O'NEILL. TLS 2 pp.

Nantucket, Mass
Sept 2nd. '25

Dear Kenneth:

I have been feeling in a much more healthy state of mind these few days, and have been carefully considering your wire and letter concerning the revised openings of The Fountain and Brown. I have

3. John L. Sullivan, heavyweight boxing champion who was renowned for his prowess as a drinker and carouser.
4. O'Neill is referring to Yank's remark to the gorilla in scene 8 of *The Hairy Ape*.

1. Walter Huston, who had created the role of Ephraim Cabot in *Desire Under the Elms* (1924), was under consideration to play Ponce de Léon in *The Fountain*.
2. Mrs. Margaret Carrington, Huston's sister and a voice teacher who had coached John Barrymore for his role in *Hamlet*.
3. Lionel Atwill, who had recently starred opposite Helen Hayes in a Theatre Guild production of Shaw's *Caesar and Cleopatra*.

several very serious objections to make. I think to put on "Brown" before "The Fountain" would be rotten bad policy for us, for both plays, and their author. I may have thought differently for a moment at times, but I am now firmly convinced of this. "Brown" needs much more careful casting, more time, and more careful preperation then "The Fountain" To me it is worth a dozen "Fountains." The masks, as you know, cannot be done until the play is finally cast; and so far, as far as I am aware, we have not got one person in mind who really fits the intended role. Then again, Jimmy would have to come back and make the masks, just at the time when the most important thing in his mind, rightly, will be his opening bill. This would be fatal. I would rather have the Fountain go on with Atwell, who is all ready to step in, and open at the former date, than have Brown sacrificed. I feel very keenly about this. As for waiting for me to do anything further to the Fountain I will polish up the vision scene, but I don't know if I will be able to revise the Bishop's scene or not—perhaps during rehearsals when my interest in the play becomes "het up" again.

Here's the way I feel about Brown—that it deserves as careful, or more careful, consideration than Belasco is giving Marco, and ought to get it. Otherwise it has no chance whatever, and might as well be withdrawn, at least for the coming season. At any rate I am emphatic in thinking that whatever plan you dope out, Brown should follow The Fountain. The reverse would be a great injury to me, I feel.

As for the Mary Blair matter,[1] I thought she was in the Co which remains in New York company. It seems to me that any question to do with the road salary should be left until it is time for that company to go on the road. In justice to her she should play the part until the company leaves New York at least. When I saw her I found her work very good—better than Mary Morris in parts of the latter part. I cannot believe that Helen Freeman can do it half so well: she was rotten in a similar part in Beyond The Horizon; but even if she is as good, it would be grossly unfair to Mary to take her out while the company is still in New York, after she has carried on for us all summer. If it is a case of what Al Jones[2] says, you can tell him for me that I have something to say about the casting of this play, as he

1. Mary Blair had replaced Mary Morris as Abbie Putnam in *Desire Under the Elms* when the production moved to Broadway.

2. Broadway producer and partner in the production firm of Jones and Green, who, with the Triumvirate, had been responsible for moving *Desire Under the Elms* to Broadway in January 1925.

would find out by looking at the contract. And I don't approve of Helen being substituted for Mary in N.Y. Also I believe that if you have a talk with Mary that you will find that she will come down off her high horse on the road salary thing.

Thank Eddie[3] very much for reading the German version of Desire. I am glad to know it is all right.

Life up here begins to look much better. I have been on the beach all day, and begin to feel fine.

All best!
Gene

---

41 • TO MACGOWAN FROM O'NEILL. WIRE (autograph version) 2 pp.
(9-5 1925 / Nantucket Mass 12 25 P)

TO KENNETH MACGOWAN
BREWSTER NY

WE AGREED UP HERE DON JUAN[1] FOUNTAIN SHOULD NOT FOLLOW EACH OTHER STOP SEEMS WORSE POSSIBLE ORDER FOR ALL INTERESTED WHY NOT GOLD MEXICAN COMEDY[2] SECOND BILL MILTON[3] COULD DO THAT STOP AS FOR BROWN I KNOW NOTHING ABOUT HARRIGAN[4] ELDERIDGE[5] LEGALLIENNE[6] SOUND FINE MACKELLAR[7] DOUBTFUL AND SHE WOULD NOT ACCEPT ANYWAY IF ALFRED LUNT[8] TIED UP WITH GUILD HE MIGHT BE GOOD PROSPECT PLAY BOTH PART AS PLANNED FOR BARRYMORE[9] AND WIFE[10] COULD DO MARGART IT IS IMPORTANT MASK EXPERIMENTING THAT CONVENCES ME AS TO AMOUNT OF TIME NEEDED EVEN AFTER CAST IS SELECTED CALL UP TONIGHT IF YOU CAN

GENE

3. Probably Edna Macgowan.

1. *The Last Night of Don Juan* by Edmond Rostand, translated from the French by Sidney Howard, which opened at the Greenwich Village Theatre on November 9, 1925.
2. *Fiesta* by Michael Gold, not produced until 1929 by the Provincetown.
3. Robert Milton, who had directed plays at the Greenwich Village Theatre.
4. William Harrigan, later to create the role of William A. Brown in the 1926 Greenwich Village Theatre production of *The Great God Brown*.
5. Florence Eldridge, who, in 1956, created the role of Mary Tyrone in the Broadway production of O'Neill's *Long Day's Journey into Night*.
6. Actress, director, playwright, producer, and translator Eva Le Gallienne.
7. Helen MacKellar. See Letter 31 above.
8. Lunt played Marco in *Marco Millions* in 1928.
9. O'Neill hoped to interest John Barrymore in playing Dion Anthony in the first half of *The Great God Brown* and William A. Brown in the rest of the play. Barrymore read the script but turned down the opportunity.
10. Lynn Fontanne, Lunt's wife, who, in 1928, would create the role of Nina Leeds in O'Neill's *Strange Interlude*.

42 • TO MACGOWAN FROM O'NEILL. WIRE (autograph version) 2 pp.
(9 5 1925 / Nantucket Ms 12 25 PM)

TO KENNETH MACGOWAN
BREWSTER

REMEMBER GODS CHILLUN MARY[1] DESERVES EVERY CONSIDERA-
TION FROM US ESPECIALLY FROM ME BOTH YOU AND BOBBY
THOUGHT HER FINE IN DESIRE TWO MONTHS AGO. IF SHE HAS
GONE BAD REHEARSE HER AND GIVE HER ANOTHER CHANCE TELL-
ING HER FRANKLY WHATS WHAT I WOULD RATHER HAVE COM-
PANY CLOSE THAN HUMILATE HER BY REPLACING HER NOW AT
START OF NEW SEASON WHILE PLAY STILL IN NEW YORK AND WE
HAVE NOTHING ELSE TO OFFER HER MIGHT TRY HER AS CYBEL[2]

GENE

---

43 • TO MACGOWAN FROM O'NEILL. WIRE 1 p. (NANTUCKET MASS
1020A SEPT 10 1925 / at foot of WIRE 1200P)

KENNETH MACGOWAN
GREENWICH VILLAGE THEATRE NEW YORK NY

CERTAINLY WILL TAKE YOUR AND BOBBIES OPINION ON HELENS[1]
ACTING FINE NEWS ABOUT TRAMP PLAY[2] MEANT TO SEND WIRE
OPENING NIGHT BUT WAS MIXED UP THOUGHT IT WAS NEXT MON-
DAY LET ME KNOW ABOUT BROWN ALL BEST

GENE

---

44 • TO MACGOWAN FROM O'NEILL. TLS 1 p.

> Saturday
> Nantucket, Mass.
> [ca. September 10, 1925]

Dear Kenneth:

Yes, "harlot" could substitute for whore and "femalin' " or "slut-
tin' " or something of the kind for "whorin'." As for the "good nights
work" that can simply be cut out by having the script jump from
"I got a new son" to the speech of the old farmer. I can't see how

1. Actress Mary Blair, who had created the role of Ella Downey in *All God's Chillun Got Wings* when other actresses had refused to play opposite a Negro.
2. A character in *The Great God Brown*.

1. Helen Freeman. See Letter 31 above.
2. *Outside Looking In* by Maxwell Anderson, which had opened the season at the Greenwich Village Theatre on September 7, 1925.

the morons will ever pick out that bit of comedy between the old men to pick on but if they do then simply cut from I got a new son" to "Fiddle 'er up, durn ye."[1]

It's grand news about the tramp play. At least the G.V. will be off to a good start this year with consequent lessening of your burden of financial worry. I meant to send a wire to you-alls and to Anderson but, not having looked at a paper in days I thought it was next Monday.

From a cable, Jimmy to Madden, Jones seems to have gone over big in London and Paul made a great hit.[2]

Tell Helen Freeman I got her letter—won't answer it now because I'll be able to talk to her in town before long. I quite see her side of it. The whole thing seems to have been a misunderstanding, at least on this end, but if its all settled now why lets all forget it.

Tell Bobby I got his note. I'm glad to hear of the successful experimenting with the masks, and am anxious to get a look.[3] Let me know as soon as you can what the dope is on "Brown" as I have to make my plans accordingly.

All best.
Gene

---

45 • TO MACGOWAN FROM O'NEILL. WIRE 1 p. (NANTUCKET MASS 22) [ca. September 23, 1925]

KENNETH MCGOWN,
GREENWICH VILLAGE THEATRE SHERIDAN SQ NEW YORK NY.

ALL RIGHT GALSORTHY PLAY IS WELL MADE SHOOT DON JUAN AS AN AUTHOR IT MAKES NO MATTER BUT AS A DIRECTOR I STILL CANDIDLY BELIEVE I IS POOR POLICY HOWEVER IF THERE IS NO GOOD ALTERNATIVE WHAT IS THER TO SAY[1] WHAT CAST HAVE YOU WHAT IS DOING ABOUT BROWN CASTING THIS LAST IS WHAT I

---

1. References are to dialogue in *Desire Under the Elms* that Macgowan was apparently censoring, in preparation for taking it on tour.
2. A London production of *The Emperor Jones*, starring Paul Robeson and directed by James Light, had recently opened to enthusiastic reviews.
3. Robert Edmond Jones was designing the masks for *The Great God Brown*.

1. Apparently Macgowan was considering a Galsworthy play after the unsuccessful run of *The Last Night of Don Juan*, which lasted only sixteen performances; but no Galsworthy play was subsequently produced, and it is impossible to determine which one was under consideration.

WORRY ABOUT AM WORKING HARD AGAIN WILL BE DOWN LAT-
TER PART NEXT WEEK PROBABLY ALL BEST.

GENE

---

46 • TO MACGOWAN FROM O'NEILL. ALS 2 pp.

Nantucket, Mass.
Sept. 28, '25

Dear Kenneth:

You needn't thank me for my wire. I meant it plumb sarcastic! In
fact, frankly, I'm feeling as disgruntled about our G.V. theatre venture as Bobby was when he hit Bermuda,—and this in spite of fine
sober, smokeless health and ideas bubbling over! (Lazarus[1] is elabo-
rately scenarioed—wonderfully, I believe—also ditto my woman play[2]
and I'm enormously excited over both—will be able to start right in
on either or both as soon as I'm unpacked in Ridgefield Also Fountain work is all done and well done, I think) So I ought to be happy
or contented or resigned about things theatrical but—

Am not! First, the Anderson opus at present succeeding in our
theatre. I've read it. It's all right—good enough stuff, turned out
well enough, meriting success—but, so it seems to me, with no
depth, not half as possible as Gold's play which has real atmosphere
and truth, and totally without significance as far as what Bobby or
you or I imagined we wanted in the theatre. Then why? Nothing
better we had the capacity or ability to produce? Then lets be honest
and either give up the ghost or give up pretending to mean anything
new or deep or significant. This start is to me worse than The
Saint—The Saint had a real idea. Late for me to be talking like this?
Maybe—but what difference would it have made when I have no actual authority in the organization except as a negotiable asset
whether I had read it before and said no or not? Bobby, according to
what he told me, never liked the play or thought we should do it.

And now a Galsworthy second-rater! What the hell are we, anyway? Why, compared to this, our first season at the P.P. was ten
years in advance of what we are now! It seems to me we're just nothing but another New York theatre. Candidly, Kenneth, I'm not in-

---

1. *Lazarus Laughed*, which O'Neill finished in 1925, was not produced until April 9,
1928, at the Pasadena (Calif.) Community Playhouse.

2. *Strange Interlude*, completed in 1927, was produced on January 30, 1928, by the
Theatre Guild.

terested in such an idea. I certainly wouldn't be interested in continuing with it next year. I'd rather go back to the P.P. The acting there might be more amateur—but so would the spirit be. We've become too professional. I think McKaig must have infected the G.V. with some of the grave mold from the Frohman office.[3]

The thing that galls me most is this—We've had "Brown" since June. "Brown" is important, we believe. Nevertheless "Brown" isn't cast yet and we don't know when it will be. Now noone can tell me that if we'd been paying half the attention to "Brown" we've been giving to all this other crap—I include in this road companies of "Desire" and recasting bickerings—we'd have had a cast for "Brown" long ago. At any rate, we *ought* to be able to do our stuff that way. If we can't it simply means we're no better than the others, and less powerful. I again say the old Provincetown idea is better. There a cast for Brown from our old group could be fixed right now and preliminary work started on masks of the cast. Perhaps the cast might not be as technically right as we'll get at the G.V. but I'm sure we'd collect more brains than Eldridge, Harrigan, etc. are liable to have. Why so much fuss about Harrigan, by the way? He may be good but the fact remains that he's been on the stage for quite a while and is still nothing much.

But no more of this beef. I'll be down and talk the rest of it in a week—leave here next Sunday—have to stop off in New London—will be in N.Y. about Wednesday.

The selections for Don Juan, except Dale,[4] I've never heard of. It requires a fine actor—two fine actors—or I feel very sorry for Rostand's ghost—and even sorrier for the G.V. for we'll get unmercifully panned.

Naturally I wouldn't permit "Brown" to go on in March or April. I believe it has a real fair success in it if done right and, if I belong in this theatre, it owes it to me to give my plays the preference in position, other things being equal. If there doesn't seem any probability of casting it adequately so it can be done by the first of the year, I'd much prefer to do it with Jimmy at the P.P. before then. If we must have poor acting lets have it there where the audience is somewhat willing to make allowances in that respect.

3. Alexander McKaig, who was serving as business manager for the Greenwich Village Theatre, had once worked for Daniel and Charles Frohman, established Broadway producers in the highly commercial Belasco tradition.

4. Possibly James Dale; but no one named Dale was in the opening night cast of *The Last Night of Don Juan.*

Eldridge's point about the mask change is no point at all it's so obvious.[5] Naturally anything so arbitrary may confuse an audience for a second but by the end of the scene they will have accepted it. It has never so far bothered anyone who read it—and lots of all kinds have up here this summer.

Well, day-day! See you soon. The crew of the good ship G.V.T. ought to have a drastic meeting then. I fear that just as the fair wind starts to blow we're liable to sink. At any rate, give an ear to my above yawp of indignant distress. I somehow feel we're going bad and have become a young organization with a brilliant past.

Gene

---

47 • TO MACGOWAN FROM O'NEILL. ALS 3 pp. (Stationery headed: Kenneth Macgowan Robert Edmond Jones Eugene O'Neill / Greenwich Village Theatre / Seventh Avenue & Fourth Street / New York City)

"Bellevue"

Paget East, Bermuda[1]

Mar. 12 [1926]

Dear Kenneth:

Have been expecting a letter from you. However, your cables have been terse and to the point and, I s'pose, have covered all the news.

5. Macgowan had sent Florence Eldridge a copy of *The Great God Brown* in an effort to interest her in playing the role of Margaret Anthony. After reading the script, Eldridge wrote Macgowan:

My dear Mr. Magowan,

The O'Neil play is tremendously interesting. I can see great possibilities in it if it is terribly well done and very clearly interpreted to those who can't see beyond the words they hear.

It seems to me almost perfect until the third act—third scene—when reality & symbolism merge to a point of (to me) confusion. But that is perhaps because I have read it only once. From the time that Brown assumes Dion's mask I become slightly bewildered.

I should like to talk to you about it. . . .

It is the sort of play I want. I've taken a solemn vow to stay away forever from "Cats & Canaries" [a thriller in which she had had great success]. There are so many who wait to earn a living in the theatre exclusively & so few who want to help it along, and I like to throw my weight on the losing side in any tug of war.

Sincerely,

Florence Eldridge

Eldridge's reservations about the play did not prevent O'Neill from seriously considering her for the role; but she was not cast.

1. The O'Neills returned to Bermuda late in February 1926 and settled at Bellevue, a twenty-five acre estate in Paget Parish.

Sixty-nine hundred doesn't sound so good for first Garrick week. Was there anything—weather or what not—to explain it? Perhaps we should have gambled on the Klaw or something really uptown? Perhaps, if possible still, we still should? The psychology of it may be that the public believes a success moves out of the Garrick but not into it. It's likely.[2]

Good old Los Angeles![3] Too bad "Desire" isn't in a real sized house there with decent prices!

Anything on Dean-Coward-London-"Brown"?[4]

Muray[5] has been down here and taken a million photos of me & us. So tell Clara[6] to get after him if she wants any for press stuff—but first let me approve! He returns on boat tomorrow.

It's strange about "Beyond T.H." There surely ought to be money for that from its fans—as a loan or gift. I can't see anyone being interested in it from the investment standpoint much.[7] You might phone Doc. Lief.[8] He has wealthy friends—Jews—who are interested in backing stuff. They would want the first money taken in—or first profits—to apply to paying their investment back first, I guess.

Will you have the bookeeper send me the gross on "Fountain" weeks? Historical interest purely! I want the figures for my morgue book.[9]

How about interesting Wolheim in an "Ape" revival for 3 weeks or 4 at the G.V. in spring when he finishes with "Glory"—if early enough. This ought to be a cash maker for the theatre, if it could be swung.[10]

2. *The Great God Brown*, after a successful five-week run at the Greenwich Village Theatre, had been moved to the larger Garrick Theatre on 35th Street. About a month later, it was moved again, to the still larger Klaw Theatre in Times Square.

3. In Los Angeles, the cast of the touring company of *Desire Under the Elms* had been arrested and forced to enact the play in court to determine whether or not it was obscene. The subsequent acquittal only increased public interest in the production.

4. O'Neill hoped to interest British producer Basil Dean and actor-playwright Noel Coward in presenting *The Great God Brown* in London; but the production never materialized.

5. Nicholas Muray, a theatrical and fashion photographer.

6. Clara A. Weiss, who worked in press relations for the Greenwich Village Theatre.

7. A revival of *Beyond the Horizon* was under consideration. Eventually, it was revived by the Actors Theatre on November 30, 1926, at the Mansfield Theatre.

8. Dr. J. O. Lief, O'Neill's dentist in New York.

9. *The Fountain* had opened at the Greenwich Village Theatre on December 10, 1925, and had lasted for 24 performances.

10. Louis Wolheim had been highly acclaimed for his portrayal of Yank in the original production of *The Hairy Ape* (1922). He also had created the role of Captain Flagg in the highly successful *What Price Glory?* by Maxwell Anderson and Laurence Stallings, which opened on September 6, 1924, and ran for 435 performances.

How is Stony Point moving?[11]

"Lazarus" is going strong! I'm going over what I've already written in the light of many new & richer notions, chiefly connected with a working out of my mask scheme. It gains significance and depth in every way daily. I'm sitting on the tops these days.

Wish I could talk this over with you. Too long to write.

You simply must come down! Must! We have a real peach of a house this time and lots of room—beautiful grounds—private beach—all at a big bargain of 150 per. It's really the nicest house I've ever seen here—or almost anywhere else—beautifully arranged as to rooms, furniture mid-Vic. somewhat but comfortable withal,—upper & lower porches, etc.—used to be one of the show places of the island, they say. Why don't you resolve to make it—with Eddy? You could, via Madden & Capt. Barlow,[12] probably get very low rates once Easter is over. It would be worth it.

Swimming every day. Much exercise. I've gained almost six pounds in the less than 2 weeks so far. Feel reborn. I was pretty low as to vitality by the time I sailed. The teeth were a final groggy blow—but I appreciate their loss on the profit side now.

Budgie[13] has accumulated the measles! Must have picked them up on the steamer somehow. Only possible place. She has one wing of this palace to herself as a quarantine island.

Outside of which we're all fine. Same to you!

Did you return Hamiltons books?[14]

Come on, you "Brown"! Daddy needs a yacht!

Gene

11. Macgowan was apparently talking with Henry Miner and Otto Kahn of "The American Operatic and Allied Arts Foundation" in Stony Point, New York. Miner had recently tried to interest Max Reinhardt in coming to Stony Point from Germany; and Macgowan may have been attempting to convince Miner to use Reinhardt's talents on an O'Neill play. In any event, there is no evidence either that Reinhardt ever came to Stony Point or that the group ever did a play involving O'Neill or Macgowan.

12. Captain of an ocean liner making regular runs to Bermuda. Richard Madden, O'Neill's agent, apparently had influence either with the steamship line or with Barlow.

13. Agnes's sister, Margery, who occasionally worked as O'Neill's secretary in Bermuda and in Ridgefield.

14. During the early weeks of 1926, O'Neill had participated in psychiatrist Gilbert V. Hamilton's research project on the sex lives and problems of married couples. In return, O'Neill, like the other participants, received free consultations with Dr. Hamilton. The latter published the results of his project in *A Research in Marriage* (1929); in 1929, Dr. Hamilton, in collaboration with Macgowan (who had also participated in the project on married couples), published *What Is Wrong with Marriage,* a popularized version of *A Research in Marriage.*

P.S. Have you some spare envelopes for this stationery? How is Nirvana going?[15]

---

48 • TO MACGOWAN FROM O'NEILL. TLS 1 p.

Bellevue,
Paget East, Bermuda,
March 15, 1926

Mr. Kenneth MacGowan,
Greenwich Village Theatre,
New York City

Dear Kenneth:

Just a line to catch this boat. I am surprised and sorry to hear that "Nirvana" only lasted three days. It certainly deserved better than that and I think it a shame for Lawson's sake it did not last. Did it get such awfully bad notices, or just what was the trouble?

I beg to remind the Directors of the Greenwich Village Theatre that they are taking a longer time to pay royalties on "Brown" than any management I have ever known, and having dealt with Arthur Hopkins, this is some statement.

I hope you will do your best to push the London production of "Brown" with Dean, and try to have a talk with Coward about it.

As for the Stony Point proposition about an option on the next three plays, it all depends. Reinhardt, Barrymore, Von Hoffman-stahl, etc., all sounds very well, but how much of it will they be able to produce? Also how much would they be willing to give me for it? With me it would be principally a question of money—and of time. You say the company will not start work until the summer of 1927? I won't say anything more about it until you have a talk with him and have written me more in detail about what the proposition would be.

Yours in a hurry,
Gene

P.S. The option on plays *might* be fine idea if you can "kid" them into offering me enough and if you're really going to be director over all—but won't this Reinhardt, von Hof. or any others of that ilk be all run as separate propositions outside your control, etc.? I don't seem to have any clear idea of the S.P. stuff yet!

15. *Nirvana* by John Howard Lawson had opened at the Greenwich Village Theatre on March 3, 1926.

49 • TO MACGOWAN FROM O'NEILL. ALS 1 p. (On stationery headed: "Bellevue" / Paget East, Bermuda)

March 25 [1926]

Dear Kenneth:

A line! I have a grand idea! Get your Stony Point people interested in options idea—then say I'm about to close with someone else but if you saw me personally—you see—trip to Bermuda in spring on Stony Point! It might work.

What is the matter with "Brown"—or is it with Garrick—or with season? Is Wilke on coast going to Frisco "Desire"?[1]

I believe Belasco will be off "Marco" on April 1st unless the fox is stalling to make me anxious.[2] How about that as first play on Stony P. option? Is there any chance getting Reinhardt on that in spite of Kummer?[3] I'm going to try out Arthur, Miller, Harris,[4] etc. Let me know anything you think or can suggest as soon as you can.

Am waiting for more from you on Stony. Still don't quite get relationship of you & permanent company to these Reinhardt, Von H. & J. Barrymore schemes.

Did Clara get after Muray on his snaps? Ought to! He ought to have some peaches! I want him stirred up so he will develope & print if he hasn't already done so, so I can get copies.

"Lazarus" coming bigger & bigger! Slow though. Have almost entirely reconstructed & rewritten 1st 2 scenes. Ten times better!

You simply must come down! It's grand here!

Gene

---

50 • TO MACGOWAN FROM O'NEILL. ALS 2 pp. (On stationery headed: "Bellevue" / Paget East, Bermuda)

April 4, [1926]

Dear Kenneth:

Perhaps there will be a letter from you on the Stony Point decision that will cross this. I am curious to know whether your deal went

1. Wilke was apparently scheduled to appear in the road company of *Desire Under the Elms* in San Francisco.

2. Belasco eventually decided not to do *Marco Millions*, feeling that it would be too costly and too great a risk.

3. Rudolf K. Kommer, Austrian journalist and translator who was Max Reinhardt's representative in the U.S. In 1923 he had been responsible for bringing Reinhardt's play *The Miracle* to America.

4. Producers Arthur Hopkins, Gilbert Miller, and Sam H. Harris. All three turned down the play.

through. They seem to take a lot of time considering things. Ask them to furnish me with a "gawgus" villa up there rent free each summer and I'll come up and participate in the theatre work provided I'm counted out of all social activities. Seriously, there's something to this, or something like it. I feel sick of all past connotations and think it behooves me to shake them—even Peaked Hill—for the next few years anyway. Bermuda is really a start on a new Tack—was last year, for that matter. The thought of going back to P'town, much as I love Peaked Hill, rather wearies me and makes me sad. The old truth is no longer true. Too many "somethin's" hide in the corners.[1] What I need for my new voyage is fresh fair winds and new ports of call. I might welcome a new scheme for the summer months that did not involve too much travel and presented an opportunity for interesting associations with new people, combined with enough water sports & outdoors.

Our home port for the next two or three years will be this here "Bellevue"! We are taking a lease on it at a thousand per—an enormous bargain as you would agree if you saw it. Agnes & I both love the house—or rather, houses! It's arranged better for our needs than any place we have ever lived in. Then again, it's not far from New York when productions go on and we expect to be here nine months out of the year, and even could stay the summer here, if put to it. So that's our latest developement for you.

Whisper! Let me knock on wood! It looks as if we'd rented Ridgefield for a decent sum for the summer! If so, I will credit the White Elephant with having one black mole, at least.

I've been lately reading von Hoffmanstahl's "Electra," Arthur Symons translation. A beautifully written thing, I think, and powerful and ought to play strikingly. Why has noone ever done it? Because the Strauss opera on it killed it? Or what? I think that it is emphatically one of the ones that ought to be done and I would be much interested in helping to do it. Marvelous speeches in it! They would take some reading.[2] Why not aim to get von Hoff. interested with us on this if he comes over—if we could cast it? At any rate, bear it

1. O'Neill is referring to Ephraim Cabot's speech at the end of part 3, scene 1, of *Desire Under the Elms*: "Even the music can't drive it out—somethin'. . . . They's no peace in houses, they's no rest livin' with folks. Somethin's always livin' with ye."
2. Austrian dramatist Hugo von Hofmannsthal's play *Elektra* (1903) was published in an English translation by Arthur Symons as *Electra* (1908). In 1909, Richard Strauss used it as the basis for an opera.

in mind for experimental production at Stony Point. To me it has wonderful possibilities for treatment. Read it again and tell me what you think. I find it the only modern play in verse that is both true poetry & true drama.

Also remember "The Alchemist."[3] I've only glanced over it but I love what I will have as the opening line of my version (to begin with strictly forewarned subscription audiences) "I fart at thee!"

McKeig evidently hasn't sent Madden any more "Brown" royalty up to last boat. Tell Alec to remember I am a Director and Directors should be paid first of all and playwrights second. Seriously, the farther behind you get the harder it is and Alec. would save a lot of bother for you & me & everyone if he would settle weekly and let someone else worry. I'm all for paying beginning at home. I hope "Bride of the Lamb"[4] is a wow.

Belasco is officially off "Marco."

Tell Clara—and for her to tell Muray—on no account to use any of Muray's except the 3 I'm sending—and they're not much. We'll get some good ones via our camera as we did last year. Muray's family groups look like Mr. & Mrs. Infra-Primate & children. He committed the crimes with a camera he borrowed down here, perhaps that's the excuse.

All our love to "you-alls."
Gene

---

51 • TO MACGOWAN FROM O'NEILL. ALS 2 pp. (On stationery headed: "Bellevue" / Paget East, Bermuda)

April 28 [1926]

Dear Kenneth:

Nevertheless, the royalty matter is acute and I am seriously peeved. I mean it! I don't think I've been getting the sort of deal I have a right to expect. No royalty from "Desire"—Coast since week ending Mar. 6th! No royalty from P.P. for "Jones" except one week and they have me on a note for 1000 which how are they going to pay? Nothing from "Brown"—which has been making money—since week of Feb 27 at G.V. two months ago! Besides which the G.V.

---

3. Play written in 1610 by English dramatist Ben Jonson (1573?–1637).
4. Play by William Hurlbut, which opened at the Greenwich Village Theatre on March 30, 1926. It was produced by Alice Brady as a starring vehicle for herself.

O'Neill with Shane and Agnes in Bermuda

owes me a thousand loan! Now where the hell do I get off at under such an arrangement? I am not Otto Kahn. I have a larger family to support, for one thing. Do you want me to begin selling the investments I made before I left N.Y. in order to pay my bills down here?[1] It is damn close to that now.

I am especially peeved at all this because I have a bug on the subject that every management should pay every author—(and particularly the G.V. with this author)—as regularly each week as they pay actors & stage hands, that royalty ought to be on the salary lists, that other debts must come after. I cannot believe, with the small royalty in dollars I get, that you have kept creditors off the doorstep only by not paying me. The sum involved per week is too small to accomplish much that way. But you have let my royalty pile up, as I warned you you would, until now it represents a real blow both for you to pay, and for me to do without. I don't blame you for this but I do blame McKaig. It is the old Grand Army game with regard to authors that he learned on Broadway with the Frohman outfit—except in this case he knows the author has no recourse whatever.

I don't want to seem hard on you, Kenneth. I know the financial worry on your shoulders, but I must still insist on my opinion that paying me weekly would not have added to that worry a damn bit, while the reverse has certainly added to my worry. I can least afford to play philanthropist just now when I'm making my first determined effort to get my own affairs stabilized so I can work steadily ahead for the next few years in peace. The amount of my income tax I have to pay in installments for last year would fair paralyze you— nearly 3000 bucks!—and yet where most of the income leaked away to is one of those enigmas. And so on.

Tell McKaig to put me on the salary list as an actor. Then paying me will be done as a matter-of-fact, without heart-ache. It is only when making good to an author that a manager feels as if God were taking back his testicles. What adds to my fury is the conviction that I'm the victim of this theatrical tradition.

I can't cheer myself hoarse over a combine with the Actors. I doubt if actors any longer respect them or want to play with them. Kahn, I think, is a two-faced tin-horn Kike whom you can trust not to double-cross you about as far as a worm can walk on its hands. A

1. O'Neill had reinvested the money he had made from the sale of some of his New London property.

complete new deal with a new deck and a new banker, that's the ideal dope! What about Stony Point? You don't mention it any more. Have you passed that up?

My advice is: Steal my royalties from the G.V., abscond on the first boat & come here! I will stake you to the fare as your collector's commission, and in spite of my professional ire will bed & feed you as if you were an honest man and not a manager.

However, joking aside, let some of the others do the waiting now for a while until the G.V. catches up with me.

All best!
Gene

---

52 • TO MACGOWAN FROM O'NEILL. ALS 2 pp. (On stationery headed: "Bellevue" / Paget East, Bermuda)

May 14th [1926]

Dear Kenneth:

A cable from McKaig arrived via phone some time since, our Semgambian[1] tells me, saying something about royalty being paid—which is cheerful news—but I assure you even before that I had decided to forgive. Pardon my impatience, in return. Not getting paid any royalty *by anyone* had gotten me as crochety as any other philanthropist.

The Actors theatre combine[2] looks fine from what you tell me. The point I felt doubtful on was whether they would put you in the saddle without loading you down with dead weight from their old organization. The idea of getting the new Channing theatre[3] sounds especially good to me. As you know, I have never been over fond of the G.V. as a theatre. One of the most important things about the new Channing, if you have anything to say about it, should be to insist on perfect acoustics. Those deaf spots are always bad work.

Why don't you amble down here on a ten day vacation once matters are set, if you're all worn out? Try to. It would be grand to see you.

1. A reference to one of the native servants the O'Neills employed in Bermuda.
2. Macgowan had proposed a merger of the Greenwich Village Theatre with the Actors' Theatre, a group unofficially sponsored by Actors' Equity, which had staged plays by Ibsen, Shaw, and Wilde on Broadway. Macgowan was to head the combined groups.
3. No theatre with this name existed in New York. O'Neill was probably referring to Chanin's 46th Street Theatre that had opened in 1925. See Letter 58 below.

"Lazarus Laughed" was finished—first draft—the 11th, but there will be lots to do on it once Budgie gets it all typed. In the meantime, I am going to get started on the lady play "Strange Interlude," if I can—and my creative urge is all for going on.

As for "Lazarus," what shall I say? It is so near to me yet that I feel as if it were pressed against my eyes and I couldn't see it. I wish you were around to "take a look" before I go over it. Certainly it contains the highest writing I have done. Certainly it *composes* on the theatre more than anything else I have done, even "Marco" (to the poetical parts of which it is akin although entirely different). Certainly it is more Elizabethan than anything before & yet entirely non-E. Certainly it uses masks as they have never been used before and with an intensely dramatic meaning that really should establish them as a sound and true medium in the modern theatre. Certainly, I know of no play like "Lazarus" at all, and I know of noone who can play "Lazarus" at all—the lead, I mean. Who can we get to laugh as one would laugh who had completely lost, even from the depths of the unconscious, all traces of the Fear of Death? But never mind—I felt that about "Brown." In short, "Lazarus" is damned far from any category. It has no plot of any sort as one knows plot. And you had better read it and I had better stop getting more involved in explaining what I can't, for the present, explain to myself.

I have many new ideas—for a play similar in technique & length to "Emperor Jones" with Mob as the hero—or villain rather!—done with masks entirely—showing the formation of a lynching mob from more or less harmless, human units—(a white man is victim of this lynching)—its gradual developement as Mob & disintegration as Man until the end is a crowd of men with the masks of brutes dancing about the captive they are hanging who has reverted (as Jones but *white*) to a gibbering beast through fear. That is, it is the same lust and fear that made him commit his crime that takes possession of them and makes them kill him in the same spirit—of enjoyment, of gratified desire. (This is a botched explanation—but you get me. Not a pretty theme—but very true! I have a fine ironic title for it "The Guilty Are Guilty.") The masks could be equally well used in a vice-versa scheme to this.

And many more new ideas. They will wait.

Your letter sounds wilted. Come down and get budding again—you & Eddy—lots of room. If it's money holds you back you can keep the passage dough back out of my royalty indefinitely and I will howl not at all!

Agnes joins in all love to all of you!

Gene

P.S. I meant to cable Clara to wait for the photos Kundren, (the steward on boat, she knows about) took. They were much better than ones I sent. Too bad.

---

53 • TO MACGOWAN FROM O'NEILL. ALS 1 p. (On stationery headed: "Bellevue" / Paget East, Bermuda)

May 28 [1926]

Dear Kenneth:

A bare line! We sail from here the 15th. Will be in and around N.Y. for about a week. Would like to invite myself out to Brewster for day or two—perhaps Aggie, too—if you'll be there then & have room. Want to duck city as much as possible. And have so much to hear & talk over.

"Strange Interlude" might be grand for Cowl.[1] At any rate, you can let her hear so. Cornell,[2] of course, would be ideal. But play can't be finished until fall. Expect to get 1st scene written before leaving here so can show you method. Am all het up over it. Also over "Lazarus," typed script of which I have been correcting & revising. Lionel[3] would be better Tiberius. Caligula in early twenties, you know—died in them. Should not be expensive scenically, way I have worked out. Needs good incidental music to be written for it. Might tell Morrow[4] if you think he's good enough. Whole raft of masks, of course, but few individual character ones.

All best!
Gene

---

1. Jane Cowl.
2. Katharine Cornell, who later turned down the role of Nina Leeds in *Strange Interlude*.
3. Lionel Barrymore.
4. Composer Macklin Marrow, who had written background music for the 1925 Greenwich Village Theatre production of *The Last Night of Don Juan* and *The Fountain*.

Bellevue,
Paget E., Bermuda,
June 3—[1926]

Dear Kenneth:

Just a line. Won't have time to answer any mail that comes by
this next boat as I believe it's a local holiday when ship gets in and
no mail distributed. We will arrive by the Fort St. George on Thursday the 17th unless something terribly unforseen occurs. If you want
to meet us and have time, fine stuff! If not, let me know somehow
where to get in touch with you at once, as I suppose G.V. is vacated
and I have no idea where the Actors Theatre–G.V. combine home
is.

Have you thought of "Marco" for the combine? If you could get
Kahn interested in script, it might be stepping off with a *daring*
foot. With the Actors, casting would be simple and I've just had an
idea that a modification of the same mask scheme I use in "Lazarus"
might make the "Marco" production even more original and distinctive. However, there is "Lazarus" and I'd let all bets rest until you've
read that. Also, for the present, Liveright[1] is "nuts" over "Marco"
and I'm suspending all hawking it about elsewhere—(Miller & Hopkins are only ones since Belasco who have said they couldn't do it.
Hampden[2] has script—and Ames[3]—but they haven't read it)—until
he finds out if he can raise the money. With him, I guess, I'd have
free hand to pick out who to direct, cast, etc.

Daring! Remember that, old Top, with this new venture! It seems
to me most emphatically a case of shooting at a star or being a dud!
The middle course also means being a dud! They will expect it of
you—us, whoever we are! (I don't even know what capacity I'm in
on it but I want to howl: Imagination, Beauty & Daring—or bust!
From a hard-headed standpoint, also, it's the only way to make a
success of it, I'm convinced!) Your program as announced isn't inspiring. Gold's play[4]—yes, late in season, provided you've knocked
'em silly first with power & beauty in the first plays or productions—

1. Horace Liveright, O'Neill's publisher.
2. Producer-actor-director Walter Hampden.
3. Producer Winthrop Ames.
4. Probably *Fiesta* by Michael Gold.

the Oklahoma play[5] (I've read it) is a good real piece of work but there's no reason why lots of other producers shouldn't do it and do it as well as you *can*. You'll never awaken them to a new vital producing principle in the theatre with that, although I think by all means you should do it. But I won't go on. More of this when I see you.

We will probably not go to Peaked Hill—at least, not until Sept. after the homos and little theatres have vacated P'town. We're bound for a lake in Maine—a camp on lake—for change. I think I may like it—canoing, fishing, rowing, tennis (of which I've played some down here) etc., etc. The place is recomended to us by Elizabeth Marbury.[6] Its high up, too, & I think I can stand a vacation from salt water for a time. I want to avoid all the P'town connotations—not that I'm afraid any more but it's no use making it harder for oneself.[7] And it would be worst time at P. Hill anyway—biting flies, much in sea by mid-July, etc. while in fall its wonderful there.

I've got a grand surprise to tell you.[8] It's neither domestic nor theatrical. In the meantime, guess about it! I promise you will be astonished—and amused!

Remember I have invited myself to visit you.

Day-day.
Gene

---

55 • TO MACGOWAN FROM O'NEILL. ALS 2 pp.
This, after living in "Bellevue"   Loon Lodge,
all winter, makes me suspect   Belgrade Lakes, Maine
God is becoming a symbolist or   July 9th [1926]
something![1]

5. Probably either *Sump'n Like Wings* or *A Lantern to See By,* by American playwright Lynn Riggs (1899–1954). Riggs, author of *Green Grow the Lilacs* (1931)—upon which Rodgers and Hammerstein based *Oklahoma!* (1943)—had recently come to New York at Macgowan's invitation.

6. Partner of Richard Madden, O'Neill's literary agent.

7. O'Neill had stopped drinking early in the year and is thinking here of his drinking companions in Provincetown, whose carousing might tempt him to fall off the wagon.

8. O'Neill may be referring here to the fact that he was to receive an honorary Doctor of Literature degree from Yale University at commencement ceremonies on June 23, 1926.

1. O'Neill drew an arrow from this sentence to the return address at the head of the letter.

Dear Kenneth:

I've been laid up with a rotten bad combination of cold in the head and sore throat for the past week—still have it—and have been feeling peevish enough to bite nails. Had just gotten started again on "Interlude," too, when it came on. Tough luck, for the damn thing seems hard to shake and keeps me from bathing and everything else. Still, it's the first bad cold I've had since around the opening of "Desire" so I suppose I shouldn't beef too much.

Your idea about Reinhardt sounds grand.[2] But will he be tempted? I doubt it. I imagine American means enormous money to him or he won't play. At any rate, try it out.

Don't waste a script in Barrymore's[3] direction unless you find out absolutely that he's definitely looking for a return from the films. Why not see if you couldn't make some team-up arrangement with Hampden? Madden says he—H—is very sore I didn't send him a script.

I don't know enough about the work of most of the men you cite to have an opinion. George Gaul[4] sounds good as an "L" possibility—Tyrone Power,[5] Conroy,[6] Hohl[7] for Tiberius—Keith,[8] Morgan,[9] Hull[10] for Caligula. Don't know Ames'[11] work—or that of any of the others except I know that if MacQuarrie[12] can play Tiberius, I can play the Virgin Mary.

What I really need to be sure of as soon as possible is, are we going to have the backing to do "L"? It simply can't be done "economically," you know that. McKaig is quite right, I think, in his estimation of its chances as written. If it were a question of sets, but it isn't. Crowds, especially when they are such an integral part of the

2. Macgowan apparently had suggested trying to interest Max Reinhardt in staging *Lazarus Laughed*.

3. Probably John Barrymore.

4. Actor who was to create the role of Reverend Light in the original production of O'Neill's *Dynamo* (1929).

5. Highly-regarded Shakespearean actor and father of the famous movie star.

6. Probably Frank Conroy.

7. Arthur Hohl.

8. Robert Keith, who had created the role of Dion Anthony in the original production of *The Great God Brown* in January 1926.

9. Probably Ralph Morgan.

10. Henry Hull.

11. Possibly Robert Ames.

12. Probably Benedict MacQuarrie, but possibly George MacQuarrie.

play-scheme as my crowds, have got to have size and volume or be absurd. Remember how vocal they are.

"Speaking of Bobby,"[13] I think it would be the wrong dope for us to urge him further. I wrote him at length from Bermuda saying how I wanted—needed is better—him for "L" etc. and I've just had a note similar to yours saying he couldn't get back before first of year and almost certainly not until long after that. Also that he feels his career is "shot," etc., and really feels his resignation is imperative for his peace of mind—not in those words but he puts it strongly. So I see nothing to do but accept what he is very evidently determined on and simply explain it on the grounds that he has to remain in Europe and isn't willing to "belong" until he can actively participate. I think to urge him further—by letters—would only make him the more obstinate. At all events, my last letter to him, referred to above, did my best. Let's wait till he "comes out of it."

The Lakes are fine and we have a good camp, good rowboat & canoe and fish abound. I had just settled down to enjoying it when this damn cold threw me out. Eugene[14] is here & Barbara[15] so we're a fat family.

Do keep me up on the financing of "L." It's important because the Guild & Hampden both want to see it—now—and if we can't swing it, I want to get in hooked up elsewhere immediately for, if I wait too long, I'll get no production next year at all,—"Marco" looking very dubious in spite of all the wonderful encomiums from Ames and others who shudder at the cost. Has Skinner[16] read "L"? Is there any latest about "Brown" on road?

All best!

Gene

P.S. Don't give too many scripts of "L" out. We want to keep "inside" talk on that down to a minimum.

---

13. Robert Edmond Jones.
14. Eugene O'Neill, Jr.
15. Barbara Burton.
16. Catholic critic Richard Dana Skinner. O'Neill and Macgowan were trying to interest religious organizations in financing *Lazarus Laughed.* In addition to the Catholics, they considered the Christian Scientists (see Letter 57 below).

Belgrade Lakes,
Maine
July 15—[1926]

Dear Kenneth:

Bobby asked me to pass the enclosed on to you. It is one of the reasons why he is "off" of our theatre—and, if the matter in the note is true—and I don't doubt most of it for I know Harrigan's[1] breed—, then who can blame Bobby for resigning? It is simply the fault of the theatre in not keeping its actors in order. I would not pay any attention to most of Leona's[2] "beef" if I didn't know the men in the cast so well. She would be pretty helpless with Harrigan running wild. Of course, I realize this happens in all plays that run long. But it shouldn't. A hard hand to check up the shows once a week is needed.

Have you sent script of "L" to Kommer? We need an answer right away. And how is the financing doing? We ought to get casting and planning right away. It's mid-July—and "L" certainly ought to be done by the first of year at latest, or not at all—much preferably by Nov. 1st or 15th.

Isn't McClintock[3] a good director? Why not consider him on "L"? Or Jimmy Light who is certainly "aces" compared to any I know and whose added self-confidence as a result of "Jones" in London and "Hamlet"[4] must have improved him immensely. And now he is "on wagon" to stay, I believe. And I know he is fine for me to work with. Perhaps, however, he too tied up down at P.P.? You see, I'm not counting on getting Reinhardt. And perhaps, except for the publicity, we wouldn't like him if we did get him.

Tell Eddy I remember I should have written to say what a fine stay I had at your place & how welcome your welcome was. But I

---

1. William Harrigan, who was playing William A. Brown in *The Great God Brown*.

2. Leona Hogarth, who was playing Margaret Anthony in *The Great God Brown*.

3. Director-producer Guthrie McClintic, husband of actress Katharine Cornell.

4. James Light had directed a 1925 Broadway modern-dress production of *Hamlet*. Produced by O'Neill's publisher, Horace Liveright, and starring Basil Sydney, it had run for 88 performances.

forgot, what with degrees & boat races & things.[5] Why don't you-alls tour across here when you go to see the children at camp?

All best!

Gene

Belgrade Lakes,
Maine
August 7 [1926]

Dear Kenneth:

My wire crossed your letter. Your wire arrived this a.m. It's hellish that everything remains so indefinite about Lazarus. It ought to be cast and the work on the masks for the crowds (so that they could be used in rehearsals of the crowds right from the start) well under way by the first of September. Otherwise, the whole thing will only be hurried and bungled as everything usually is—for you can't produce Lazarus later than the first of the year, hardly, with any fair chance of return. I feel very much as Bobby does that it's pretty hopeless to attempt to accomplish anything fine under these conditions in a theatre. I feel very discouraged about this Actors combine. Combine? As far as I can see the G.V. has been simply swallowed up by a vastly inferior, quite brainless organization! You made one grand mistake when you let them keep the name of Actors theatre and all the paraphanalia of their ridiculous letter-head staff![1] What have we gained, for Christ sake? We have no money to do any real work with, we haven't even got a theatre to plan ahead with, and we've lost our absolute control! Who has gained by this? Certainly not Bobby—if he had elected to stay in, for he would be more cramped than before. Certainly not I! On the contrary, I feel deeply humiliated by being swallowed by an organization for which I have no respect and which gives me nothing in return in the way of advantages for production of my plays! What authority have I in this "combine" of a theatre—the G.V.—which sprung from the P.P. and which my plays certainly did a big part in creating? I tell you can-

---

5. After receiving his honorary degree at Yale, O'Neill had stopped in New London for the annual Harvard-Yale crew races.

1. The Board of Directors of the Actors' Theatre, which was listed on the letterhead of the new combine, included Ethel Barrymore, John Barrymore, Laurette Taylor, John Drew, and Jane Cowl, among others.

didly, Kenneth, if it weren't for our friendship I'd be out of this Combine—script of "L" and all—as fast as I could get to the telegraph office! And what have you gained? More money, perhaps, which undoubtedly you ought to have, but no added prestige. Director of the G.V. was more than this is. And you have to beg for coin as insistently as before. So what the hell? I'm not denying the G.V. was finished financially and that something had to be done but I think we have been cheated into giving our good names for nothing, and that the wherewithal to achieve new things has not been placed at our disposal, and therefore we are doomed to artistic failure before we start—just another of those theatres a good deal inferior in possible scope to the Guild and many others.

What can be done? Well, I think if you start to raise a howl—in my name, which will let you out of the responsibility—it may have some salutary effect. Tell whoever should be told that my decision, as laid down in this letter to you, is that if the Actors Theatre, with which I am supposed to be combined for mutual benefit, cannot raise the money to insure time and material for a proper production of either "Marco" or "Lazarus" (Simonson[2] claims "M" can be done beautifully at not-too-great cost), then I feel cheated and I wish to be publicly announced as out of it, just as Bobby is.

As the Director of this new theatre, I can't see why it is up to you to shoulder the responsibility of raising the money. A Director isn't that, certainly.

And I might go on and on indefinitely, for a deep sense of "insult and injury" has been growing & brewing in my mind ever since I've realized how little we've got in exchange for the G.V. labors. I'm sick of your having to beg money from these tin-horn bastards, Catholic or Jew, for my plays. I'm sick of your submitting them to them, whose opinion is worthless. Its humiliating for you and for me. It cheapens us both and it cheapens the plays in the minds of cheap people—and the less they respect us the less money you'll ever get from them, you can bank on that, human nature being what it is. This putting my stuff up for auction in the slave-market spoils the game for me. The regular commercial managers have their lousy disadvantages but I'm not sure if they're not less insulting to one's self-respect. Certainly our dealings in a money way with the Selwyns[3]

2. Designer-producer Lee Simonson, who was on the Board of the Theatre Guild.
3. Arch and Edgar Selwyn, coproducers with the triumvirate of *Welded* (1924).

(Welded) and with Jones & Greene[4] (Fountain) proved that, compared to Kahn, say, they were generous gentlemen, good losers, and much more sincere patrons of the "best in the theatre," whatever that is. I am sure, if we were what we were, or independent, we could get backing from the commercial theatre itself for "Marco" or "L"—somewhere—perhaps not—at any rate, it would be a clean-cut business, with no favors asked.

But enough. Only it occurs to me that our progression from the P.P. to the G.V. to the Actors to—what? is not any progress toward the sort of theatre we want and should stand for but rather a reversion to show-shop Type. And like Yank in the "H.A,"[5] I question the moon above Broadway dolefully "Where do I get off at? Where do I fit in?"

And in fairness to a friend, I think you should set me free to submit "L" to the Guild now so that I may get quick action there in case, as it seems to me quite possible, you can't raise the coin at the Actors to do it. For, unless the improbable happens, "Marco" is out of it for next season and, even if you get the backing and a possible route booked for "Brown" & "Beyond," the road is too uncertain to count on for anything—in which case, with "L" tied up by contract or held up until too late for production elsewhere, I would be "in the soup." This would not be nice. Of course, it will probably not be greeted with howls of acceptance elsewhere. But there is a chance with the Guild and Hopkins and a few others.

The decision of the Catholics, I knew all along, having once been one myself. Skinner must be a dull boy—or a bad Catholic—to imagine, after he'd read it, that they'd fall. If they are not stupid, it should hit them as a flat denial of all their fundamental dogmas. So after all—! As for the Christian S.[6] I fear they will feel the same, old Top, although I'm not familiar with their particular brand of salvation-hootch. The point is that if "L" is anything, it's absolutely non-sectarian. And to the members of a sect that's more anathema than even the doctrine of a rival creed. As for Wall street, I imagine they're not good enough judges of plays or religions or what have you down there, to see it as a profitable stock gamble.

What would set me more "in the soup," in case of the failure of

4. Producers A. L. Jones and Morris Green, who in 1925 had underwritten the costs of moving *Desire Under the Elms* from the Greenwich Village Theatre to Broadway.

5. *The Hairy Ape.*

6. Christian Scientists.

an "L" production, is that there is no chance of "Strange Interlude" being ready for next season. My experience with it so far—I did most of a second scene two separate times and tore them up before I got started on the really *right* one!—is that there's going to be more work on it than on any previous one—much more—with no end to the going over & over it, before I'll be willing to call it done. If I get it—and the 1st draft of some new one—done by next June I'll think it a good year. The point is my stuff is much deeper and more complicated now and I'm also not so easily satisfied with what I've dashed off as I used to be.

Naturally, until I hit my stride—or rather found *the one* action & place for the 2nd scene—I felt rather sour (one reason why I haven't written before, but don't blame this letter on that for I'm "all set" now.) on life generally. But the swimming & boating, etc. are grand and we all love the lake. Also motoring about this interesting Maine country is pleasant. Perhaps I could do with less progeny about for I was never cut out, seemingly, for a pater familias and children in squads, even when indubitably my own, tend to "get my goat." However, they have their recompensing sides too. But I do feel that A.[7] & I could do with more real friends to talk with—especially I feel that I could for, my days of rum being, I am quite confident, over forever in this world, I rather feel the void left by those companionable or (even when most horrible) intensely dramatic phantoms and obsessions, which, with caressing claws in my heart and brain, used to lead me for weeks at a time, otherwise lonely, down the ever-changing vistas of that No-Mans-Land lying between the D.Ts and Reality as we suppose it. But I reckon that, having now been "on the wagon" for a longer time—a good deal—than ever before since I started drinking at 15, I have a vague feeling of maladjustment to this "cleaner, greener land" somewhere inside me. It is not that I feel any desire to drink whatever. Quite the contrary. I rather wonder that I ever had sought such a high-priced release, and the idea of it is (what must be fatal to any temptation!), dull and stupid to my mind now. But it is just like getting over leprosy, I opine. One feels so normal with so little to be normal about. One's misses playing solitaire with ones scales.

I have been pondering over the theatre and I have tentatively worked out a scheme that I want to put up to someone—Jimmy L.

7. Agnes.

or someone who is foot loose. This would solve for me the problem of my permanent relationship to the theatre both as writer & worker-in, and I believe might be profitable, if given a decent stake to start with. It's an idea founded upon an O'Neill repertoire and a permanent co. for chief roles as follows: Start Oct. 1st with a revival of "Anna Christie" (with Lord,[8] if possible—perhaps with last act revised, or playing alternate last acts for novelty) for three to four weeks—then "The Straw" for 2 weeks—then "Emperor Jones" 3 weeks until last week in Nov.—then opening of my new play each year whatever it was, this to run 4 wks or less if only half-liked and, if a big success, not more than 8 wks (1st of Feb) at our theatre before being moved—then an experimental new production of a[9] classic with the emphasis on the acting, for four weeks—then four weeks of either an original modern play or a revival of a modern play with the emphasis on originality of production. (This would take the season to either Mar 1st or April 1st, depending on how long my new play had run.) Then two to 3 weeks of "All God's Chillun," (with it being played on alternate nights by an all-white and all-colored cast, or some novel touch like that), followed by 4 to 5 weeks of "Hairy Ape," with a chance of getting Wally[10] that late in season. The next season would be

Beyond the Horizon	—3 to 4
Gold	—2 to 3
Great God Brown	—3 to 4
New Play	—4
Classic Revival	—4
Welded	—1
Glencairn cycle	—2
Desire Under The Elms	—4 to 5

I would work for this theatre all during summer with whoever was Director for certain hours outside my writing daily and would be at all rehearsals practically from start of season until 1st of year, by which time everything would be planned to last detail for remainder of season. New and original productions of all these old plays, in the

---

8. Pauline Lord, who had created the title role in the original production of *"Anna Christie"* (1921).

9. O'Neill deleted "foreign" here.

10. Louis Wolheim, who had created the role of Yank in the original production of *The Hairy Ape* (1922).

light of past errors, would be in order and this, together with the entirely new productions, would give the Director his chance. And the actors would certainly have theirs.

Now I may be dumb but it seems to me such a theatre would pay for itself, once given a fair start, and it is an even business proposition. Also I can see how, from it, by gradually including more of other people's plays in future years, while sticking to my proven standbys, by gradually sticking in split weeks, then a week with a different play each night, a repertory theatre might finally grow from it. And also, I feel this is absolutely—as things appear now—the only possible chance for one growing up as a self-supporting unit. And Jimmy L. I feel, is certainly the best available man for a Director (not connected with raising the money)

What do you think of this? You see, I've got to have a chance to grow in the theatre and make it grow. I've got something I ought to contribute beyond plays. This Actors Theatre promises no such opportunity—much less than I have enjoyed hitherto—and I can't help being convinced that, for me, it is a backward step. I also feel you are going to find that your absolute dictatorship will be double-crossed the moment you step on their prejudices. Honestly now, you simply *can't* believe that anything can evolve out of a theatre where the Director has to give consideration to what Francis Wilson and similar people have to vouchsave?[11] And if you think you *don't* have to give consideration to such birds if you don't want to, then just try it a few decisive times!

But that's your affair, of course, and none of my business. I merely state it as a prophecy.

No more of that stuff. I sure hope the "Brown-Beyond" Tour will go through somehow—that "Brown" will at least get a Chicago chance. Aren't Jones & Greene interested at all? Eldridge[12] or Mary Ellis[13] would be fine. Who is Clifford Sellers?[14] Helen Freeman wouldn't do. I saw her toward the end in "B.T.H." She was bad. Also, she always felt miscast and I doubt if she'd want to do it. You

11. Author, actor, and manager, Wilson was the first president of Actors' Equity and also served as president of the Actors' Theatre. O'Neill deleted "old" before "people."

12. Florence Eldridge.

13. Actress who later appeared in a 1931 London production of *Strange Interlude*.

14. Actress who had appeared as William A. Brown's mother in the original Greenwich Village Theatre production of *The Great God Brown* (1926) and as Harriet Williams in the 1925 revival of *Diff'rent*.

want the same woman for Marguerite & Ruth,[15] don't you? Hogarth would be ideal.

Sorry but I think your swell idea of a prize play is a bad hunch. Prizes are another way of becoming banal and, besides, I doubt if you'd get anything worth 2500 out of it. And it's bad advertizing, this offering prizes. It "places" you.

Here's something important. Of that 1500 borrowed from Mrs. S.[16] 1000 remains to be paid. It must be due now and I think Bogue[17] will soon be on my tail about it. Now the organization still owes me 500 advance of Gold's play and 500 of the 1000 I gave at the "Brown" opening. So will you take up this note for me with her? Undoubtedly, you can exchange a note of the New Co. for it and thus avoid paying me the 1000, which I should presently be clamoring for, and at the same time get me out of her debt. How about it? It looks to me a good solution for all of us.

The Prague—"Desire" pictures were amusing. Did the "Hairy Ape" ones ever come out in World, as you said they would?

This seems rather a tough letter to be imposing on you—but, as a friend, I know you want to know just how I feel about things.

Agnes sends her love to Eddy and the kids—and mine also—why don't one or all of you come up in the Ford to visit? Eugene Jr. & Barbara are leaving on Wednesday next.

All best!
Gene

P.S. Will you give enclosed to Clara and ask her to have B & L[18] send the lady the book she asks for and Clara send her the mimeoed data (which I haven't) she asks for?
(over)

P.S. I don't think there's a chance with Reinhardt really. If he could read English, yes—but not after it's been transposed through Kummer's cropped bean, whether his report be good or ill!

---

15. O'Neill means Margaret Anthony, the leading female character in *The Great God Brown*, who was intended to resemble Marguerite in *Faust*; Ruth Atkins is the leading female character in *Beyond the Horizon*.

16. Mrs. Willard Straight.

17. Mrs. Straight's secretary.

18. Boni and Liveright.

Brewster, Aug. 12, 1926

Dear Gene:

Well, I started out being peeved as hell over your letter, and
calmed off as I got more and more of it read, and ended up with
pretty full understanding of your angle. And also understanding how
difficult it is for you in Maine to understand the true in'ards of the
new layout. I want to try to cover all you've written about, but I'll
start on some of the things you don't start with.

To start at the beginning, any kind of producing on the lines
we're interested in costs money and is pretty risky. The Guild is the
only one that has got by, and it has done this by having a theatre
(the Garrick) for $25,000 a year that they ought to have paid forty
for, and by exploiting the foreign plays that had already proved
themselves, and by generally skinning pretty close to the line that
just divides the desert of bunk from the sown. Saddled with the two
disadvantages of being downtown and not having enough capital
we've lost money on everything but "Desire," "Brown," "Fashion,"
"Love for Love," & "Bride of the Lamb." And we lost enough on the
others to show a deficit on them all. We've got things down mar-
velously economical now, but it's a damned risky game anyhow. This
is all babytalk, I know, but I put it down.

Now where are we with the Actors' Theatre? You object to the
name and the letterhead staff. I don't give a damn about the name;
I never did about the G. V. or the P.P. What we did was the only
thing that mattered; and that will hold this year. Taking the A. T.
name is just the way to get the A. T.'s finances. The letter head staff
means nothing either. Or the most it means is that if 36 actors can
make up their minds to abolish the A.T. by firing me they can do
so. There is going to be no question of who runs this theatre, because
I've had just enough of three hellish seasons of worry and struggle to
make me extremely ready to spit in anyone's eye and go off in the
woods and enjoy myself. And that's exactly what I'm going to do if
I meet up with any trouble. The plain fact of the matter about the
staff is that just one employee of the old A. T. remains—the book-
keeper who borrows money at the banks. The rest is G. V.

As for advantages from the A. T. First of all, instead of starting
a season on a capital of $7500, we've started on a capital of $50,000,
all got together in May and June, and I feel sure of $35,000 more
in September, October and November. I shall have to do some work

on this, but that is the price of control. If Digges[1] or Duncan[2] or one of the old directors of the A. T. had been responsible for getting the money in, he could have bossed the ranch. My advantage here, too, is that raising the money for the A. T. is about a third the trouble it was for the P.P.-G. V. because Wilson, and a lot of other people got 75 or 80 men in the habit of writing a thousand dollars for the theatre into their charity lists every year.

Now what shape are we in to operate this year? We haven't hired a theatre yet, but only because we're trying to get the right one at the right price. Right in size and not saddled with a useless profit to the owner. We could have the Little[3]—an ideal house—for $60,000 net, which means $75,000 without the staff, but a 600-seat house isn't worth that. The same for Chinan's new house.[4] The Shuberts offered the Bijou[5] or the Forty-Ninth[6] for $60,000 for 30 weeks everything in, but I think Lee[7] will make better proposition when he gets back from a sick spell in the Adirondacks. Meanwhile the Guild is dickering over the Garrick. Personally I doubt that we ought to do Lazarus in so small a house as any of these. We need a small house for all the rest, but Lazarus needs the feel of a bigger place and the whole thing ought to be scaled for a big public. So the question of what house L gets is a question of the ordinary booking business six or eight weeks before production.

For the rest, we are set to be able to do five plays at an average production figure of $7500 to $10,000 with $7500 or $5000 ready for running losses. Five shows at $15000 each—$75000. If Lazarus was something short of $50,000 then it would go in without a question. But obviously it's got to have a lot of money spent on it and this money has got to be found outside, which is just what would have happened at the G.V. or would happen with any theatre of ours. If you want to put your plays out in large form, then the risks

1. Actor-director Dudley Digges, a director of the Actors' Theatre before the combine.

2. Augustin Duncan. He had created the role of Curtis Jayson in O'Neill's *The First Man* (1922).

3. The Little Theatre, 238 West 44th Street, opened in 1922 and owned by Winthrop Ames.

4. Chanin's 46th Street Theatre, 226–36 West 46th Street, opened in 1925 and owned by the Chanin Construction Company.

5. The Bijou Theatre, 209 West 45th Street, opened in 1917 and owned by J. J. Shubert.

6. There was no 49th Street Theatre in New York in 1926; Macgowan may be referring to the 48th Street Theatre.

7. Lee Shubert, producer and theatre owner.

for you as well as for any theatre—and the delays—are going to be considerable. There's Marco to prove it. If the plays were hokum and still had your rep behind that would be different. But in any case a huge production with a hundred and twenty people doesn't slip onto the American stage very quickly or easily. This, obviously again, is babytalk.

Where to get $50,000 and up for Lazarus. I'll grant the Catholic angle was pretty hopeless and the Christian Scientists will probably be as bad. The Reinhardt hunch is the best, because that will automatically bring in Kahn and money to spare. Kommer hasn't cabled yet, however; I suppose on account of that Salzburg festival. Our own guarantors may come through along with Griffis,[8] who has backed McClintic. They've been away vacationing, but three of them are in town Friday and I have appointments with them.

Now where do you get off? I know, of course, that you've got to have some play running to keep the wolf off. I think the Beyond revival and the double tour can be negotiated, I'll know that Friday (Eldridge will play in both, she wired me). (And Ralph Morgan could play Beyond for four weeks, then we'd have to replace.) The Guild would grab Lazarus I'm sure, and they can afford to. But do you relish having Moeller[9] direct it? I just throw out that disquieting idea because the A. T. has got to have Lazarus. It can't string you along indefinitely on it, though any other management would pay an advance, talk about dates and then look round for the money or for partners to split in, and probably do a Belasco[10] on you at the end. I think you ought to give me two weeks to round up a production. If I can't do it by then, sell Lazarus to the Guild. (Incidentally Helburn and Wertheim and Moeller, too, I think, along with Simonson are abroad).[11]

You ask—to shift to another point—what authority have. You have just as much as with the G.V. That was always my dictatorship in the end. You insisted on one-man control when we first talked

8. Investment banker Stanton Griffis.

9. Philip Moeller, who directed most Theatre Guild productions and was later to direct the original productions of *Strange Interlude* (1928), *Dynamo* (1929), *Mourning Becomes Electra* (1931), *Ah, Wilderness!* (1933), and *Days Without End* (1934).

10. David Belasco had dropped his option on *Marco Millions* after holding it more than a year.

11. Theresa Helburn, Maurice Wertheim, Philip Moeller, and Lee Simonson were all members of the Board of the Theatre Guild.

P.P., and we managed to get along in pretty close harmony in spite of that. This is the state of affairs with the A. T. What advantage do you get as a playwright? Besides more say-so on every element, physical and time, in production, you get a chance at a better cast than at the G. V., and you get a play hitched up in such a way that it can run along and turn royalties in to you without doing a land-office business. If the same actors had played Brown for Harris,[12] or Desire, either, it would have run about half as long. You know how Welded folded up when it was playing at a figure that the G. V. could have made profitable. And if Welded had run along we could have fixed up the production and the lights and pulled the acting into better shape. But if you honestly think you aren't getting enough of a break to make it worth while helping this theatre to live, then I can't beg you to help it.

For myself, I'm getting tired, but I do see that from the abortive idealism of our first attempts at the P.P., we've worked slowly towards more rep., more money, and a chance in a year, I think, to have the opportunity of moving steadily into real repertory.

It might be done with the scheme you outline. Then again—Eight productions a year, most of them new, will cost a heap. There may be an angel to finance them. But Jimmy won't find him. I'm for a new O'Neill and a revived O'Neill each year, and three or four new Americans, and, if fortune smiles, a revival too. Barring the high cost of Lazarus, we can start this season and work it more and more repertory-like as we go along.

But Jimmy! Well, I may as well spill my spleen on him! Intelligent, yes. But, in my humble opinion, and judged by us and not by Woods,[13] Harris and Golden,[14] a total loss as a director or a stage director. He's done things over pretty well—watched. That means Emperor, Hamlet (which he saw in London), S. S. Glencairn. The rest is silence. He hasn't got vitality and power and he's sloppy and irresponsible and incapable of inspiring confidence. Look at the P.P. this year if you want a sample. He's got just one virtue—I'm still judging him from a real standard and not by comparison with the Broadway sisters—you could boss the life out of him. Gosh! I feel better for saying all that.

---

12. Producer Sam Harris.
13. Producer A. H. Woods.
14. Producer John Golden.

And now let me say something for old Francis Wilson. He *is* 72, but if anybody's got any more admiration for you, and if anybody ever stood up better for Desire to the dear old conservatives, I don't know him.[15]

The $1000 has been on my conscience for some time. It's part of about $9000 unpaid bills left from the G. V. I've been trying to fix up the A. T. legally so that we could pay off about half of these, and fund the rest onto some kind of benefit in the fall. The A. T's old lawyer has been away vacating for about four weeks, and we're due to sit down with him Wednesday and work this out.

There wasn't any enclosure in your letter for Clara to tend to. The envelope had been re-sealed by the Post Office so maybe it fell out. Do you remember who the lady was and what she wanted.

We've had three good plays—or good plays in the making come in lately. A dramatization of the Negro novel of Charleston called "Porgy."[16] A play about the apple pickers of California by Totheroh,[17] who wrote Wild Birds. A tragedy of Minnesota farm life, with a fine situation and good characterization spoiled by too much plot and "theatre."

The managers are frightfully leary about the Road (they're leary, too, about Broadway, and aren't starting in August this year). I can't find any enthusiasm to risk Brown out. We've got to do it ourselves with some outsider like this Griffis man. Helen Freeman came back yesterday, and talked about Beyond with her. Frankly. I said that Ross,[18] who wanted to put up the money, liked her, but that I was sure you wouldn't see her in it, and she said she didn't think she could play the beginning now, anyway. She hinted at a desire to team up with me in directing it. Mary Ellis wished herself out. I think Eldridge very much the best bet—a perfect temperament for it, not so good for Margaret, but not bad. Clifford Silers[19] played the other girl in Diffrent. She's worked into Brown pretty well.

Well, between your letter, and mine, and a sultry day culminat-

15. As president of Actors' Equity, Francis Wilson had supported Macgowan's proposal of a citizens' play-jury to decide whether or not *Desire Under the Elms* ought to be closed. See Letter 29 above.

16. *Porgy*, by DuBose and Dorothy Heyward, was produced by the Theatre Guild in 1927.

17. Possibly *The Breaking of the Calm*, by Dan Totheroh.

18. Probably Sidney Ross, who, in 1927, coproduced Noel Coward's *The Marquise* with Macgowan.

19. Clifford Sellers.

ing in a thunderstorm as I write, I feel pretty groggy and disgusted with existence. The only spark is your news that Strange Interlude is striding along. The weather will be fine now that the lightening has landed, and maybe our own little thunderstorm will leave things clearer. I hope to God it does. If it doesn't there isn't much in the theatre life to sit up for.

As ever,

P.S. There's something terribly deadening in the way time and troubles, even though they get passed through, can eat into patience and courage and people that have worked together with so much in common as Bobby and you and I.

---

59 • TO MACGOWAN FROM O'NEILL. ALS 4 pp.

Belgrade Lakes,
Monday
[After August 12, 1926]

Dear Kenneth:

All right, old Top! The Ayes have it! Still and all, my principal grudge remains—against this or any other old theatre—this particularly because I belong to it which I assure you I wouldn't to any other—that we ought to be able to start work on "Lazarus Laughed" far enough ahead, with the full certainty of where, how, when & with whom. Such a play demands that from any producer. (Belasco was going to give it to "Marco," no? I mean, when he meant business.) If we'd been able to start as soon as I got back we'd have had six months (or five) to work on masks, etc. *knowing* "L" would be the second bill or third bill. I'm not claiming under the circumstances it *was* possible. But it ought to be where such a play is concerned. And you know as well as I that no theatre in America will be worth bothering one's bean about until such a step in advance can be made for it is obvious that without that step nothing new or old can be done except in the established hit-or-miss way. I give you two examples from our past. Do the masks in "Brown" do what the script requires of them? They do not. They only get across personal resemblance of a blurry meaninglessness. Whose fault? Noone's! Not enough time to see them. Perhaps the result the script calls for is impossible to attain by the method by combination masks the script describes. I think I see this now. With more time on masks in their proper lighting, I—we—would have seen it then. Then again, "Desire." Has it ever been produced as I wrote it? Never! (I'm leaving acting out of this dope, as a necessary uncertainty). There have never been the elm trees of my play, characters almost, and my acts were chopped up into four distinct scenes through lack of time to get the changes perfected in black-outs, the flow of life from room to room of the house, the house as character, the acts as smooth developing wholes have never existed. You know this.

Now these two plays were well done, as things go. But if you are "getting tired" of conditions in the show-shop from your end as a director, I am certainly getting God damn tired of them—of eternally putting up with inexcusable—in the sense of avoidable in a true theatre with more time and preparation—*approximations* to what I've written. Put yourself in this playwrights position. I stand for the playwright's side of it in this theatre. What's the use of my trying to get ahead with new stuff until some theatre can give that stuff the care and opportunity it must have in order to register its new significance outside of the written page in a theatre? It makes me feel hopeless about writing except for my own satisfaction in a book. (and, as in the old past, never going near rehearsals or taking any interest—except financial—in the production). What I want now— when I'm able and eager for it—is a theatre I can give my best to in every way. I'm sick and tired of old theatres under old conditions, of new theatres handcuffed by old conditions, of "art" theatres with fuzzy ideals and no money or efficiency—in fact, of *the* American theatre as it exists. I've had exactly ten years of it as a playwright— considerably more than your three as director—and my ambition to see my stuff performed on any stage I know (never very avid!) is beginning almost to cease, and this at a time when I *know* I have most to give to a theatre.

I write the above principally to a friend, a good deal to a co-idealist and fellow-worker, hardly at all to the director of a certain old (G.V., P.P, A.T. what matter?) theatre. So don't get your managerial back up! From your angle, you might kick in almost the same words. We are both tired. And no wonder. But where I claim the right to be especially concerned is that "Marco" has already passed by the few who might do it even adequately, that the theatre I'm in can't do it at all, that "Laz" is uncertain, that I'm deep in a new one even more difficult, if not so costly, that still more difficult ones— except for a *new* theatre—are in my brain, and that, looking this over, it seems I as an artist have a lot to "view with alarm."

My objection to *your* position is most certainly *your own*. You are—and have been, except a little that 1st P.P. year—not getting any chance to give what you have to give toward a new theatre, you are not getting any chance to work creatively with me in the art of the theatre, to dream and plan the executing of dreams, you are not becoming what I urged you—(how you must bless my interference there, at times!) to take over the P.P. & dictatorship for, you are being forced into the job of a manager instead of a European director, it seems to me, and I hope you can give me credit for being unselfishly resentful against conditions because of this in addition to my resentment against them on my own account.

And therefore your postscript is unjust, I think. "Time & troubles" have not affected my courage as a playwright and are hardly liable to, and although my patience frequently bogs down it has an elastic quality yet. And my feeling for you and confidence in you as a co-worker for and in a new theatre remains as unsinkable as of yore, and then some! So what have you? All I ask is that we be able to work together and let someone else do the roll top desk stuff. And *all* I ask in addition is new actors, new directors and a new theatre for my new plays to be worked by and with!!! Surely a simple matter! There must be a Maecenas somewhere in the U.S. if we could but find him who would have the faith and generosity to gamble artistically for a few years on my new plays & revivals of old ones as a basis and give us the chance to start clean, clear of old people & old conditions, and "do our stuff." I may be a fool but I believe in this. I believe if we knew how to go after this opportunity, we'd find it. (Baker found Harkness)[1] In fact, I don't believe much in anything in the theatre but this dream. It is this theatre I'm writing for.

Consider "the thunderstorm" over. If it has brought back a little ozone of our old idealism, it was a good one. It has to me.

Why don't you try and get up over a week-end? Bar Harbor X'press—sleep & you're here at 8 a.m. Great fishing, swimming, canoeing, rowing—golf course ¼ mile off only. Plenty of room now. Eugene & Barbara gone.

Luck!
Gene

1. Professor George Pierce Baker, in whose "47 Workshop" O'Neill had studied at Harvard in 1914–15, had recently moved to Yale to head a newly formed drama department. Edward S. Harkness, an heir to the Standard Oil fortune, had given Yale one million dollars for a new theatre center.

P.S. Who do you think of for directing "Lazarus" if Reinhardt out?

(over)

P.S. I think your idea of 50000 or over for "Lazarus" is not necessary. Seems to me it should not cost more than 25000 to get on—sets severely simple, costumes are inexpensive, depend a great deal on arbitrary lights. The running expenses of crowds will be high, of course, but the play will be on a week before this starts. Will masks be very expensive?

We don't want any "spectacular," as such is usually termed, quality to this. A severe simplicity of outline, a formalized grouping—no hint of excess—if you get me, it's hard to explain.

If "Fountain" only cost 18000 to get on—

---

60 • TO MACGOWAN FROM O'NEILL. WIRE 1 p. (1926 SEP 3 PM 12 30 / BELGRADE LAKES ME 3 1200P)

KENNETH MACGOWAN
ACTORS THEATRE 45 WEST 47 ST NEWYORK NY

IMAGINE REINHARDTS PLANS ARE COMPLICATED BECAUSE HE MUST DO SOMETHING FOR GEST[1] STOP GEST WOULD SEE TO IT THAT LET US OUT STOP ADVISE YOU CABLE HIM I CANNOT WAIT THAT LONG ON SUCH AN INDEFINITE POSSIBILITY STOP YOU KNOW I CANNOT STOP HAVE YOU GOT BACKING FOR IT YET STOP THIS MUST BE DECIDED AT ONCE REGARDS

GENE

---

61 • TO MACGOWAN FROM O'NEILL. WIRE 1 p. (1926 SEP 12 PM 8 25 / BELGRADE LAKES ME 12)

KENNETH MACGOWAN
ACTORS THEATRE 45 WEST 47 ST NEWYORK NY

DO NOT PAY MUCH ATTENTION TO LATTER PART OF LETTER I MAILED YOU YESTERDAY THIS WAITING GAME HAS GOT ME ON EDGE WRITE ME WHAT YOU THINK OF REINHART PROBABILITY NOW ALL BEST

GENE

1. New York producer Morris Gest, who had worked with Reinhardt and had produced the highly successful production of *The Miracle* in 1924.

62 • TO MACGOWAN FROM O'NEILL. WIRE (autograph version) 2 pp.
(Received at 430 PM 9 28 1926 / Belgrade Lake Me 3 30 PM)

KENNETH MACGOWAN BREWSTER NY

GOOD NEWS ABOUT DANCHENKO[1] HOPE HE CAN ARRANGE DO IT
AS PICTURE HE CAN HAVE IT FOR MOSCOW TELL FITZI I HEARTLY
APPROVE BERKMAN[2] AS TRANSLATOR BUT SHE MUST NOT SEND
SCRIPT UNTIL I HAVE FINISHED REVISION. I LIKE HOGARTH BETTER
THAN ELDRIDGE ESPECIALLY IF BROWN IS TO BE DONE LATER BY
SAME COMPANY WILL TALK THIS OVER WHEN YOU COME. AS PER
YOUR LETTER WILL EXPECT YOU EARLY NEXT WEEK WIRE WHEN
MEET YOU BELGRADE ALL REGARDS

GENE

---

63 • TO MACGOWAN FROM O'NEILL. ALS 1 p.

Belgrade Lakes,
Maine
Friday
[October 1926?]

Dear Kenneth:

Here's a proposition: I've applied for 2 tickets for Yale-Dartmouth
game, New Haven, Oct 16th (my birthday, by way). Why don't you
plan now take day off, go with me? I'll be in N. Y. Thursday a.m.
on same train you took, I expect. We could leave N.Y. Sat. a.m.—
see game (which ought to be one of high spots of year)—stay New
Haven evening, see Baker & his theatre, take up "Marco" with him
if we decide to, at any rate see what he says about any plans for it.[1]
It would be good outing and at same time we'd be getting something done. What say? Perhaps I won't get tickets but guess I will,
all right. Old Doc. O'Neill, the Yale grad, has his rights![2]

1. Vladimir Nemirovich-Danchenko, Russian director who had split off from the Moscow Art Theatre and was apparently interested in doing a Russian production of *Lazarus
Laughed.*
2. Alexander Berkman,, Russian expatriate intellectual and anarchist, who was also a
translator. Mary Eleanor Fitzgerald (Fitzi) had worked with Berkman on the anarchist publication *The Blast* before coming to the Provincetown.

1. O'Neill hoped to interest George Pierce Baker in producing *Marco Millions* for the
opening of Yale's new Harkness Theatre in December 1926.
2. Reference is to O'Neill's honorary Doctor of Literature degree from Yale.

See you Thursday a.m.

Gene

P.S. When you stop at Harvard Club will you ask them if they've reserved room for me from Thursday a.m.? Am writing them but want make sure. Don't make special trip but if you happen in.

See if you can stir up any definite dope on Tiffany films. Their man came—attractive offer in some ways.[3]

---

64 • TO MACGOWAN FROM O'NEILL. ALS 2 pp.

Hamilton, Bermuda
Dec. 7th [1926]

Dear Kenneth:

Glad to get your letter. It looks hopeful for "Beyond," if the right theatre can be got. Here's hoping to Gawd! I still think it was bad dope not to have got the Mansfield at a two dollar top, if possible.[1] I think we'd be getting them in droves. The criticisms were better than I expected. Even Smart Alec on the loud basoon![2]

The news from Chicago sounds good.[3] I'm hoping for more of it on the next mail. Let them understand, however—you might tell Madden this too—that if the bonus thing goes through I don't want it paid until after January 1st. Income tax, get me?

I was tickled to see that the critics gave you credit for quitting the Actors on a high spot.[4]

The steamer schedules to here are all scrambled—only one boat a week, irregularly. So watch that.

We're still sort of living in trunks, half unpacked. Our smaller house is ready but our furniture isn't. But we'll be in soon. We're

3. Tiffany Film Company may have expressed interest in purchasing movie rights to an O'Neill play or plays.

1. The Actors' Theatre revival of *Beyond the Horizon* had opened at New York's Mansfield Theatre on November 30, 1926.
2. Alexander Woollcott's favorable review of *Beyond the Horizon* appeared in the New York *World*, December 1, 1926, p. 17.
3. The Goodman Theatre in Chicago had apparently expressed interest in producing *Lazarus Laughed*.
4. Macgowan had resigned as producing director of the Actors' Theatre during the week preceding the opening of *Beyond the Horizon*. He was succeeded by Guthrie McClintic.

all fine—in health. Agnes has received bad news about her father. His condition is much more serious than they had thought—can't get him into my old T.B. Alma Mater.[5] Will have to be a bed patient, for a long time, at best. She is very worried.

I'm starting to go over "Marco M" for publication. Hard to work, as unsettled as we are now. Want to go over "Laz," then. Then on to "Strange Interlude." With all that's inside me now I ought to be able to explode in that play in a regular blood-letting by the time I get to it.

Any little errand? Yes, while I remember it—and much obliged. Enclosed is a card and a check. Have the same roses sent to Carlotta,[6] 20 East 67th to get to her on Christmas a.m. Don't forget this now, old top! I rely on you.

All best!
Gene

---

65 • TO MACGOWAN FROM O'NEILL. ALS 2 pp.

Spithead,
Warwick, Bermuda
Thursday
[December 1926]

Dear Kenneth:

Well, here we are—stopping temporarily at a cottage near our place, the smaller house of which is not quite ready for occupancy yet nor the furniture for it yet arrived. Our Spithead will be a wonder of a spot once it's done.[1] It's ideal for me. I've been in swimming every day and the sea is the same old sea.

Yet I'm not what you could call perfectly at peace with God. The two days voyage was a beautiful little minor hell. The high cost of living seemed horribly exhorbitant. One was tempted to refuse to

5. Gaylord Farm Sanitorium in Wallingford, Connecticut, where O'Neill had been a patient from December 24, 1912, until June 3, 1913.

6. Actress Carlotta Monterey, whom O'Neill had first met in 1922 and with whom he had become reacquainted in the summer of 1926, when she was a guest at the home of Elizabeth Marbury in Belgrade Lakes, Maine. He had continued to see Carlotta at her New York apartment in October and November, while he was in town overseeing rehearsals of *Beyond the Horizon*.

1. Early in 1926 the O'Neills had bought a two-hundred-year-old house on Little Turtle Bay and were restoring it.

pay the bill. I envy those simple souls to whom life is always either this *or* that. It's the this *and* that, the this-that desire,—more than desire, need!—that slow-poisons the soul with complicated contradictions. Vague? Well, you get me, I hope. But be silent about what you get, I need not warn you. And do not mistake my nebulious cries for whinings. Beauty, either here or there, is worth whatever price one has to pay for it, here or there. Yes!, as friend Lazarus says. Oh very much so!

Your wire about "Beyond" was encouraging. Let's hope the business will keep step.

Be sure and have Clara have Muray send me those photos of me as soon as possible. I liked them so much and I'm anxious to have Agnes see them. She is fine. So are the heirs. And it is good to be home again. And lucky I left when I did—for I love her and them and my home and nothing could ever take their place—but oh Christ, there are also other things—"on the other side of the hills"[2]—the curse of being an extremist is that every ideal remains single and alone, demanding all-or-nothing or destruction.

Oh balls! "What haunted, haunting ghosts we are."[3] Pardon my getting maudlin. But it relieves me to tell someone—I mean not someone but that rare privilege, a friend.

Let me know about Chicago—and anything you may hear. Are the gossips on my trail? I am a poor intriguer. Everything I do always seems—for the moment—so proudly right I never dream of concealments.

Try to get me a letter as soon as you've leisure. One ship is laid up now and for the next 2 weeks there's only one mail per.

And try and get down!

All best!
Gene

---

66 • TO MACGOWAN FROM O'NEILL. TLS 1 p.

Hamilton, Bermuda,
December 16, 1926

Dear Kenneth,

Just a note in answer to your own. Never rely on Madden to write fully about what I want to hear about. I have a long letter from him

2. O'Neill is referring here to his developing infatuation with Carlotta Monterey.
3. A line of Dion Anthony's in act 2, scene 2 of *The Great God Brown*.

but it is mostly play-agents rhetoric, and he fails to mention anything about "Beyond" except the gross for the first week. I judge from your note that Ross and you are taking it over from the Actors Theatre and bringing it to the Bijou. How this all came about I don't know, but more power to your arm.

Here's something in which you can be of the greatest help to me. The First National Bank and Trust Company of Ridgefield are again after me to reduce the $20,000 mortgage on Ridgefield to 10, being forced, as they claim, to do this because of a recent ruling of the Federal Reserve Bank of New York, in which the limit of mortgages to be taken by member banks should not exceed 10 percent of its capital and surplus. In their particular case the limit is $10,000 they say. Will you tell Ross that if he ever wants to do me a good turn this is the time. Could he not do something about this for me in the way of advice as to who would take over the entire mortgage from this bank?

It is a first rate investment, paying 6 percent, as you know, and we could have raised the mortgage to 25,000 if we had wanted to at the time we took it out. It is a Mr. Davis, the Vice President and Cashier, who has been taking this matter up with me direct, and Harry Weinberger knows all the details of the mortgage.

Madden's letter to Gering[1] is so verbose that I have a hard time getting the exact drift of it. It seems to be about my making an agreement with them that Reinhardt must take over $5,000 worth of their scenery and wardrobe. It seems to me that this is not anything that I can do anything about. Any arrangement of this kind would have to be made with Reinhardt, and I suppose he would not be willing to make it until he had seen their production—although if as I gather from Madden Bel Geddes[2] is to design the Chicago sets I suppose Reinhardt would be agreeable. You can explain this both to Gering and Reinhardt. If Madden attempts to explain it we are all going to have to hire lawyers to decode his explanation. I wish you would write me about this. I don't think Madden understands what it is all about, so don't rely on him to give me any information or on me to take any direct action on the kind of information he does give.

1. Marion Gering, who was apparently scheduled to produce and direct the Goodman Theatre production of *Lazarus Laughed*. It never materialized.
2. Norman Bel Geddes, who had designed the American production of *The Miracle* for Max Reinhardt.

The water is grand and the kayak has just arrived. I am almost finished going over "Marco Millions." I am about to start on "Lazarus," and all is pipping with Pippa. Will you send me any "Lazarus" script you can get hold of.

Have you any ideas to make now that the Cohen[3] thing is off? How about Patterson, McNutt and Mitchell?[4]

Yours,
Gene

P.S. Don't "understand" in your letters. They are read not only by me![5]

---

67 • TO MACGOWAN FROM O'NEILL. TLS 1 p.

[December 1926]

Dear Kenneth:

Just a line in much haste in answer to your last. I hope you got the script O.K. and liked what I had done to it. I am sorry—somewhat—about the snag about Hale,[1] although I am by no means sure he could do anything with it. I feel the same about Chalmers[2]—a bit more optimistic about him, however. Has he read the play? As for Didur,[3] isn't he the bird with the Polish accent? Not so good! Has anybody even tried to see Chaliapin?[4] Or get him to have the play read to him? I still have a hunch in his direction. Why not have the part of Laz translated into fine Russian—by Bulgakov,[5] say—and let Chaliapin do it in his own tongue, rest of cast in English? It would be a wonderful strange effect. And as far as most of an average audience understanding what Lazarus means, why it would probably be a lot clearer to them in Russian! Does this sound like pessimism?

3. Possibly either producer Harry I. Cohen or producer Albert J. Cohen.
4. Producers Patterson McNutt and Charles E. Mitchell.
5. O'Neill is cautioning Macgowan not to divulge anything in his letters regarding O'Neill's relationship with Carlotta Monterey, as Agnes Boulton O'Neill read Macgowan's letters.

1. Probably singer-actor Richard Hale, who had played the title role in the Provincetown Players' 1926 production of *Orpheus*.
2. Thomas Chalmers, then playing Andrew Mayo in the revival of *Beyond the Horizon*.
3. Polish actor-opera singer Adamo Didur, who was then a member of the Metropolitan Opera Company.
4. Famed Russian opera singer Feodor Chaliapin, who was also an exceptionally fine actor.
5. Playwright, producer, and director Michael Bulgakov.

Well, it is and I am. No director in the world can make anything of my play but a horrible, humiliating fizzle—for me!—until the right Lazarus is found. Any other supposition is only the usual blind theatrical-game hoping for a miracle where there is plainly no god. I do not, frankly, look forward to this Chicago thing with any confidence except in your ability to get the best out of what's at hand. I know you will do this. But, between us, I am hellish sorry I need that five thousand so badly—that Ridgefield didn't sell—for I'm terribly afraid it's going to be a five thousand I may regret for a lifetime. Not that I doubt Gering or anyone. But without a great Laz, what have you?

Yes, make-up like a mask, might do for Caligula, etc.—but it would have to be better make-up than I've ever seen.

Try to keep "Beyond" on at the Princess or somewhere—Mayfair[6]—anywhere rather than close. IT's damned important.

How about Walter Huston for Tiberius?

Again I implore, give the Chaliapin thing a chance without taking for granted agents tales about him. The play, you know, might get him to agree to much that his agents, working on a percentage of what he gets, wouldn't like to see him do. I'd rather have him do the part in Russian a hundred fold than anyone else in English

Gene

P.S. Why don't you try get down here consultation mid-way rehearsals—get them to pay your fare—or I would. This is good dope.

---

68 • TO MACGOWAN FROM O'NEILL. TLS 2 pp.

Hamilton Bermuda
Dec. 30 [1926]

Dear Kenneth:

Your letter with the news about the new Gering arrangement I had proposed, going through all right was welcome. I had begun to think from Madden's silence that the deal was all off—and I sure hated to see that five thou. get away from me, what with the high cost of renovating houses in Bermuda. I hope there will be no further hitch

6. Both New York theatres.

Now here is something that is damned important—*damned* important! I have been laboring for the past two weeks like hell on "Lazarus" and I have made what are very grave alterations and cuts—especially in the first scene which I have taken out of the Bible—all the Saint John Gospel stuff out, etc—and most of Lazarus talk, relying on a few sentences of his and his laughter. The scene has now, I think, real mystery and power—is much shorter, of course. It was always, to my mind, the weakest in the play. There was too much in it that reminded one of a regular Biblical play—a bad start for Laz. I have also paid particular attention throughout to getting the chants of the Chorus and Crowd into a more definite sound pattern. And I have cleared up Caligula at the end and trimmed all the loose ends throughout. It is now, I think, a much better play. But you know me when I get after my own stuff—after I've had time for perspective and you will know what to expect. Now this new script *must* be used for the Chicago production. So will you have Madden cable me the moment they sign the contract and I will get this script off to you by the first boat thereafter. I don't want to send it until I am sure they are on. I have only the one. When you get the script will you have copies made at once? They will have to be done by a damn good careful stenographer, and the copies gone over afterwards for errors. How about that girl who used to be at the Actors office? At any rate, put someone you can trust on it, who will take an interest and be absolutely accurate. I am so tired of getting scripts through Madden that are full of the most absurd errors afterwards. I have to go over them line for line—its as much of a job as typing them myself. And hang on to the script when you get it as you would your life. I would go entirely nuts if anything happened to it after the hard work I have put in on it. Send two scripts to me. Let the Chicago crowd get their own made. Send one at once to Kommer to show Reinhardt, and give one to Fitzie to send Berkman for his Russian translation.

I am intending to start work on "Strange Interlude" tomorrow—the 31—hunch—one year on the wagon, my boy! I am going to drink fifty lime squashes watching the new year in and, at least, put my lunch in memory of the good old days.

It is good news about "Beyond." I sure hope it holds up and runs along. As for The Straw and Pauline Lord, that sounds like a damn good idea, if you can get her. But if "Beyond" holds its own why not do the Lord thing separately—not close Beyond to do it? I am sure Straw with Polly in it would make money. And I could go over it again, if the proposition goes through.[1]

Did you get my check for twenty-five I sent you some weeks ago?

I have sent Marco to Liveright after thoroughly going over it and cutting. The next to last scene I cut out entirely and I switched the whole scheme of acts, scenes into a much better plan. The play now is much shorter and more wieldy.

I do not know just what to make of the Reinhardt situation. It seemed from both your letter and Maddens to be fairly uncertain as far as New York is concerned. Perhaps when he gets the play in detail things will be different. For I think this new version is some play! I have a real swelled head about it.

Well, I guess that's about all—except to say that we are having a hell of an overcrowded time of it in the little house, that I am working in a bedroom with children, carpenters, plumbers, masons and whatever else you have doing all sorts of telling chorus work in the near vicinity, and it doesn't bother me much which proves that I can't really be as artistic as the prints would have it. Also we are discovering that the average Bermuda artisan more than makes up for his lower wages by the longer time he takes. It is a scream to watch them doing "stills" of men at labor—but the scream is of laughter only when they are working on the place next door. But the place will be a wonder when it is finally fixed up—absolutely ideal for me and will surely pay me big dividends in the work I shall do here. I love it. Shane and Oona and Agnes are all fine. You and Eddy *must* come down and see us once we get settled and have a house—or at least half a one to place at your disposal.

All our best to all of you! Happy New Year!

Gene

P.S. I'm worried about something. I sent you a check for 25 to get roses for Carlotta for X'mas. Did you ever get it? The letter was addressed care of Mansfield Theatre or to Charlton St.—was mailed two weeks or more ago. Hope it's O.K.

There is lots I don't write. Emotionally I'm still up in the air. Perhaps this will be good for "Interlude" (author's thought!) but otherwise it hain't purty.

---

1. Macgowan had apparently proposed reviving O'Neill's play *The Straw* (1921), starring Pauline Lord.

Jan. 12 [1927]

Dear Kenneth:

Just a line. I'm deep in "Strange Interlude" again, groaning in spirit and sweating blood at the immense amount of labor in it still before me. But it will be a great thing—if it comes off.

As for number of people, I'm pretty helpless without any script. I should say 150 or thereabouts for the Greek scene would be the greatest number you'd need. I meant it to be elastic, according to size of theatre.[1]

I cabled you yesterday. To reduce to five ages is O.K. but I think the seven types should be kept.[2] Also the intermission after 2nd Act *must* be kept. It's the most important intermission of all and all are important. As for Geddes scheme to simply mask designing by using costume & make-up for races in general, I'm willing.

I rely on you to curb Geddes' enthusiasm for sets. It's dangerous to this play—any hippodroming. With a Lazarus you can play "L.L." with a spot light, a couple of tables, two soap boxes, a black curtain & the Hudson Duster gang.[3] The less prominent the sets are, the better for the play. They need absolute austerity—which I doubt if Geddes has—and I think trying to fit the play into a revolving set (what for, in God's name, there's plenty of time and there *should* be intermissions to give people a chance to recover, digest & think for a minute or two), or sliding sets, or a unit set, is all designer's non-sense. I still think the simple scheme I worked out fits what I wrote better than any. My watchword to you here is masks, people, lights, and a Lazarus—and as little set as possible. I wasn't at all keen for Geddes' Joan of Arc idea[4] (I was for it for Joan)—as applied to Laz. Didn't seem to me to belong to Laz. at all.

I hold no animus toward Polly[5] for not having read "Straw." She's

----

1. Macgowan must have asked how large a cast O'Neill wanted for *Lazarus Laughed*.

2. The chorus in *Lazarus Laughed* was divided to represent the seven ages of man. Each "age" was divided into seven general types of character.

3. A band of truckdrivers and stevedores who terrorized Greenwich Village during O'Neill's "Hell Hole" years (1915–16). John Wallace's Golden Swan saloon was the Dusters' hangout as well as O'Neill's.

4. In Paris in 1925, Norman Bel Geddes had directed and designed a production of *Jeanne d'Arc* by Mercedes de Acosta, starring Eva Le Gallienne.

5. Pauline Lord.

a great gal & actress but I never suspected her of being a voracious reader.

All best!

Gene GET *CHALIAPIN*!

P.S. (over) *This is important!* For God's sake, cut out the giving away of the Clark book at "Beyond." I've meant to write about this long ago. It's a cheap stunt with a poor book and it reflects on me. In no theatre of mine would any stunt like that ever be pulled, you can bet your life on that. It doesn't help me, it hurts me with the only people I care a damn about. So can it, will you?[6] Every time I see your add I feel like Channing Pollock.[7] You shouldn't let Ross introduce these brilliant, revolutionary ideas into the theatre. I can see where he is going to be a regular cut-up! Seriously, I appreciate his good intentions but I feel my worst enemy couldn't do worse by me! I don't need that sort of ballyhoo! And I doubt if it sells a single seat.

---

70 • TO MACGOWAN FROM O'NEILL. ALS 2 pp.

Hamilton,
Jan. 21 [1927]

Dear Kenneth:

I got your cable but I can't seem to locate the Laz. drawings I made. Everything is still in such a mess, so much of my stuff is still in boxes and trunks that, although I've been through them all, I must have stuck the drawing in some special spot which I was to remember especially and have forgotten. However, thinking it over carefully, they were not so good. They were at best only a suggestion for a keynote of austere simplicity. What my letter about Geddes meant was my fear, in spite of my deep and genuine respect for his talents, that he would overemphasize the sets, make them too *pronouncedly* abstract and thus make an abstract play even more difficult to understand. For instance, if the set for the first scene in Lazarus house hits an audience in the eye as too startlingly unlike a house the

---

6. Macgowan had instituted the practice of giving out free copies of Barrett H. Clark's brief critical biography, *Eugene O'Neill* (published in 1926 by Robert M. McBride), at performances of *Beyond the Horizon*.

7. Popular American playwright of the day.

attention will be immediately concentrated on this and on the *queerness* of the masks & chorus and away from the humanity of Lazarus. The dramatic effect of this scene ought to be an arrowhead of concentration directed at the one man who is real and true and alive in the midst of false, dead people. It is hard to explain. Laz. is a play for a director, for sets composed of people arranged by that director, an actors' play and especially the actor's (Laz) play, and the playwrights play. It is not a scenic designer's. It should be made plain on the program—this is *important* to me!—that masks, chorus, etc. are all in my script, that they are in my design of this play for an imaginative theatre. I want to be known as having done this, for better or worse, so there can be no mistake in people's minds as to the materials I work with. (You remember "Bobby's" house in "Desire" and the confusion that led to)[1]

All this fear about the set may be absurd of me. I'm waiting to see the drawings you're sending me. I couldn't make anything of your sketches. But if I were sure of a fine casting for Laz—and for Tib, Cal,[2] Miriam & Pompeia—there would be no question. The sets then could be anything. The actors & play & director would be sure to dominate. But I'm afraid you're going to be forced to go on with a weak cast, things being as they be and a Chicago production in an Art theatre meaning little to an actor. So it seems to me that right now *all* the best efforts of everyone concerned should be concentrated on one thing—the casting of Laz. Until that is done, and well done, everything else is simply futile and the question of this set or that set is meaningless to me. Neither Gering nor anyone can *teach* an ordinary actor to play Laz. A big, imaginative striking personality must be there first for a director to inspire.

And that's why I again hope to hear from you in your next more about what is being done on this point. The loss of Hale[3] seems to me unimportant. He is all right for a regular Little Theatre production, maybe, but he isn't a big enough personality. I hope you will have considered what I wrote about C. doing Laz. in Russian. It seems to me *the most important* thing of all that someone get to see Chaliapin in person, (with a sympathetic interpreter), no matter

1. Robert Edmond Jones's set for *Desire Under the Elms* had included the simultaneous presentation of several rooms in the Cabot house, an innovation that had confused some audiences.

2. Tiberius and Caligula, major characters in *Lazarus Laughed*.

3. Probably Richard Hale (see Letter 67 above), who apparently had decided not to play Lazarus.

where he is. Bulgakov would help here. If this is not done I shall always feel that the big opportunity—the logical opportunity—for doing the play justice was neglected—and deliberately neglected in favor of unimportant—by comparison—details.

Remember, I'm saying all this after going over and studying every line of the play for weeks. C. may be a chance in a million (according to his agent) but the play hasn't been read to him and until this is done and you have his reaction as an artist, noone has a right to think they know his position or his contracts or anything else. Would anyone take Madden's commercial word as final about my possible reaction to a great artistic chance—or his opinions about my unamiable temperament.

I'm only repeating old stuff. You know all this. Without a Laz, the play—and you & I as connected with it—are sunk, and the only consolation will be that Chicago isn't a very deep ocean and it's easy to swim ashore again from there.

Malc Williams[5] couldn't do Tiberius. That's out. He would be nothing like my idea. Waldron[6] I don't know anything about. Huston[7] is the man if you can get him. Pompeia? Ann Harding[8]—or Helen Gahagan[9]—or Carlotta[10] might do it. Miriam—Blanche Yurka[11]—Mary Morris[12] might do. Caligula—Ralph Morgan?— Charley Ellis,[13] at a pinch—or Teddy Ballantyne[14] (this isn't bad idea. Teddy *can* read lines & has a presence & a touch of mad quality)

Enough! All best from us all

Gene

4. The text of the holograph letter is unclear for this word; a conjectural reading has been supplied.

5. Malcolm Williams, who was then playing James Mayo in the Actors' Theatre revival of *Beyond the Horizon*.

6. Charles Waldron.

7. Walter Huston.

8. Actress who had performed with the Provincetown Players.

9. Actress who had performed with the Provincetown Players, most notably in Walter Hasenclever's two-character play, *Beyond* (1925), with Walter Abel.

10. Carlotta Monterey.

11. Actress who, among many other roles during a long and distinguished career, had played Gertrude to John Barrymore's Hamlet (1922).

12. Actress who had appeared in several Provincetown Players productions, including *Desire Under the Elms*.

13. Charles Ellis, another of the Provincetown Players, who had created the roles of Benny Rogers in *Diff'rent* (1920), Shorty in *All God's Chillun Got Wings* (1924), and Eben Cabot in *Desire Under the Elms* (1924).

14. Edward J. Ballantine, who had created the role of Cocky in O'Neill's *Bound East for Cardiff* and had also appeared in many Provincetown Players productions, and on Broadway with John Barrymore in *Richard III* (1920) and *Hamlet* (1922).

Hamilton, Bermuda
Jan. 23 [1927]

Dear Kenneth:

Seven in the chorus I would stick to. You need the volume of seven voices, seven people can be arranged by a director to give a definite dramatic effect, etc. I picked out seven for a number of such reasons. Five is too meager to impress. In the case of the Maenads the Chorus is more important than the crowds. As for the size of the masks I picked double-sized rather tentatively. My objective was to approximate the effect of the Greek masks and give plenty of room for a megaphone effect inside the mouths that would give a distinctive volume & sound to the chanting and help to carry across each word distinctly. This last is important. My notion was that the masks should be double in every sense—the Chorus as utterly distinct (visually) from the crowd, no chance of confusing them with members of crowd, a strange & unreal intensification of the crowd. Your drawing of double-size is my idea. How do you mean, it would look bad? Why would it? It ought to look entirely strange. But this is something I would have to see to be sure of—but I think I'm right. But remember the megaphone—a la Greek—for the inside of mouths. The Chorus chant must sound different from the chant of Crowd—or what my ear heard won't come off.

If Ross won't go into the O'Neill theatre thing deep enough, there's no use his coming to see me. In fact—confidentially—he's not what I want for that, money or not. He's too interested in himself connected with a theatre. And he struck me as too—Jewish—and a bit of a piker. Has he done anything on the Ridgefield mortgage thing yet? If he doesn't come clean with me on that, he's never going to be associated with another play of mine, you can let him know that. That's in his own line, it isn't any question of money or any kind of financial gamble, he can easily do it if he goes to a little trouble, and if he doesn't care to be troubled he'll find I won't be troubled with him in the theatre. At any rate, I've got to know something on the mortgage thing soon. I'll have to sic Harry W.[1] on it, if R. doesn't do anything.

I don't think Ross is your bet—nor the McAvoy thing[2] either. I

1. Harry Weinberger.
2. Probably a reference to playwright-director-producer J. P. McEvoy, whose play *God Loves Us* had been Macgowan's first production for the Actors' Theatre in 1926.

have what I think is a damn good idea—or hunch. Why don't you try to hitch up with Sam Harris? Don't laugh. From his reactions to some of my stuff, I'd say he was the most deeply sincere of those who want to do something real but feel keenly (and confess) that they don't know how and haven't any one with them who does know how. You might go to him with some strange & startling proposal that, under his banner and your dictatorship, he give you an outfit to do two or three things yearly—one of mine, say, you could guarantee— etc. etc. Its too long to write. We'll talk it. The more I've thought of it, the more points I've seen in it for you. The Greenwich V.-P.P. stuff was fine for your standing. You've established yourself as Art. The fringe stuff—half-commercial—is no good for you. The Actors always seemed this to me. The association with Ross is sort of would-be commercial. What you want now—if possible to get—is definite 100% association with—and of—the commercial theatre doing *artistic* things—that is, being yourself but commercially not to be scorned. Do you get me? The only chance is with a man like Harris who might let you fulfill yourself to fulfill himself. With Ames, Arthur,[3] etc. you would be under the shadow. Oh balls! Those aren't the words. I'll tell you later. I haven't one-quarter said it.

No, I didn't say anything against his Joan set at that luncheon because Geddes wasn't through telling about it when I had to beat it, if you'll remember.

Try hard to come down Jan. 30th. Seems to me then would be just about right time for us to get together.

Send me some drawings of movable set. I have the vaguest idea of just what you mean.

All best!
Gene

P.S. "S.I." is coming along fine.

---

72 • TO MACGOWAN FROM O'NEILL. TLS 1 p.

Hamilton, Bermuda,
February 10, 1927

Dear Kenneth:

No, I am strong for Fritz Lieber.[1] I think he might just hit this right, and I would certainly like to see him do a fine piece of work

3. Broadway producers Winthrop Ames and Arthur Hopkins.

1. Shakespearean actor Fritz Leiber, who had apparently been proposed to play Lazarus.

for his own sake as well as mine. I liked him very much personally when I met him.

I hope my Harris hunch worked out well. I am anxious to hear what he had to say to you.

Bob Milton[2] wrote me about a play. I told him if he had not read "Marco Millions" to get a script of that and read it. You can explain to him when you see him that I have since cut the play down about a half an hour—one scene out entirely—as he will see when the book is published.

It is too bad about "Beyond." I think Ross played the damned fool. I am off of him for life.

I have a howl to make to you. You did not send me back my cut script with the new script. This is very bad work. How am I to check up? Will you see that this is done at once? Also remember that the five scripts I asked you to have made were for me, and me alone, each one for a definite purpose. Did you give the one to Fitzie to send to Berkman, and was another sent to Kummer?[3] I expected you to send me two. Will you send the other one I should have gotten to George Jean Nathan.[4] He wants to write something about it and he has never had a chance really to read the play. This seems to me particularly important. He got a poor impression of it through Madden forcing him, like a damned fool, to read it in snatches the day before he sailed for Europe, in between farewell calls and packing, and I want this bad impression corrected. Promise me you will do this for me, will you?

When do you think you will be able to get down here? I think you ought to be able to make it as soon as things get really on their way out in Chicago. I don't know whether I shall go up either for the rehearsals or the production. It all depends on Strange Interlude. I expect to finish it by March the first, but I am not sure. It is a very costly trip from here to Chicago and return. With "Beyond" dead, and Spithead still building, and Ridgefield still not selling, I don't know that I can afford it.

All best to you. Don't forget this thing about the scripts now, will you?

Gene

2. Robert Milton, who had directed plays at the Greenwich Village Theatre.
3. Austrian journalist and translator Rudolf Kommer, Max Reinhardt's American representative.
4. New York drama critic and editor, with H. L. Mencken, of the *American Mercury*. Nathan had been one of O'Neill's earliest champions, and they became intimate friends.

Hamilton, Bermuda,
February 24, 1927

Dear Kenneth,

I was sorry to hear about the mix-up in Chicago. I was beginning to hope from your letters that everything would go fine out there and we would get a good production out of it that might run on for a couple of months. I have not cabled Madden yet about the extension. I really don't know exactly what to say. Candidly, from the way things look I would much rather they gave the whole thing up. However, in justice to Mrs. Ryerson,[1] who certainly acted fine, I think, I will be willing to extend the time until November first, provided they do "The Great God Brown" in place of "Lazarus" this year, at the same scale of royalties which I would have gotten for the "Lazarus" production while at the Goodman Theatre. And provided also that the clause in the contract calling for the first six weeks' performances without royalties be cancelled and my royalties start with the opening performance.

If, however, they insist on not doing "Brown," then I shall have to ask them for a thousand dollars advance to be paid me on the expiration of the present contract, this advance to apply on royalties which would likewise begin with the opening performance next fall. I think this fair enough. In holding up the play they are ruining my chance for getting any money out of it this spring as I had confidently expected.

Has Milton read "Marco Millions"? It will be published before very long now, as I have read the first set of proofs and will get the page proofs within a few days[2]

I hope you have gotten the script of "Lazarus" to Nathan. It might be a good thing if you would have the same party who made the last script make five more for me, and I will pay the bill.

I am also very anxious to get a script to Alfred Kreymborg. They want something of mine in this new yearly magazine "The American Caravan" which he and Van Wyck Brooks and Rosenfeld are getting out. I thought maybe they might use a scene or an act from "Lazarus." I am writing Kreymborg to get in touch with you.[3]

1. Probably the producer or angel for the planned Chicago production of *Lazarus Laughed*.
2. *Marco Millions* was published by Boni and Liveright in April 1927.

Yes, we are all fine, and the house is coming along in great shape. When are you going to pay us your visit?

All best.

Sincerely,.
Gene

---

74 • TO MACGOWAN FROM O'NEILL. ALS 1 p.

Hamilton, Bermuda
Feb. 28th [1927]

Dear Kenneth:

Just a line to get back to you on this same boat.

It's all very well about Reinhardt wanting to work with me but that pays no bills—of which there are and will be a multitude. Why the hell doesn't he buy the play if he's so keen? I'll really have to start right away submitting it elsewhere. Madden has sent a script to the Guild already—without my authorization, be it said—the old version, I suppose—that's a shame. Will you send them a copy of the new version as soon as the new copies are made?

And I feel the same way about the Habima.[1] It may be all for the glory of Jehovah but I can't convince the butcher of that.

"Strange Interlude" is finished. It's the biggest ever! It's a "work." I'm tremendous pleased with the deep scope of it. Nothing like it has been done before. After which, I'll sign myself up as my own press agent, what? I'm going over last of it now. The first play is already typed. But keep anything about "S. I" under your hat.

All best! Come down as soon as you can.

Gene

3. Poet, playwright, and editor Alfred Kreymborg was about to publish the first issue of his new yearly anthology, which he coedited with Van Wyck Brooks, Lewis Mumford, and Paul Rosenfeld. Act 1 of *Lazarus Laughed* appeared in the September 1927 issue, in a version very different from that in the published text of the full play, which appeared two months later.

1. A Hebrew-language, Jewish theatre group that had been founded in Moscow in the early 1900s with advice and help from Stanislavsky, whose pupil, Eugene Vakhtangov, was their director for a time. After surviving both Czarist persecution and Bolshevik oppression, the company toured in America and Europe and in the late 1920s settled in what was then Palestine. They had apparently expressed interest in doing *Lazarus Laughed*.

Hamilton,
Mar. 24 [1927]

Dear Kenneth:

The news from Chicago is good—financially speaking! Otherwise, I would rather they dropped it. But I am glad Gering is out. Who will be their new director? I have a hunch in this respect. If Dantchenko is through with his movie stuff by that time, why don't they try to get him to direct it? According to Lawrence Langner,[1] who is down here on a trip, he will surely know enough English by that time. And it would be just such a boost as the Chicago people need after "Ragged Edge."[2] Also, if I cannot get a definite agreement from Reinhardt soon, I intend to get after Dantchenko about doing "Lazarus" in N.Y. I suppose there would be no difficulty in getting backing for him. What do you think of this? When do you expect definite word from R.[3] about your own situation? I suppose when you do that you'll be in a position to get this "Laz" matter settled one way or another. Did R. ever hear Lieber read? I'm looking forward to seeing the photos of Geddes' sets.

As for the Chanim matter and Jimmy, all I know is that Jimmy was working tentatively on sounding out different people on the O'Neill theatre idea.[4] But it was all very tentative and I haven't yet gone into the matter fully with him. I simply told him, as I told you, what my own outline for the scheme was—when he was directing "Beyond." I don't see what play of mine anybody could be asking backing for—with "Laz" sort of mixed up with R.—unless it were a revival. Jimmy was interested in reviving "Anna C." Maybe that's it. "Strange Interlude," although finished, I won't regard as absolutely ready for production until I've let it rest and gone over it again some months hence. In the meantime, I'm getting "Dynamo" ready to write and may start actual work on it soon. I'm also trying to write an original story, around my idea for "The Squarehead

---

1. Playwright, director, and producer who was on the Board of the Theatre Guild.

2. Play translated by Marion Gering and George Abbott from the German of Francis Langer, produced in Chicago in the first week of February 1927 by the Chicago Play Production Company.

3. Sidney Ross, with whom Macgowan apparently contemplated coproducing.

4. Reference may be to Chanin's 46th Street Theatre and to James Light's attempts to interest its owners in letting him use it as a base for an O'Neill repertory theatre.

Saga," for the films.[5] Needs must when the devil drives! I also have my financial worries at present. The Tiffany people are still very hot after me but, so far, their proposition isn't good enough.

I wish our old triumvirate were still alive. This being without any sympathetic outlet for my "Strange Interlude"—unless the Guild or Arthur get interested—isn't so good. There aren't many managers I'd want that submitted to.

I had a note from Bobby but no address. Why is he so mysterious?

We sure enjoyed having Clara around. She is a peach. Isn't there some chance of your paying us a visit soon? There is so much to talk over.

Eugene is down on vacation—six feet tall now! We're all fine, as you'll hear from Clara.

All best!
Gene

P.S. (later) I've let Lawrence Langner read what is typed of "Interlude" and he is all steamed up about it—thinks it's the best I've done, etc.—so there may be a strong chance of the Guild there. I hope so. I need something definite settled for next year. I'm in a bad way with no prospects. But keep this strictly under your hat! They are again considering "Marco" at the present moment and I hope they will sign on for it this time. I want to get "Marco" off my hands before "Interlude," naturally.

Is Cornell really signed up for the Maugham play, do you know? In which case, I won't bother letting her read "Interlude"[6]

---

76 • TO MACGOWAN FROM O'NEILL. TLS 1 p.

Hamilton, Bermuda
April 1st [1927]

Dear Kenneth:

What is all this that has been happening to you? Or is it something that can't be told? Clara had said you were fat and beaming and your last letters have come as a surprise.

---

5. O'Neill's notebooks, dated 1926, contain a narrative of a plot for "The Saga of Ollie—'Squarehead Saga' " and the notation "Made into farcical movie scenario 1927."

6. Somerset Maugham's *The Letter* opened in September 1927, with Katharine Cornell as the star.

I'm damn sorry your financial situation is so rotten but I suppose that will soon buck up once the Reinhardt thing is settled. I would offer you whatever in the way of assistance I could give except that my own status is at present so precarious. But of course I could always come forward with something if you got in any desperate pinch. The O'Neill family in mass is at present praying for the sale of Ridgefield which would settle my mortgage mess there, which is crucial, and give me capital to continue down here with.

It's too damn bad about that Indiana blow-up.[1] It's diabolical the way the unexpected turns up black like that just at the worst moment. It's happened to me so often I sort of look forward to it now.

There's also an unholy mess about the Spithead mortgage which the mortgagee is trying to call in on me this spring—ten thousand, my boy, at this time of all times! But I'm not worrying much about it as the lawyers down here say he hasn't got a leg to stand on, and has simply misunderstood the peculiar form of archaic Bermuda document.

"Strange Interlude" is almost typed now. I wish you could read it. Of course, I intend to go over it again later on but I think the present version can stand without any changes but cutting.

Much love to you from us all.
Gene

P.S. Any news from Kommer about Reinhardt reading "Laz"? I wish we could get this set and an advance paid on it. He ought to say as soon as he's read it whether he wants it or not.

---

77 • TO MACGOWAN FROM O'NEILL. ALS 1 p.

[April 1–May 2, 1927?]

Dear Kenneth:

Just a line. You will have seen Aggie by this[1] and heard all the dope. Two scripts of "S.I"—there are only 3—are up—one to Cornell, as I promised her—one to Guild as I promised Langner when here. I want you very much to read it—but not submit it to anyone

1. Macgowan had assumed the post of advisory director with the Chicago Play Producing Company early in 1927. Fourteen midwest cities were organized into a circuit for the company to tour; it is possible that O'Neill may be referring to an incident that occurred on the tour.

1. Agnes Boulton O'Neill was visiting her dying father at the Laurel Heights Sanitorium in Shelton, Connecticut.

yet. Last I heard Burton[2] wanted Chanin's to do "Marco." Let them laugh that off first. You can get script from Bobby after Miss. Sergeant[3] gives Cornell one to him and he has read it. Or perhaps Aggie will send it to Nathan first, if she gets it from Cornell.

All best in haste.

Gene

P.S. Sure I want that Chicago grand! Where is it? Don't know anything about Iden Payne[4]—but no matter.

---

78 • TO MACGOWAN FROM O'NEILL. TLS 1 p.

Hamilton, Bermuda

May 2nd [1927]

Dear Kenneth:

I am sorry Aggie didn't get to see you. She says she tried to get you on the wire a couple of times in a hurry but you were either busy or something. She was in a pretty hectic state, what with jumping out to the San and to her family and worrying about her father generally and she had to pass up most of the things she was supposed to do for me—which included having a talk with you. However, I expect to be up within a couple of weeks and it all can wait till then.

As for the script of "Strange Interlude," that fell through because Cornell walked off to Europe with one I wanted you and Bobby and Nathan to read. Where she's going to send it back to, I don't know—and with her signed up for "The Letter" I can imagine no more useless thing than having it in her hands. But so it goes. The other script is with the Guild and there is a strong possibility that they may take it, judging from reports. However, there's a hell of a lot of cutting to be done on it yet before I shall call it ready for anyone. I would not have sent scripts out to anyone except that I knew that Cornell was leaving soon and I had promised to let her see it before she did, and that Langner was so enthused with the draft of

2. Possibly director David Burton.

3. Elizabeth Shepley Sergeant, who had interviewed and become friends with O'Neill in Maine during the summer of 1926. She spent six weeks in March and April 1927 in Bermuda at the O'Neills' new house, recuperating from an auto accident.

4. B. Iden Payne, playwright, producer, and director, who was at this time director of the Goodman Repertory Theatre in Chicago.

the acts he read down here and thought it advisable I send it in at once. There is also a strong probability that they will do "Marco."

The fourth script of "S.I.," due to the stenog's dumbness, is so faint and blurred as to be unreadable and a total loss. And the only other is my own script that I can't send anyone. This will explain why I don't send you another, and haven't before this.

I will certainly be glad to see you soon. There is a hell of a lot to talk over.

I have been feeling like the wrath of Christ for the past ten days—laid up with tonsils, sore throat, cough, cold in the head and all the fixings. It has meant keeping out of the briny and that has peeved me no end.

I wish you and Eddy could make the trip down.

All best.

Gene

P.S. I'm not so stuck on the Geddes sets. They may work out very ingeniously but I still stick to my Appia notion[1] as the right thing for the play. However, this isn't fair. I'm open to be shown. It is just that I don't seem to visualize "Laz" in them. What news from Chi? Who is their present idea for director? Suggest Ben-Ami to them. He did a pretty good job with goat song.[2]

---

79 • TO MACGOWAN FROM O'NEILL. ALS 1 p.

Hamilton, Bermuda
May 30, 1927

Dear Kenneth:

Here is the check for that typing. I had it all made out to give to you that morning on the boat—and then of course forgot all about it. But better late than never!

I didn't see half as much of you as I would have liked to nor talk over half the things I wanted to. But the situation I was in was a bit exceptional and nothing better could be done in a short week. I know you understand this. Better luck next time. I would have

1. Swiss scenic and lighting designer Adolphe Appia (1862–1928), whose work was marked by extreme simplicity.

2. Jacob Ben-Ami, who had created the role of Michael Cape in O'Neill's *Welded* (1924), had directed a Broadway production of Franz Werfel's *The Goat Song* in January 1926.

stayed longer if it could have been done.[1] However it's grand down here and Aggie and the kids are good to be with again—and the sea. It's a bit lonely though and I feel isolated at times now that everyone we knew who was the slightest bit intelligent or amusing has blown for the season.

Connecticut, from what I saw of it at Wertheims,[2] is wonderful now too so I can't be snooty about our superior climate. I suppose you're now out at Brewster for good.

I'll get one of those two scripts of "S. I" to you soon. I'm very anxious to have you read it but this business of only having two copies complicates matters with Nathan and the Guild hanging on to them for the moment.

Let me know whatever you may hear from Chi. All best from us all to you all.

Gene

---

80 • TO MACGOWAN FROM O'NEILL. TLS 1 p. (On stationery headed: Spithead / Bermuda)

July 4th
1927

Dear Kenneth,

Just a line to enclose a check for you which I had all ready to give you that day you came down to see me off, which of course I forgot all about. It is for the typing of "Lazarus."

How is everything with you? How is the book with Macdonald[1] coming along? How many gallons of it has he got written? Do you hear anything at all from Chicago? I am rather anxious to know if there is any chance of their doing it out there or not.

I have decided to hold off "Strange Interlude" from you until I get the revised script finished, which will be within a couple of weeks. This will be better.

What do you hear from Bobby? Where is he now? Jimmy Light

1. O'Neill had gone to New York in mid-May to discuss possible productions of *Marco Millions* and *Strange Interlude* with officials of the Theatre Guild.

2. During his visit O'Neill had spent some time with Guild director, stockbroker Maurice Wertheim at his home in Connecticut.

1. Presumably Charles Blair Macdonald, author of *Scotland's Gift—Golf*, published in 1928 by Charles Scribner; Macdonald had substantial help from Macgowan in writing this book.

and his frau are down here visiting us. I wish you and Eddy could get down sometime before we leave, but I suppose there is not much chance. Well, do it next winter!

All best from us all.

As ever,
Gene

---

81 • TO MACGOWAN FROM O'NEILL. ALS 2 pp. (On stationery headed: Spithead / Bermuda)

August 7th [1927]

Dear Kenneth:

I've been meaning—as usual!—to write you for the past few weeks. But this time my excuse is genuinely not laziness. I've been laid up with summer flu—Bermuda brand—and a rotten bad cough which had me worried until a strange doctor, who had written me a letter or two from Boston, happened to call, happened to have some anti-flu vaccine with him, shot me full of it a few times and I made a brilliant recovery—except that I'm pretty pepless yet, but that may be only the climate, which is 85 to 90, night and day, all sunshine without a let up. You get so you pray for a good old grey New England murky 24 hours.

I was damn glad to hear the Chanin thing has gone through all right & Ross,[1] and that you have a theatre nailed down. As for a revival of mine, if you come to consider one, I still think "The Straw" is the dope—"Anna Christie," of course, if you could get Lord.

I haven't got to actual dialogue on "Dynamo" yet, as I had hoped to. Going over "Strange Interlude" has been a longer job than I anticipated—a thinking about every line. And I've spent considerable time on "Lazarus" getting it ready for fall publication—cut out most of the "Ha-ha" on a new scheme and got the masks, etc. chorus throughout a good deal more definite.

I'll get a new script of "Interlude" to you soon. I'm sorry now you didn't read the old one—all of it, I mean—so you'd see how I've improved it by paring and selecting. But you know me, Al![2]

1. Macgowan and Sidney Ross had apparently made an agreement with the Chanin Theatre Corporation to produce plays in theatres owned by the Chanins (brothers Irwin S. and Henry I. Chanin) in New York.

2. This popular slang phrase originated with Ring Lardner's collection of short stories, *You Know Me Al* (1916), which was a series of letters written by rookie major-league baseball player Jack Keefe to "Friend Al" back home in Bedford, Indiana.

My brain has sort of gone dead on me for the nonce but if I get any brilliant thoughts about plays you might do, I'll hand them on.

I'll be up the last week of the month. I want very much to see you and talk. There didn't seem to be much chance this last time in N.Y.

Agnes joins in all love to all of you. The climate has sort of got me licked temporarily but Aggie & the kids eat it up.

Hasta luego!
Gene

P.S. Any news from Chi.?

---

82 • TO MACGOWAN FROM O'NEILL. ALS 2 pp. (On stationery headed: Spithead / Bermuda)

Oct. 27, '27

Dear Kenneth:

I'm taking advantage of your kind proffer of aid. Herewith is a check and a note. With the one will you purchase flowers—roses— or use your own judgment or the florist's as to what would be best— I don't know flower lingo—and send to Carlotta at 20 East 67th Street with the enclosed note attached. Many thanks!

Back around the fifteenth. I'll hope to see a lot more of you this next time than the last now that you're settled in town. In the mean-time, here's wishing you "all the breaks"![1] It seems as if that were about the best wish one friend could make another in the show-shop game. (Let us not add, in the game of life—we who are trying so hard to believe in something hidden in either flesh or spirit—oh dear me, no, let us not admit, for another twenty years at least, that life is merely—and perhaps at its highest and holiest!—a game in which the best winning of the greatest winner is in regarding with a self-contempt the pain of his inevitable loss—a game of greater and lesser losers!

Selah! Daddy's Bedtime Secret for Today! I need a little of the glue of God, I'm afraid—a bit broken.[2]

See you soon.
Gene

1. Macgowan and Ross's first production, Noel Coward's play *The Marquise*, opened at New York's Biltmore Theatre on November 14, 1927.
2. Reference is to a line spoken by William Brown in act 4 scene 1 of *The Great God Brown*: "This is Daddy's bedtime secret for today: Man is born broken. He lives by mend-ing. The grace of God is glue!"

3: Le Plessis

3: Le Plessis

Euphoria and paranoia—moods of supreme elation giving way to violent protestations of guiltlessness, hatred, vengeance. Both O'Neill and Carlotta Monterey stand revealed in pathetic nakedness in the letters written to Macgowan from Europe. At first the lovers attempt to clothe themselves in ecstatic protestations of undying love, peppered with flurries of exclamation points and, from her, italicizations to the third power. Suddenly ecstasy turns to vicious calumny about Agnes O'Neill and her life prior to their marriage. Private detectives are brought into play, presumably at the urging of the lawyers, and O'Neill, to stop what he called Agnes's "legalized blackmail," himself threatens blackmail. Carlotta inveighs against many of O'Neill's oldest friends, lumping them with Jews, Bohemians, and other undesirables—reporters, "gossips," and the like. Then, as suddenly, the birds sing, and the lovers wander hand in hand as if they had not yet become aware of their nakedness.

There is nothing, really, that can be said in defense of many of the letters in this group. The O'Neills appear here at their worst, but they are not much different from the participants in any drawn-out and painful divorce action. The scum that arises in the letters may well have been occasioned by boiling, nocturnal conversations as the two, defying the guilt they felt in their illegal sexual union, reacted to real or imaginary wounds. Louis Sheaffer reasonably suggests that the adoration of Carlotta was an essential balm to O'Neill's sense of guilt at leaving Agnes and his children, just as the defamation of Agnes was a way of justifying his affair with Carlotta.[1] The point is well made. Certainly some spiritual uplift was needed to balance the degradation of spirit in the divorce, but the love duet did little to dissipate the bad taste left by the petty hauteurs, which are in origin essentially bourgeois.

The situation eased when Agnes told reporters that she would seek a divorce. Her announcement was made in June 1928, but not until February 1929 did she agree to the terms of a settlement. She was to receive between six and ten thousand dollars yearly, depending on O'Neill's income from royalties, and she was to have a lifetime interest in Spithead. This assured, she went to Reno. The divorce be-

1. Louis Sheaffer, *O'Neill: Son and Artist* (Boston, Toronto: Little, Brown, 1973), p. 323.

came final on July 3, 1929. Carlotta and O'Neill were married on July 22.

By that time the euphoria had diminished somewhat, and a domestic routine had been established. In the thrill of the first moments, in February 1928, the lovers had journeyed from London to Paris and then had taken the Villa Marguerite at Guéthary, near Biarritz in the Basses-Pyrénées. In September they left for a cruise to the Orient. In this restless, itinerant state, O'Neill was unable to work. He began to drink—his first major lapse, fell ill, as did Carlotta, and they quarreled. Separations and reunions and further separations followed. The press discovered them and made them international copy. They returned to Europe by separate ships, but when, with that kind of coincidence the bemused call "fate," the two ships docked at Port Said at the same time, he returned to her, and together they came back to France to rent a château at Le Plessis, ten kilometers from Tours.

The château was run down. Carlotta ordered repairs and new installations—a bath, a swimming pool, and other amenities. With Carlotta's independent income and O'Neill's royalties from the long-running *Strange Interlude*, the couple could afford to live in style. She took him to cobblers and tailors; he bought a Bugatti roadster and dashed about the countryside. There were cheap servants; the exchange was in their favor. Nevertheless, the letters reveal a concern for money and a kind of new-rich wonder at having life by the financial tail.

Inevitably, there was gossip chastising O'Neill for high living while deserted Agnes and her children were left in supposed penury. Seeking to counteract the rumors, Macgowan fell briefly out of Carlotta's graces by releasing to *The New Yorker* a glimpse of their life at Le Plessis that stressed its simplicity:

> A friend of Eugene O'Neill's just returned from a visit to him says that all reports about him have been exaggerated for a long time. It seems that the first wild items about him and his activities in the Far East were caused indirectly by his well-known aversion to publicity. The reporters were startled to find his name on a hotel register and concluded the signer must be an imposter—they didn't believe O'Neill would use his own name. This excited them to begin with, and then O'Neill was elusive, and they got all worked up. This really started the hullabaloo which has been kept going ever since. Flamboyant descriptions

of the château he has rented in France have exaggerated its grandeur. It is not a show place, simply an old residence on an estate owned by three noble ladies who rented it to the O'Neills furnished, for about half of what a four-room apartment rents in New York. It is without electricity and has but one bath. The former occupants retain the farming and gardening privileges on the estate, which comprises about seven hundred acres.

O'Neill has dammed up a stream for a swimming pool, because he has never been without one on the grounds of any house he has owned or lived in. He still owns Peaked Hill, near Provincetown, the first house he bought after fame and fortune took him out of Greenwich Village; his house on Hamilton Harbor, Bermuda, goes to the second Mrs. O'Neill under the divorce arrangements; and the other one he owned, near Ridgefield, Connecticut, has been sold. The Provincetown house is two miles from that town and hard to reach, through sand and mosquitoes. Even so, a delegation from a women's college once grimly made its way there to petition him to write a play for the college girls with eighteen women's parts and no men. The playwright once said, possibly just after that visit, that his ideal home would be an estate in Siberia with a fifteen-foot wall and Russian wolf hounds inside and out.[2]

Macgowan hoped that the information would put an end to the rumors and misstatements that had been spread about the O'Neills, but Carlotta flared up at the implicit apologia in the article.[3] In the end, their friend was reinstated in grace, and at Le Plessis the two settled into a kind of calm while the ugly past, characterized by so much inhumanity and self-betrayal, faded. Work began.

When he left for Europe, O'Neill had in hand the draft of *Dynamo*, which he then saw as the first play of a trilogy whose subject would be the crisis of faith in the modern world. The trilogy was

2. From "The Talk of the Town," *The New Yorker*, September 28, 1929, p. 21. Reprinted by permission; Copr. © 1929, 1957 The New Yorker Magazine, Inc.

3. Carlotta's letter to Macgowan no longer exists, but something of its tone can be gathered from her letter dated May 24, 1930 (Letter 94), in which she inveighs against apologizing for their way of life. Sheaffer quotes her letter to Saxe Commins on the subject of Macgowan's breach of discipline, where she stated that she forbade anyone's giving publicity about the O'Neills without her consent: "I need no apology to the public or Gene's old friends . . . whether I am living in *30 rooms* or *3*. I pay as I go—& it's nobody's damned business" (Sheaffer, p. 334).

never to be completed. *Days Without End,* the second play, was finished after much struggle when O'Neill again returned to the United States. The third, *It Cannot Be Mad,* generated ideas that merged into the cycle of plays on American historical themes, "A Tale of Possessors, Self-dispossessed." *Dynamo* was completed in 1928, although it was in plan as early as 1924 and had originally been intended for production by the Triumvirate. The Theatre Guild's production in February 1929 was not successful, and O'Neill blamed himself, partly because announcements of it as the first part of the forthcoming religious trilogy seemed pretentious and partly because he could not be on hand to oversee rehearsals. Later he would disparage the play and write in an in-house letter to Carlotta, "I feel 'Dynamo,' in a sense, wronged us—not because the critics panned it, that means nothing, they have panned some of my best stuff, but because I felt myself it was a step back, not a step forward, and so did not represent what you are to me."[4]

That the marriage and his writing would become deeply intertwined was inevitable. The inscriptions on the manuscripts and gift copies that he gave her continually refer to the plays as their children. One, dated April 23, 1931, presented the manuscripts of *Mourning Becomes Electra* to her in terms that reveal much about their life at Le Plessis:

To Carlotta

In memory of the interminable days of rain in which you bravely suffered in silence that this trilogy might be born—days when I had work but you had nothing but household frets and a blank vista through the salon windows of the gray land of Le Plessis, with the wet black trees still and dripping, and the mist wraiths mourning over the drowned fields—days when you had the self-forgetting love to greet my lunchtime depressing, sunk preoccupations with a courageous cheering banter—days which for you were bitterly lonely, when I seemed far away and lost to you in a grim, savage gloomy country of my own—days which were for you like hateful boring inseparable enemies who nagged at nerves and spirit until an intolerable ennui and life-sickness poisoned your spirit—

In short, days in which you collaborated, as only deep love can,

4. Eugene O'Neill, *Inscriptions: Eugene O'Neill to Carlotta Monterey O'Neill* (New Haven: privately printed, 1960). The letter is dated December 4, 1929.

in the writing of this trilogy of the damned! These scripts are rightly yours and my presenting them is a gift of what is half yours already. Let us hope what the trilogy may have in it will repay the travail we've gone through for its sake!

I want these scripts to remind you that I have known your love with my love even when I have seemed not to know that I have seen it[,] even when I have appeared most blind; that I have felt it warmly around me always, (even in my study in the closing pages of an act!), sustaining and comforting, a warm secure sanctuary for the man after the author's despairing solitudes and inevitable defeats, a victory of love-in-love,—mother, and wife and mistress and friend!—And collaborator!

Collaborator, I love you!

Gene

Le Plessis—April 23, 1931

In the end, it is the writing that gives substance to sentimental passion, just as it justifies in part the indecorous outcries, the notoriety, and the delirium of the early years of their life together. At first, as O'Neill traveled, his writing faltered. The peripatetic restlessness of his youth, which had finally spiraled to a center in his workroom at Peaked Hill Bar, began again as he made the grand tour through Europe and the Orient. Such voyaging was the dream of younger versions of O'Neill's heroes—Robert Mayo of *Beyond the Horizon,* for example, or Edmund Tyrone. For the dramatist, however, wide-ranging physical movement was not the way. Movement impeded creativity, and in Europe it was not until the château at Le Plessis provided him with a point of rest and sanctuary that he again began to write. The melodrama of many of the letters from Europe suggests disturbance in the inner creative life, just as it perhaps anticipates the ultimate problems of Carlotta's mental condition that occasioned the nearly fatal separation in later years, when the two lived at Marblehead in Massachusetts.[5]

---

5. The story of that separation has been often told. A closehand account of Carlotta's violent rejection of O'Neill and of their subsequent reunion is recounted in the words of Saxe Commins in Dorothy Commins, *What Is an Editor?* (Chicago: University of Chicago Press, 1978), pp. 62–86. In his account Commins, who, as O'Neill's close friend and editor, was one of the most assiduous of the caretakers, calls Carlotta "evil." More revealing are O'Neill's words with which he forgave her and returned to her: "She is ill."

What is not fully reflected in the letters here published and what is often misunderstood is the significant truth of the marriage: Carlotta, to fulfill her commission to set out the guest towels, had to build a "Siberian" wall around O'Neill and his work, leaving him undisturbed in the silence he required to write. As she discovered, she was to become the ultimate caretaker, replacing Macgowan as O'Neill's protector.

The pattern of life that began at Le Plessis was to continue until O'Neill was no longer able to write. The work diary for *Mourning Becomes Electra* reveals that he had had vague ideas about a tragedy in the Greek manner and on Greek themes as early as 1926, when the production designs with choruses and masks for *Lazarus Laughed* and *The Great God Brown* were being conceived. In 1928, during the trip to the Far East, the idea became firmer, and after the two had settled in Le Plessis, in late May 1929, work on *Mourning Becomes Electra* began in earnest. The writing was to continue through 1931, when O'Neill revised galley proofs on the published script. Between November 1929 and August 1930, he spent 225 full working days with scarcely a respite on the script, pouring out the vital energies of his being in incessant devising and revision. The diary reveals his experiment with asides and masks and other art theatre contrivances, but, as his letter to Macgowan of June 14, 1929, states, he came to the point where he threw out all art theatre paraphernalia in favor of a greater literary integrity: "Constructivism and such stuff is all right for directors but its only in an authors way. . . . Greater classical simplicity, austerity combined with the utmost freedom and flexibility, that's the stuff!" (Letter 91).

One more play of the canon, *Days Without End,* the unsuccessful companion play to *Dynamo,* remained to be written in the art theatre manner; but, in effect, with *Mourning Becomes Electra* O'Neill put behind him the days when he would devise schemes offering "imaginative opportunities for Bobby" and turned again toward the realistic style of his youth, the style that was to be the hallmark of the last, greatest plays.[6]

The days of collaboration came then to their ending. When Carlotta and Langner arrived, Macgowan had no further function in O'Neill's life, except as a distant friend. When he no longer traveled

6. "Bobby" never designed better than in the simple, classic, realistic mode he found for the settings of *Mourning Becomes Electra*.

in O'Neill's wake, Macgowan fell on troubled times. The productions with Reed were critically respected, but no more. Money was tight. He was considering writing a detective story. He dined out on O'Neill by writing articles on the playwright and by leaking information about his friend to *The New Yorker*. Shortly, however, he would find the new direction that promised a substantial career. Thereafter, as Macgowan's life was consumed by Hollywood and as O'Neill isolated himself to plan his most massive works, the correspondence thinned and entered its final phase.

Feb. 22, 1928

Dear Kenneth:

Well, we've been in London now for almost a week[1] and I must
confess—it is a confession for an O'Neill—that I certainly like this
town better than any city I've ever been in. There is something
so stable and solid and self-assuredly courteous about it. It's like a
soothing bath for the nerves after the frazzle of New York. And I've
been very much incognito. Noone knows that a notorious Yank is in
their midst. The "eminent dramatist" is very much on vacation and
Eugene O'Neill, the man, is at last given his chance to spread himself and live. And, as in the story of the dinasauras who only cohabits
with his mate once in every thousand years, "Christ, how he does
enjoy it!"

God, I wish I could tell you how happy I am! I'm simply trans-
formed and transfigured inside! A dream I had given up even the
hope of ever dreaming again has come true! I wander about foolish
and goggle-eyed with joy in a honeymoon that is a thousand times
more poignant and sweet and ecstatic because it comes at an age
when one's past—particularly a past such as mine—gives one the
power to appreciate what happiness means and how rare it is and how
horribly grateful one should be for it. And dreaming it all over in
these days when the dream has become flesh and flesh the dream, it
really seems to my mystic side as if some compassionate God, looking back at Carlotta's unhappy life and mine, had said to himself,
well, they deserve something from me in recompense for all my little
jokes, they deserve each other if they have the guts to take the gift.
And we did have—and here we are!

I know the tale of another's love is always sappy to a guy's ears—
nevertheless I continue to impose mine on your friendship knowing
that even if you think me quite "nuts" you will be glad I enjoy being

1. O'Neill had gone to New York in November 1927 to oversee rehearsals of the Theatre Guild productions of *Marco Millions* and *Strange Interlude*. He had also resumed his
courtship of Carlotta Monterey, deciding in December to divorce Agnes and marry Carlotta.
Accordingly, after the openings of *Marco Millions* (January 9, 1928) and *Strange Interlude*
(January 30, 1928), O'Neill and Carlotta, installed in separate cabins and the former trav-
eling under an assumed name after telling the press that he was going to California, had
sailed for England on the *Berengaria* on February 10, 1928.

that way! I felt freed the moment the boat left New York and although it was a rough trip and we spent most of the time in our cabins—(there were several on the passenger list who would have recognized us)—we managed to have a happy time of it. And these days in London have been perfect. To say that Carlotta and I are in love in the sense of any love I have ever experienced before is weak and inadequate. This is a brand new emotion and I could beat my brains out on the threshold of any old disciple of Aphrodite out of pure gratitude for the revelation! It is so damn right in every way! We "belong" to each other! We fulfill each other! "The world is round and perfect. I am living a dream within the great dream of the tide————breathing in the tide I dream and breathe back my dream into the tide!"[2]

But you've had about enough of my raving I suspect.

We're heading for the south of France on Sunday and will motor around until we find what we want either on the coast of France or Spain or Italy—a villa not too isolated and not too near, not too farmy and not too swank, where we can have a car and a boat and so forth and be close enough to a town to mingle in when we need a change. We've got people—agents—in Paris already looking up all sorts of places and it will not take long, I think, until we are settled.

Then for "Dynamo." I feel full of work and creative energy—new ideas have come—others are filling out in my mind. In short, old chummie, I bloody well burgeon a bit!

c/o Guaranty Trust, Pall Mall, London will be the address until I write you I'm settled. Drop me a line and let me know what you hear and all the dope on Langner's play.[3]

When we'll return to U.S. I don't know—and somehow I can't seem to care. The Guild, if they take them, can very well put on my stuff for a couple of years without me. Of course, a lot depends on what Agnes does or doesn't do—on whether she has the honor to keep the pledge we have always made to each other and the promise she made to keep that pledge when she was in N.Y. I think she will. She is fine and sound at bottom. But the influences she is under in Bermuda with that Phila. Social Register bunch of futile women with money is about as far removed from fundamental human being-

2. The quotation, slightly altered (for "round" read "whole"), is from a speech by Nina Leeds at the beginning of act 5 of *Strange Interlude*.

3. Langner's *These Modern Women* had opened on February 13, 1928, at the Eltinge Theatre, produced by Macgowan and Robert Rockmore.

ism as one could get—and A. is easily swayed by the rich and the social. So one never can tell. But it doesn't matter much any way as long as I can live and write where people mind their own business and approve of love without moral didacs. We may stay away for a long time in any event. Now I'm started I want to keep going. There's Greece & Egypt and the East—and South Africa where I've always wanted to go and where I need to go for the new negro play I've doped out and will write in the next few years—and the South Seas. There's a good bit of the old Gene O'Neill, A.B.—his spirit refined and minus the spirits that kept it going—reborn in me. I *feel* life again—without fear this time. It isn't a battle now—it's the end of the war, I hope—and the dawn of a new appreciation and evaluation.

Well, all best to you—and Carlotta joins in. You have been a fine friend to us both—when friends to both were almost nil—and we both are deeply grateful. You must try and get over and see us this summer.

As for all my pseudo-friends, you will have my commendation when you hear any of them "viewing with alarm" if you infuriate them by saying you have heard from me and that for the first time in my life I am really happy!

> Adios, amigo! Write,
> Gene

---

83 • TO MACGOWAN FROM O'NEILL. ALS 3 pp. (On stationery headed: Hotel du Rhin / 4 et 6, Place Vendôme / Paris)

> Feb. 27, '28

Dear Kenneth:

We arrived here last night after a wonderful trip by motor from Calais—a fast trip, for the French chauf. was hitting the high spots and making over seventy at times—and that in a big closed car! It was grand weather and I got a good eye full of the French country side and the villages through which we passed. It was great stuff. We're only going to stay in Paris a couple of days and then beat it—again by motor—to the South along the Bay of Biscay side and look over villas in the neighborhood of Biarritz (not in Biarritz itself, of course. That is too resorty)

This is a grand honeymoon! Astonishing cheap too—considering. I won't bore you by telling you again how happy and alive I am.

Carlotta is marvelous. I really feel as if I had never been in love before. Even in the matter of sex where I have had, God knows, sufficient experience hither & yon in the past. I have come to the conclusion that I never even dreamed of what it could be in the way of a physical & spiritual expression before. This is a true revelation to me!

But there I go again!

We hope to be settled within a week or ten days and I'll then get my teeth into "Dynamo." I'm enjoying myself hugely and feel that I'm entitled to this first vacation away from the burden of myself that I've ever had, but still I'll be glad to get to work after a week or so resting on a beach.

I see by the Paris Herald that "Maya" is being run after by the police.[1] It brings back "Desire" days. Perhaps old pal Banton will drag in "Interlude."

All best! I'll hope to hear from you via the Guaranty Trust, London before too long.

Gene

---

85 • TO MACGOWAN FROM O'NEILL. TLS 2 pp. (On stationery headed: Hotel du Palais / Biarritz)

[March or early April 1928]

Dear Kenneth:

We have been here for a couple of days and it is a grand place now in the off season—not the sort of thing it is in the summer when it becomes "swanky" but quiet and peaceful—grand country with a fine beach and the Pyranees mountains in the background. We have already rented a villa in a little village called Guethary about seven miles from here and will move in the end of the week. It looks like the right place for work—has a private beach of its own, a small wood and grounds and tennis court and row boat. The house is an old French one—not like the damned modern Basque villas for the rich which have sprung up all over the place. It has old stone balconies where one may sunbath and is altogether charming. We have taken it for six months and can at last consider ourselves "put." So the address from now on will be Villa Marguerite, Guethary, Bas

---

1. *Maya*, translated by Ernest Boyd from the French of Simon Gantillon, had been closed by order of New York district attorney Joab H. Banton in late February 1928.

Pyranees, France. The Spanish frontier is not so many kilometres away and we expect to take trips down into Spain. Altogether the prospects are bright and we are both very happy. Carlotta has so far done all the talking in French for the firm but I find that a lot of my five years of it in prep school and college comes back to me and I can usually understand all that is said—if they go slow—although when I come to reply I find myself automatically stumbling into Spanish! A queer combination of having once learned to read one language and to have picked up a jabbering knowledge of another. Well, I suppose it will gradually straighten itself out and my Argentine lingo will be a help when we go to Spain—if they can understand it there! In the meantime, what with Carlotta's English accent and Spanish appearance and my own God-knows-what-but-not-typically-Yank mug and my inability not to say "Si" when I ought to say "Oui" and the general supposition that we are both Montereys—well, we puzzle the folks a bit but agreeably because they see we are in love and so it must be all right whatever it is.

The motor trip down here from Paris was wonderful—the weather mild and balmy. We came down through all the chateau country along the Loire in Tourraine and stopped off and went through quite a few of them—Chambord, Amboise, Loches, etc.—the most beautiful and dramatic places I have ever seen. It was an unforgetable experience. So was Paris, for that matter. In fact, so much has happened since I left New York in the way of new experiences that it seems as if a long time must have elapsed and I simply cannot believe the fact that I was still in New York four weeks ago.

I wonder what has been happening in N.Y. and Bermuda—if anything. I haven't been able to send any permanent address to the Guaranty Trust in London and so haven't had one piece of mail or a cable since I sailed. I hope all is fair weather both in the commercial and domestic fields of drama but I must say I haven't lost any sleep over the dearth of news.

[Autograph]

I find Carlotta's Corona rather a trial to write with on a high table so I'll conclude this in pencil. We both hope you may take it into your head to come over this summer—that there may be a "break" that will enable you to do so—in which case you must come down and visit us.

Carlotta has been marvelous to and for me! Quite outside of her beauty which is an enduring delight she has proven so wonderfully kind and considerate and "sympatico"—such a grand pal! And she is so deeply in love it fills me with a humble awe and gratitude. Well—! I am a bit in love myself, what?

I hope the mail when it comes in a postponed flood won't be an avalanche of the disturbing and worrying—but I guess I can stand up under anything now.

Splitting fifty-fifty on all expenses as we are doing our expenses, although we have done it pretty much de luxe, has been astonishingly inexpensive. The dope certainly is to do Europe in the off season! Our rooms at this hotel—the best in Biarritz—would cost five to ten times as much in the season but amount to very little now.

All affectionate best from us both! Write once in a while!

Gene

---

86 • TO MACGOWAN FROM O'NEILL. ALS 5 pp.

Villa Marguerite,
Guéthary, B.P.
France
April 27th [1928]

Dear Kenneth:

A belated Sunday Times came containing your letter defending "Laz"[1]—for which many thanks!—and served to remind me that I haven't written you in a dog's age.

There's not much in the way of news. "A fortunate people has no history"—or whatever that saying is—and we are quite uneventfully happy and more in love than ever. That this happiness has stood the test of an absolutely secluded life in which we see noone but each other, in which noone even speaks English, in which for six weeks it did practically nothing but rain day after day, in which the strain of uncertainty about what Agnes would do has been—and still is—

1. Macgowan's letter had appeared in the New York *Times* on April 15, 1928, section 9, p. 4. *Lazarus Laughed* had received its first staging on April 9, 1928, at the Pasadena (Calif.) Community Playhouse and had been described in the *Times* as "several notches below the author's best work."

particularly trying, in which the fear of being recognized and landed in the Tabloids is ever present—that our love has waxed under a trial that would have turned a great many into a series of destroying brawls is something we are mighty proud of, and in years to come I'm sure we'll look back on it with a feeling of gratitude. It is a good thing to face all possible music at the start. It gives you a good measure of the living—with worth of the other. Carlotta is a brick!

Agnes seems to be going ahead with her plans for going West— but she is also developing a most ungenerous and, taking into account all I have done for her, most dishonorable greed. It is funny how soon an aching heart turns into a greedy gut! Evidently some of her worthy Society drunken neighbor-friends have advised her to "take me for all I've got." She is demanding Spithead for life—although she knows its too pretentious for her to keep up and she only wants it for snobby reasons, and that I have 45000 tied up in it which I badly need as an income bringer—and she wants in all other ways more than I offered her in an agreement more generous than Sinclair Lewis wife got from him, considering he must have been making three times my income! Can you beat it! It takes these ladies who hadn't a pot to piss in before they met you to elaborate the style to which they are accustomed! She threatens not to get a divorce unless I buy it at this price. There seems little difference to me between the blackmail they give you the Big Iron House for and this legalized brand. However, I am too old to start in being a sucker, and Carlotta has agreed with me that I should put up a battle, so I've written Harry[2] to tell her to go to hell if she won't take what I offered. She'll never get as much out of any court. And if she refuses to get a divorce I can eventually starve her into it. It would, of course, entail sacrifices. I'd have to keep my plays to myself for a few years—try and get them translated and done in Germany and Russia and C-S.[3]—no money but recognition. As far as finances go I can hold out indefinitely. I've gathered a stake together over here, but quite outside of that Carlotta has enough income to keep us both in very decent comfort over here where living is cheap.

But what a rotten mess to have wished on one by a person who is really bound in honor by a pledge made repeatedly during our years together that if either fell in love the other would divorce at once!

2. Harry Weinberger.
3. Czechoslovakia.

There was even a no alimony clause to the pledge! It's sickening to one's opinion of human nature! I've staked all the members of her family—who won't approve of what she's doing now, be it said in fairness to them!—repaired their houses, paid their doctors bills, sent Cecil[4] to Italy for a year and a half for her health, paid for the father's last sickness, his sanitarium bill, his funeral—I've supported her child[5] and I've always let her run bills regardless. But you know all this. I'm not boasting of what I've done—but wouldn't you think she'd take it into consideration? It saddens me that a woman I lived with for nine years, that I once loved, should try to double-cross and blackmail me in a way that no whore I've ever met in the lowest dive would ever have done! And Agnes is dead for me now and that's her epitaph in my memory! I had hoped to remain her friend and help her—but I don't want yellow friends! And there is a lot of other stuff she has done in a lousy rotten cheap revengeful way that makes friendly relations impossible. And perhaps it's better so. At least, it's wiped the past from my mind as nothing else could have. There's nothing like a kick in the ass!

I've got half of "Dynamo" about finished. It has developed wonderfully in the doing and planning and is far deeper and richer than it was in scenario. In structure and method of staging it will be an onward development deriving from the Ape and Desire. The dialogue will be à la "Interlude" but, as it deals with more simple people psychologically, it will have more of syloloquy and less of the quick aside thought. And it will, I hope be full of intense dramatic story from start to finish. But I'll write you in detail about it later. I'm working on it slowly and carefully in the hopes that I can get it done in first writing and not have the grinding thankless job of rewriting and cutting I had on "Interlude"—a job that wore me to the bone.

I've had lots of new creative notions—the old bean is in the pink that way. The grand opus of my life—the autobiographical "Sea-Mother's Son"—has been much in my dreams of late. If I can write that up to what the dreams call for it will make a work that I flatter myself will be one of those timeless Big Things. It has got me all "het up." It should be a piece of writing not like any that has ever

4. Agnes's sister.
5. Barbara Burton.

been done before the way I plan it. My subtitle is to be "The Story of the Birth of a Soul"—and it will be just that![6]

How is everything by you? I hope the breaks are turning in your favor. Is there any chance of your getting over this summer? Carlotta says to tell you there is always a room here for you and Welcome on the mat. It would be wonderful if you could come.

Tell Doctor Hamilton[7] I often think of him—as always with gratitude and affection—and that I'm going to write him one of these days. Read him this letter, too. I want him to know I'm happy and going strong—because I know he'd be pleased to know it. Has he ever finished the play—the one he read me the first part of? He certainly ought to. It was grand stuff. But I suppose he's "up to his ears" on his own job.

What do you hear of "Laz" in Pasadena? I've had a little news from Madden and it all sounded good—as if Pitchell[8] had done the stuff! I sure hope so!

Here's a favor I'd like to ask. Will you get me three hundred Parke & Davis 1/2 grain Thyroid Tablets and mail them to me here? Better get Hamilton to give you a prescription as I used to have trouble getting them without one. Let me know how much and I'll reimburse you pronto.

And here's another favor: Will you noise it abroad that you've heard from me—*most happy* and well!—from Prague, that I had taken a house near there for a month and was then probably going on to Russia for "Laz" and then coming back to Italy to finish "Dynamo"? I want to cover up all tracks that lead to France, since I was recognized in Paris and the Herald there was trying to locate me. It would be bad stuff if we were spotted here now in all our peace and quiet—just when the swimming is getting good!

This is a beautiful spot and a very comfortable villa. Our plans after the end of summer are not fixed yet. We'll probably go to Ger-

---

6. A plot summary for this never-undertaken play appears as a 1928 entry in O'Neill's work diary. The play involves a forty-year-old man, lying near death in a hospital, who hears a doctor say that his survival depends on his will to live—whereupon he re-examines his life in a series of flashbacks, deciding ultimately that he can accept the suffering he has been through, can "say yes to his life," can "conquer his death wish."

7. Dr. Gilbert V. Hamilton, New York psychiatrist who had had a few sessions with O'Neill in early 1926.

8. Irving Pichel, who played the title role in the Pasadena Playhouse production of *Lazarus Laughed*.

many for a while, get married there (if A. does the decent thing), then to England, then to South Africa for the winter (I've always wanted to go there) and up as far in the interior as Lake Tanganyika, with a permanent house at Durban in Natal wonderful spot & climate (where I once touched as a sailor) where I'll write another play. Then in the spring up the opposite (East coast) to Suez and the Mediterranean—then in Greece for six months and on the Bosphorus where I'll write me another drama—or maybe all of this writing time will be on the "Sea-Mother's Son" (keep this title to yourself!)—then, stopping at India, to Hong-Kong and Peking where I'll do more writing, then to Honolulu and finally, two years from this Spring, back to California where C. and I expect to make our home for good. Of course, there may be changes in the sequence of this itinerary but we want to go to all these places—and will go. So, divorce or no divorce, productions in New York or no productions, the States probably won't see me again for two years. I'm sick of being "put" and so is Carlotta. Enough of the old Gene O'Neill has been reborn in me to put me in the mood "for to admire and for to see" the world I've missed. I'll take care that none of this wandering interferes with my work but, on the contrary, does it good. And, splitting fifty-fifty, all the travelling won't amount to any impossible burden.

Unless you have a damn good hiding place for my letters, you'd better destroy them. Frankly, I wouldn't want Eddy to come across them. I have a hunch that her sympathies—as woman with woman—might be with Agnes, that poor forlorn deserted wife to whom my agreement—which she thinks is too little!—only guarantees from six to ten thousand a year!

Write me! And try to make the break and come over. You'd like Guéthary and the Basque Coast!

All affectionate friendship!
Gene

P.S. I inclose a note from Carlotta to you. I discover it is a glowing tribute and I blush becomingly as an undeserving one should. It is only too easy to be a "man" with Carlotta.

P.S. II You'd better address all future letters care of Guaranty Trust Co., 50, Pall Mall, London. I may have to pull up stakes and blow out of here if the newspapers get too hot on the scent. And I needn't warn you not to confide this address to anyone anytime on any excuse!

Villa Marguerite,
Guéthary, B.P.
France
July 3rd [1928]

Dear Kenneth:

Well, I know this is the hell of a long time to hold up an answer to your letter but I've just been lazing along in one of those periods when writing a letter seems almost more than one can bear although one is able to do one's daily stint of playwriting.

That is, on some days. I was laid up for ten days with the flu. And then there are other series of days after the mail has come bringing news of the fair Aggie's vaccilating plans, new antics and new exhorbitant demands by way of the price of a divorce, that work becomes impossible for a while. So then Carlotta and I pack our little bags and hop in the car (yes, we've got a Renault and an expert chauffer at forty a month, five a week apiece—living luxurious over here comes low!—keep this about the car dark or Agnes will want fifty thousand more!) and take a short trip. I now know the Basque country, the French part of it, by heart and I sure love it and its people. So much so that, after all the storms are over and the travelling we intend to do done, it is quite possible that we may make our home here. I am beginning to think that is the only sane thing to do. The cheapness of living on the franc outside of the big cities is incredible. Our chauffer—and he is not ordinary but extra good—gets forty dollars a month, our extra good cook gets twenty-eight, our maid eighteen, and a little girl to help the other two twelve—grand total ninty eight, which means forty-nine apiece for C. and me. Can you beat it? And believe me they work with a will and seem to enjoy it and feel their jobs are well paid for they're singing and laughing all the time. The chauf., for example washes the car and will do anything else of any sort around the place with a glad grin—and he has papers of a first class mechanicien. But enough. I don't want to make you too envious.

I have passed my exam for a driver's license and go banging along the roads with much satisfaction—and what roads they are for driving, most of them! I now consider myself a really expert driver with an all around experience second to none. The Dupont was left hand drive with right hand shifts, of course—the Renault I had to drive during the exam which isn't such a joke here was a right hand drive with left hand shifts—and our car, which hadn't arrived at exam time, is a right hand drive with right hand shifts! In addition, one day when the car they were letting me practice on was out I drove one with a four speed in advance arrangement. So am I not right in feeling full fledged? As a final word let me say that the big Renault is some car! But keep it dark, kid, keep it dark! A Renault sounds so damn wealthy in the U.S. And the car again was a fifty-fifty break.

To return to the disagreeable topic of the Aggie, I have just received a clipping of an interview she gave to the News which strikes me as fairly tawdry stuff under the belt.[1] I opine she had a few shocks down the gullet. She seems to have managed this whole publicity business with the greatest possible amount of bad judgment and poor taste—with her exclusive interviews! And to pick out a tabloid to confess to! The lady is shamefully gumming her own game with all real people; I should think. She shows herself up as a damned bad loser—and so damned ill bred to boot. People with any decency certainly don't manage such things that way, or I'm a fool. Do you ever catch any opinions on this matter? If so, I'd like to hear them.

I won't go into detail about her antics. Suffice it to say that her lawyers up to date are trying their damndest to force an agreement on me that would make me her financial slave for life. So I've got to put up a battle in self-preservation, divorce or no divorce. Carlotta and I have discovered that as long as we stay over here the legal tie is by no means necessary and we're quite reconciled—not to add happy!—going on as we are. That is where I have the bulge on Aggie who will never be able to believe that Carlotta is not a scheming vamp who will make my life a hell on earth until I bestow my notorious name upon her, and is so evidently relying on that pressure forcing me to accept any exorbitant agreement she offers. Aggie is going to discover different, if she keeps on. In fact, she is going to find out a lot of new things about me, one of which is that when the last straw is piled on I can become a pretty ruthless enemy to have, even at the cost of keeping all my new plays to myself for some years

1. Agnes had announced, in an "exclusive" interview with the New York *Daily News* on June 21, 1928, that she was suing O'Neill for divorce in Reno or Mexico.

to come. She has pulled some pretty rough stuff, Kenneth, since you last heard from me.

But what the hell? She is so damn dead for me now that it doesn't matter—and she realizes this and it infuriates her more than anything else because she knows now that her power to hurt is gone. What she has pulled lately has been really a good thing for it has wiped her memory off my slate. I think of her only as a rather yellow-hearted female who is trying to "take me."

And that will be about all of my woes! Let us turn to the bright side, which is that Carlotta and I are more in love than ever and serene in the confidence that our future together is assured of happiness, no matter what comes up. Also, despite the worries and the interruptions Dynamo is two-thirds completed—first draft—and I think it will prove to be one of my plays. I should finish it within the next two months, no matter how Aggie tries to hinder. Whether I shall submit it to the Guild for production next season is another question, all depending on that frau's procedure. If she keeps on her present tactics, no. The sooner I am legally incomeless in that event, the sooner she'll have to wake up. I can well afford (I know the lady well enough to have foreseen what is happening and get well heeled over here) artistically as well as financially to skip a season or even two—especially as, production or not, I won't return to the States for a year from this fall at least. The plans now call for a trip around Africa by steamer with a four months settling down in a house in Cape Colony or Natal and an inland journey to Lake Tanganyika to visit the lions at home—then to Hong Kong and get a house there for four months or so. During these house periods I will write. Does it not sound grand? Well, I honestly hand it to myself that it's coming to me. I anticipate a thrill when we hit Durban in Natal and I look at the harbor and remember that eighteen years or so ago I arrived there on a catal steamer from B.A.,[2] ragged and broke 5 (this french Underwood[3] has just developed the jumps and I had to play mechanicien) But is not the above a better prospect than sitting at rehearsals watching the premium sugar cured ones work out their little notions? Yes!

Speaking of those ones, have you seen Judith Anderson cavort as Nina?[4] I know nothing about the lady other than that she was once

2. Buenos Aires.
3. O'Neill's typewriter.
4. Judith Anderson had succeeded Lynn Fontanne as Nina Leeds in the Broadway production of *Strange Interlude.*

enamoured of Louis Calhern[5] according to rumor. This I consider quite the equivalent of Nina's holding intercourse with a Polish-American private with shell shock and trench feet, so perhaps she will play the role with understanding.

Your dope about having a whirl at the detective story and your plan for same deeply intrigue me. It seems to me that might be the real way to sandbag your financial stresses. There is certainly lots of room at the top in that line, take it from one who has waded through a lot of them and found most of them incredibly lousy. Van Dine[6] certainly deserves the money he's made. And if you hit one off that brought home the bacon, then you're a nut if you don't come over here to live and do your stuff, spending only such time in New York as the occasion arises to do something in the theatre you want to do. A dollar is really mighty over here.

Tell Doc Hamilton I know I ought to have answered his fine letter long ago and that I'm going to as soon as I have read his play the second copy of which arrived three days back. The other never did get here although I wrote the Guaranty in London about it. I think it must have gone by mistake to the Paris office, which I have no dealings with, and been sent to some other O'Neill. I'm looking forward to reading the Docs book.[7]

How is Bobby these days? Do you ever see him?

For Gawd's sake go ahead with the solid articles on me! I am as sick as you of the other whim-wham.

Carlotta joins in all affectionate best to you. She says I may confide in you that she has blossomed forth into luxuriant bosoms and gained ten pounds. There is nothing serious back of this, however—it is only love. I declare that the aforesaid twins add infinitely to her beauty but she says that is only my author's pride.

Give my best—from Vienna, Berlin or whatever town you'd like me in—to anyone that ought to have it.

We're both damn sorry you can't come over. Promise you will next year!

All the breaks, Kenneth!
Gene

---

5. American stage and movie actor.

6. S. S. Van Dine, pen-name of Willard Huntington Wright (1888–1939), highly successful writer of detective fiction and creator of the character Philo Vance.

7. *A Research in Marriage* (1929), Dr. Gilbert V. Hamilton's study of the sex lives and problems of married people.

Aug 10th 1928

Kenneth dear,—

Your letter yesterday was a joy to me as well as Gene. I am happy to know your heart sings! *So does mine!*

I enclose two wee snapshots,—not so good & not so bad,—but look deep into my lover's eyes—& you will see *how HE is!*

We are both walking thro' some nasty bogs for happiness—but, dear Kenneth, *it is ours!* A richness of *understanding, depth,—strength,—gentleness,—joy*—the *ecstasy of Life,—simplicity* and *healthy passion*—all these *are ours*—& I, for one, am *humbly grateful* and *proudly rich*! Now & then the "Miasma" chokes me—but not for long—because I know that WE ARE! Each day brings us closer together—and each worry ties us more securely.

When you next see Gene you will understand—you will see the knots are gone & he has gained *freedom & loves & is interested* in *Living!*—I could *shriek* to the Heavens my joy in his liberation!—*Now,*—Life is before him & his desires *are my happiness* & I *never* will be able to repay him for *what he* has *given to me!* Bless him!

Forgive my outburst—but I want *you* to know how *I* feel!

Love always,—
—Carlotta—

---

address) c/o Guaranty Trust Co.,
50, Pall Mall, London
Guéthary, Sept. 21st [1928]

Dear Kenneth:

Well, this is the farewell before the Big Hop to the East. We're leaving here in a few days—then to Paris for a few more—then to Marseille to board the good ship. We're bound first for Hong Kong—a little over a month's voyage. I've written you before about our other plans but everything beyond H. K. is as yet tentative and will depend on what we find when we get to the East.

I sure am looking forward to getting away! I've been pestered to death lately on the domestic wrangle—cables from Harry[1] every few

---

1. Harry Weinberger.

days to answer, all sorts of decisions to make—with the only result, so far, that the miserable affair remains deadlocked. . . . [2]

And so I'll have to wait more or less on this strange lady's whim. I can only shadow box and pull the punch. It's bad on my nerves—and upsets Carlotta! But, believe me, Kenneth, once I'm free of that baby I'm going to arrange my life and affairs so I'll make her pay for this!

Outside of the above, life is happy! That sounds like a joke but isnt. What I mean is that, while I'm worried and enraged by this, it doesn't touch me inside and I'm not hurt by it. I repeat, she's too dead and I've too much real love inside me to protect me.

"Dynamo" went off to the Guild two weeks ago. I'd been working like hell on it and just managed to get it gone over before this new aspect of mess began to avalanche on me. I'm dead tired—there's been all the packing etc. to get done too. So I won't attempt to tell you any more about the play than I've already told. I'm much too on top of it and full of the reaction to know what it's all about, anyway. Madden will have scripts made from his. Get one and read it, if you like. I feel its damn good.

In this rather bewildering domestic contretemps I've missed my few real friends a lot—their advice—and expert legal advice on this side has been wanting when I've needed it. I've had to devote a hell of a lot more thought and energy to it than its worth. That has been exasperating. However, in spite of all, I'm full of new creative ideas and pep. So what the hell! But I did hope she'd get started on a divorce before I embarked so I could sail with an entirely free mind and not waiting for stabs in the back.

I deeply sympathize with your struggle with the Shuberts over Young Love.[3] What a hell of a game they've made the show shop! Did I tell you Carlotta and I ran plump into Lee Shubert & Kline[4]

2. At this point, the editors have deleted the details of O'Neill's charges against Agnes. Although, half a century later, they are not accusations that amount to very much, they remain unproven calumnies against which the subject has no defense. Because Agnes's daughters are alive, the editors have chosen not to include this material.

3. A controversial play by Samson Raphaelson, which Macgowan and Ross were trying to produce on Broadway. Apparently they were having trouble finding a theatre.

4. William Klein, lawyer for the Shuberts. When the New York district attorney closed the Shubert production of *Maya* (see Letter 84 above), the Shuberts and Klein demanded publicly that *Strange Interlude* be closed also. The official censor sent by the district attorney to view and judge O'Neill's play was unable to obtain a seat, and the matter was never resolved.

in a hotel in San Sebastian, Spain where we had motored to see the Grand Prix auto race? Has he told you that one? We shook hands smilingly as though neither had ever heard of a play called "Strange Interlude." It was a funny scene.

I'm sure damn glad to hear you're really going ahead with the detective stories! It looks to me as though that might be the easy route, as you say, to break into financial ease and so on to what you want to write.

I wrote Doc. Hamilton last week. So the Bureau of S. H. had a fit and withdrew its name, eh? What bastards! No, you hadn't told me about his introduction. That's fine stuff![5]

Yes, it is too bad Aggie didn't trust it to my generosity—but, idiotically I, with no reason, have trusted her and she, with every reason, has always suspected every move I made to be one against her! You'd think by the agreement she offered that I was lying awake nights thinking up schemes to deprive Shane & Oona of every conceivable right! And the big hitch is that she hangs on like death to a clause that gives *her* twice as much apiece for Shane & Oona as I give Eugene's mother for him—this, in case she remarries, you understand! She's dead set, it seems, that I'll have to support that next husband of hers through the medium of the childrens allowance—or keep supporting Barbara!

Can you tie it? Honestly, it's incredible!

Well, good luck, Kenneth! All the breaks to you! They're about due your way! My love to Eddy & the kids! C. joins in all affection to you. Write me—the Guaranty, London will always be forwarded. I'm glad "the grand" was a help. I'll send you cards & things from the East and let you know how we are—and where. I'm in the pink physically—but tired of nerve and a bit spiritually nauseated by this Aggie's ride around.

Again, luck!
Gene

5. Possibly a reference to *What Is Wrong with Marriage*, which Macgowan and Gilbert V. Hamilton published in 1929. Although the title page listed both as coauthors, in his introduction Hamilton indicated that this popularized version of his earlier *A Research in Marriage* was largely Macgowan's work. At this time, Hamilton was director of the Division of Psychobiological Research of the Bureau of Social Hygiene in New York City, which apparently had refused to allow its name to be used in either volume.

March 26th 1929

Kenneth—my dear—,

We rec'd your stingy wee note today enclosing clippings & a pho-
tograph of Tora Teje[1]—gorgeous woman—*thats* the kind of Nina *I'd*
like to see!—

Kenneth, let your Scotch brain work & get some kind of job that
brings you to Europe after June—to come & stay with us in Tour-
aine.—When we leave here—we go there—lovely, peaceful old
France. No Americans—English or Dutch! And *I* want you (apart
from being the gracious hostess for Gene!) & hope above hope you'll
manage somehow,—bring Bobbie too & Miss Serg*eant*![2] No one else!

We'll have so much to say—or will we? Talk means so little after
all—but we'll be happy & you'll understand.—And it will be
peace—dear Kenneth—& I want *you* there,—dear loyal you—to feel
happy with us & we'll laugh & laugh!—I am all plans for a real *home*
for us.—We really do deserve it.—Gene looks so well & deep in
work—& his soul *rich*!

Hope you found Dr. Hamilton well. I hope to meet him some
day—

Love to you—& bless you—

Carlotta

June 14th 1929

Dear Kenneth:

The above is the permanent address for the next few years—to be
kept strictly under the old hat! We are still in process of getting
moved in but already I feel soundly at home here. It is a beautiful
place as we hope you will some day prove with your own eyes. There
are acres and acres of farm and wonderful old woods attached, a

1. Swedish actress who later played in 1933 productions of *Mourning Becomes Electra* and
Desire Under the Elms.

2. Robert Edmond Jones and Elizabeth Shepley Sergeant, two of the very few persons
trusted by O'Neill and Carlotta with details of their romance.

stream running through in which I am arranging a swimming pool—and what not—everything! Its the sort of house I've always dreamed about but never could have achieved in our U. S. The life of the farm can be observed and absorbed on all sides—and yet at a proper distance from the sweat of it. There are chickens and ducks and a large herd of prize cows and a flock of six hundred sheep and wheat fields and vegetable gardens galore. From all of which we get the benefit without any responsibility since the proprietors retain the farm end of it. In all the place comprises about seven hundred acres and its quite a bike ride around its private roads. The house itself is a fairly large chateau, with tourelles, with grand old carven wood furniture. I have a corking study—and, believe me, there is going to be some real work done in it! The price per year of all this grandeur amounts to a little over fifty dollars a month apiece! Think of it! Of course the place is old—a virtue for us!—and we have to use oil lamps and there is only one bath room, etc. But we love that too! And, of course, we have to have quite a few servants—but their wages don't count up to what we'd pay two good ones in God's country. Altogether the grandest bargain—this Le Plessis—that I've ever heard of! And we pay no taxes except the French income tax which doesn't amount to much. The low rental is explained by the fact that we're in real French country, undefiled by the usual rich expatriates, and the natives here won't stand for the high stuff. But at that we were incredibly lucky. This is the one spot in this section of the few that were available that we wanted at all. People don't rent their places around here, particularly furnished. They stick or sell. Our landladies are three sisters of the provincial nobility, the Vicomptesse de Banville, the Marquise de Verdun and another title. The old story of the parents dying and none of the heirs being able to keep up the place separately accounts for its being rentable. These nobilities were inclined to eye us with misgiving at first but they immediately approved of Carlotta who knew how to treat them on their own plane, having been educated over here, and when they found out I was an eminent member of the Institute (U.S.)[1] they accepted me as non-barbarian. And since then they have been the most considerate and courteous people you could wise for landlords. It is a pleasure to deal with them. They are anything but the grasping

1. The National Institute of Arts and Letters. O'Neill had received its gold medal for drama in 1923. Apparently the three French women considered the Institute the equivalent of the French Academy.

O'Neill and Carlotta at Le Plessis

French one hears so much about from Americans and whom one so rarely meets except in the resort districts.

That's enough space to devote to our new home—but I can't tell you how enthusiastic I am about it or how deeply at home and at peace I feel here already! And my inside needs just that. God knows I've had enough of hopping about in temporary shelters since I left N.Y. Here there is a sense of permanency.

I've been working like hell for the past week on Dynamo—second set of proofs which I've again done a drastic job on—cut the minister entirely out of the last part, etc., etc. It will be a much better play when you read it in the book.[2] The new scenes, one entirely of thought soliloquoy, help a lot in clearing up and emphasizing.

Yes, I am off of the rest of the trilogy[3] for a year or so. First because it isn't really a trilogy anyway and I now want each play to stand as a separate entity. Secondly because my messiness and bad judgment about Dynamo and its resulting sacrifice has had its reaction in making me temporarily cold toward the two ideas connected in my mind with "D." Thirdly because I wouldn't want to write the Catholic "Without Ending of Days" now any way because of the queer coincidence that its story, although I had it written out long before I thought of breaking with A, would be sure to be misinterpreted (especially by you psycho-sharks!) as thinly-veiled autobiography where the wife and two young children of the play are concerned. And I wouldn't want that for the sake of anyone involved.

But fourthly and most importantly, my whole urge is toward the new large idea I've been doping out for some time now. It arouses my creative enthusiasm as the thing with the biggest scope to turn loose my intensest effort—and that's what I need now. I won't go into details. Suffice it that it will be the biggest thing I've yet attempted.[4] No, don't guess! It has nothing to do with my Grand Opus founded on autobiographical material.[5] This is something entirely new.

And here's another thing I'm off of for good! No more sets or theatrical devices as anything but unimportant background—except in

2. *Dynamo* had opened on Broadway on February 11, 1929, and lasted only 50 performances. O'Neill, upset by what he felt was the critics' inability to understand the play, was making numerous revisions for the published version.

3. *Dynamo* had originally been conceived as the first play in a trilogy exploring "the sickness of today." The plan was never completed.

4. O'Neill is referring to what later became *Mourning Becomes Electra*.

5. "The Sea-Mother's Son" (see Letter 86 above).

the most imperatively exceptional case where organically they belong. To read "Dynamo" is to stumble continually over the sets. They're always in my way, writing and reading—and they are in the way of the dramatic action. Hereafter I write plays primarily as literature to be read—and the more simply they read, the better they will act, no matter what technique is used. "Interlude" is a proof of this. I don't mean that I wouldn't use masks again in the writing if a Lazarus or Brown should demand it—but I do mean that my trend will be to regard anything depending on director or scenic designer for collaboration to bring out its full values as suspect. Brown & Lazarus, of course, don't. They will always convey more to a readers imagination than any production can give. But I'm fed up with the show shop we call a theatre in the world today and I refuse to write any more which uses it. Constructivism and such stuff is all right for directors but its only in an authors way. At least that's the way I feel now. Greater classical simplicity, austerity combined with the utmost freedom and flexibility, that's the stuff! But more of this when I can talk to you. It's too long.

June 20th (cont.)

I stopped this letter intending to go on with it the next day but there has been so much doing in the way of work in the a.ms.—getting my new stuff thoroughly doped out on paper before I get down to actual dialogue, and doing a lot of reading in connection with the theme that will take me a month or so yet—and getting stuff around the house settled in the p.ms and swimming and biking and walking and what not, that I have had no chance for correspondence.

The papers in England seem to have got hold of some weird story that I am dying of T. B. in Switzerland and I suppose it got relayed to the States. How the hell it got started I don't know. This is the second time this year the reporters have Camilled me and it comes at an inopportunely healthy time when I never felt better! Why is T. B. so romantic to the news folk, I wonder? Haven't they heard yet that Dumas Fils is dead?

What do you think of my plagiarism suit?[6] Wouldn't it nut you! But I suppose I'm lucky to have escaped so long from such swine—

6. On May 27, 1929, a woman who wrote under the pen-name George Lewys had filed a suit in a New York court charging that *Strange Interlude* was plagiarized from her novel *The Temple of Pallas-Athenae*, which had been privately published in 1924. After a week-long and much publicized trial in March 1930, Lewys's suit was dismissed as "wholly pre-

or fools. What gravels me is that this bitch is getting a million bucks worth of publicity—all she's really after, probably!—and I'm bound to loose in the matter of trial expenses no matter how much I win! Our laws in this regard certainly encourage blackmailers and exhibitionists! Such a case would be impossible any where else. It makes me sore. And her fool book—which I haven't yet seen—was privately printed at that. It's like accusing a drunkard of stealing marshmallow sundaes.

Your description of the Pasadena Lazarus production sounds surprisingly good. I agree with you about the double-sized masks. I'm going to change that in the script sometime when I get a chance. It doesn't seem to mean anything special to me any more—the double size idea.

I don't imagine you'll get Norman[7] to back any O'Neill road rep. He isn't really much interested in the theatrical game. But somebody ought to glimpse a chance for return in it. I think it would make money, don't you? Why don't you try Lee Shubert on it? I'm serious. Tell him I seriously suggested it.

I hope nothing in my last put you off the O'Neill book. I wish to hell you would do it, you know that! I'll feel much different about it as soon as all my present publicity is over—about divorce & plagiarism. Did I mention in my last Mickle's book published by Cape in England "Six Plays of E.O'N"?[8] It has received some good write-ups there.

Speaking about "Jones" & movies, have you seen Dudley Murphy?[9] He was speaking to Madden about some scheme he had for it.

Tell Doc. Hamilton he's right about marriage, Take it from a good Catholic! But free love, as I've bitterly learned from all the humiliating dodges we've had to go through in the past year even in Europe & the East, is a worse form of slavery to convention when you're in the public eye with "the boys" after you and people beside yourself to be protected! But, come to think of it, that's all an effect of marriage too! Yes, the Doc is entirely correct!

---

posterous" and she was ordered to pay O'Neill $7,500, the Theatre Guild (producers of the play) $5,000, and O'Neill's publisher $5,000—none of which was ever collected, as she had no money.

7. Probably Norman Winston, a successful New York shoe manufacturer who had backed the Provincetown Playhouse and who was a friend of both Macgowan and O'Neill.

8. Alan D. Mickle's *Six Plays of Eugene O'Neill*, published in 1929 by Jonathan Cape in London and Horace Liveright in New York.

9. Director of the 1933 film version of *The Emperor Jones*.

I'm sorry about the book. I had imagined it was booming.[10]

C. joins with me in all affectionate best! Find some dodge that will bring you over here!

> As ever,
> Gene

---

92 • TO MACGOWAN FROM O'NEILL. ALS 2 pp. (On stationery headed: Le Plessis / Saint-Antoine du Rocher / (Indre-et-Loire))

> July 26th 1929

P.S. Write some news!

Dear Kenneth:

Much gratitude from us both for your cable! We feel all fixed now—and happy![1]

Wish you could come over. It's grand here at Plessis. I'll send you some snaps—when I've taken some!

Not much work done in past few weeks, as you can imagine. This, that and the other to be attended to—plus plagiarism suits—can you beat that!—and other stuff. But from now on expect to be hard at it.

Eugene[2] is coming to visit soon—is at present in Germany. I look forward to seeing him.

All best to Doc. H. when you write. Is there any chance of his ever coming to Europe? Would love to have him here.

My best to Norman[3] when you see him. I've meant to write him but have been so on the hop haven't written anyone but Harry W. on legal stuff. Too many of those letters!

Carlotta joins in all love

> Gene

P.S. Am I posted at Harvard Club?[4]
P.S. II Love to Eddy & the kids.

---

10. *What Is Wrong with Marriage.*

1. Eugene O'Neill and Carlotta Monterey had been married in Paris on July 22, 1929.
2. Eugene O'Neill, Jr., who had graduated with high honors from Yale and was now taking postgraduate courses at the University of Freiburg.
3. Norman Winston.
4. O'Neill wonders whether his name is posted at the Harvard Club for nonpayment of dues.

93 • TO MACGOWAN FROM O'NEILL. ALS 2 pp. (On stationery headed: Le Plessis / Saint-Antoine du Rocher / (Indre-et-Loire))

March 28th '30

Dear Kenneth:

We've been off on a long motor tour vacation and I didn't get your letter until we returned a few days ago. Reason for the vacation was I'd finished my first draft after 4½ months of the most concentrated labor I've ever put in and felt all washed up and in need of a change of scene to get a little perspective on what I'd done.[1]

I'm disappointed to learn "Children of Darkness" didn't bring home the bacon.[2] Judging from what I'd seen of the notices I was hoping you had a big success. Hard luck! But it was a real smash artistically, wasn't it, and it did put the new firm on the map in the right way. So what the hell. You're off to a fine start. I sure hope the Wilbur Steele opus[3] will connect. Apart from your end of it I've always thought Wilbur was one grand guy and real friend of mine and anything he does has my loudest cheers. Also I've always been keen on what he wrote. Give him my best when you see him and let me know his address. I'd like to write him when the mood is on.

I'd like to meet Reed. Tell him to drop in here—give me plenty of warning so I'll be sure to be here. If he's going to tour around France he'll be sure to visit Tours and the chateau district and we are only ten kilometres from Tours. He's due to be disappointed if he expects to see anything interesting in the European theatre. From all I've seen and heard of, it's all pretty cheap and dull.

As for my own opus, I'll let you in on this in the strictest confidence (for the present)—it is a trilogy but one quite apart from the loose "Dynamo" trio—entirely different, no connection whatever. This is a real trilogy carrying on the same characters, etc.—not just a general theme resemblance between plays. I've finished the first draft of all three. It was some job! But I'm pleased—in fact, enthusiastic. Of course, there's a hell of a lot still to be done. I intend to write it over twice more in long hand, with spells of letting it rest

1. O'Neill had finished the first draft of *Mourning Becomes Electra* on February 21, 1930.
2. Play by Edwin Justus Mayer that had opened on January 7, 1930, at Broadway's Biltmore Theatre, produced by Macgowan and Joseph Verner Reed as the first venture of their new partnership.
3. *When Hell Froze*, adapted by Wilbur Daniel Steele and Norma Mitchell from a Steele short story. Macgowan and Reed opened the play, starring Jane Cowl, in Boston in late September 1930.

up in between, before I even have it typed; so there isn't much chance of it being ready for production for any time next season. Some labor! But it's the biggest thing I have ever tackled and I aim to give it every chance to become what it ought to be.

In the way of personal news, there's nothing much. I'm fit and so is Carlotta and we're a happy married couple and life is pleasant here in our chateau. Damn sorry you're not coming over. You'd like this Le Plessis home. It's the goods!

Have you seen the Garbo "Anna C"?[4] Is it good. And what is this "Green Pastures" play[5] really like the press boys are making such a fuss over?

All affectionate best to you, Eddy, and the kids!

As ever,
Gene

---

94 • TO MACGOWAN FROM CARLOTTA O'NEILL. ALS 8 pp. (On stationery headed: Le Plessis / Saint-Antoine du Rocher / (Indre-et-Loire))

May 24th 1930

Dear nice Scotch Kenneth,

I love the Scotch & I *know* them—I've lived in Scotland—& I was married to one![1]—Dear *loyal* souls—such a rare thing in this life of parasites and weaklings.—

But—will you tell me *why*—in the name of Heaven—Gene & I should apologize to anyone in this world if we have *thirty* servants or *no* servants?[2] Will you tell me *why* you get fussed because a lot of *failures, sore heads, drunks,* and *would-be artists* (in one line or another) thro' envy, disappointment and jealousy criticize a man because he lives in the manner that all middle class people (have they the money!) live? It is too absurd. As far as *my friends* are concerned & their criticism of me—my dear Kenneth I have *three friends* in N.Y.

4. The second film version (the first was a 1923 silent film) of *"Anna Christie,"* starring Greta Garbo, had been released in February 1930.

5. Play by American playwright Marc Connelly (1890–1981), which had opened on Broadway on February 26, 1930, and had aroused controversy—due to its depiction of biblical figures, including "De Lawd," using black actors and actresses—as well as almost universal critical praise. It won the 1930 Pulitzer Prize.

1. Carlotta's first husband was Scottish lawyer John Moffat.

2. Macgowan had apparently written expressing dismay at stateside gossip about Eugene and Carlotta.

& *they* only criticize me to my face!—The rest are parasites who borrow money of me (& hate me afterwards—[Gene has suffered from this same strange experience])—& people who invited me to their houses & I never accepted etc. etc.—Now, when they are left behind with their speakeasy life they hate us all the more!—I never knew people before who discussed other people's financial affairs. I was always brought up to look upon that as the *height* of bad form!—But these would-be friends of Gene's confuse Gene's third wife with his second. . . .[4]

I have always lived on my own. Outside my first husband (Gene is my fourth!) no husband has ever purchased a rag for my back—I have never asked for alimony—& consider myself much too decent a person to bleat my troubles to the world. I have gone thro' hell—but few have known I was capable of suffering. I don't give a damn for anyone in N.Y. outside of three people,—and am happy, content & busy. I have given Gene, for the first time in his life, a decent home. I have introduced him to Beethoven, Bach, Franck & all good music from which he derives great pleasure.—I have taken him to good tailors, bootmakers, shirt makers, etc.—so that he feels a well being & pleasure in dressing. I have done everything possible to make him forget the self conscious, uneasy, slovenly atmosphere in which he lived.—I was crucified for eighteen months nursing him body, soul & mind—being called a harlot & other pleasant names—by the so-called friends of Gene's—while they were sympathizing with the "dear little woman" who had been left behind, . . .[5]

If you hear that I refused to have Mrs. Light[6] in my house it is true. Mr. L. was here for one night (his excuse to talk business!) but he will not come again. None of those sympathizers will ever walk in *my* house while I am in it. And G. explained *why* to Mr. L. & he asked G. to see Mrs. L. just for a moment!!! We were in Paris—at the hotel. I arranged tea & went out to an Art Exhibit. And she *knowing* how G. felt forced herself upon him! That is the Jew of it! The jews in N.Y.—that man Winston[7] (or whatever he calls himself)

3. Carlotta O'Neill inserted square brackets in the text of this letter.
4. The editors have deleted here a brief passage referring to O'Neill's unsubstantiated charges against Agnes.
5. Another brief deletion has been made here.
6. Provincetowner James Light's second wife, Patti.
7. Norman Winston.

even G.'s attorney[8]—I never, in my long & varied experience, have come across such tactless, thick skinned, stupid people.—

But—what they say or think means nothing to me.—Gene's work & comfort is *my* job! I pay *one half of all our expenses. I am under no obligations to anyone & never have been*—.

Now—we understand each other. And I *beg* of you,—no matter *what* they say,—to never apologize for us. We *have* a huge château,—we *have* 10 servants,—we *have* a concrete swimming pool,—we *have* three cars! And *I* nearly *bought* a château (*with* MY OWN MONEY.). Thank God, Gene talked me out of it! Because we will eventually buy a home in America.—

This letter is vulgar—but the superb is vulgar! Most of those people think of nothing but money.—They rarely earn any so must always be a parasite on some one. God give them success in some line & us peace!—

You're a dear.—but much too mild—. CUSS! it would you good.—Open up & let the spirit flow,—don't let these male & female chestnut worms annoy you!

Our love always—dear Scotch Kenneth—

Carlotta

---

95 • TO MACGOWAN FROM CARLOTTA O'NEILL. ALS 1 p. (On stationery headed: Le Plessis / Saint-Antoine du Rocher / (Indre-et-Loire))

[June 1930?]

To Kenneth—love from Gene & "Blemie" & "Bess"[1] and Carlotta

You can send those of the house etc—back to me as I simply send them to you to give you an idea of Plessis & grounds![2]—

Some day I'll take a good snap of the whole of the front of Plessis & send it to you! It is quite lovely—

8. Harry Weinberger.

1. "Blemie" was the O'Neills' Dalmatian dog; "Bess" was apparently another pet, possibly an Irish setter.
2. Enclosed with this letter were snapshots of Le Plessis, O'Neill, and the pets.

Hotel du Rhin,
Paris, France
Feb. 4th 1931

Dear Kenneth:

I was damn glad to get your letter. You are quite right about it. I do owe you one, but there has been very little news to write about. I have kept on working steadily and now have all three plays typed. The work was held up somewhat by both Carlotta and myself getting the grippe almost simultaneously—and we didn't just get it, we really got it! Carlotta has been in the American Hospital for two weeks taking a rest recuperation. She was all in. She got up too soon down at Le Plessis in order to nurse me and the come back keeled her over, but she is out now and feeling much better and we expect to light out for the Canary Islands in a couple of weeks and stay there a month and get some hot sun. The damn weather here has been incredible and I have had all of winter in France that I ever want to have. I think it has been either raining or gray nine days out of ten for the past year. I am going to do my final going over of the plays at the Canaries.

I was damned sorry to get the news about Wilbur's play.[1] I had hoped for all of your sakes that that one would be a knockout. I have read fine things of your Twelvth Night[2] and wish I could see it. You are undoubtedly right in thinking that it has done your firm a lot of good—even if it hasn't made much money.

If you are going to be in London in March, I will perhaps still be at the Canaries then. Anyway if you have only a week over here, you certainly would not have time to come to Tours, and frankly I would not invite a dog down to Tourraine in this weather. The grounds of our rented estate make very fine frog ponds, but they are not much use unless you are amphibious. Even a New England winter begins to look good after our experience down there this year.

I have not heard the news from London yet although Interlude was

---

1. *When Hell Froze*, which never reached Broadway.

2. Macgowan and Reed's production of *Twelfth Night*, starring Jane Cowl, had opened on October 15, 1930, at Broadway's Maxine Elliott's Theatre and had been hailed by Brooks Atkinson of the *New York Times* as "the finest Shakespeare New York has seen for many a day." It lasted only 65 performances, however.

supposed to open on Monday, but I have a hunch that the news will be bad when it comes. I can't imagine the "limies" getting very steamed up about that play. And I am not much excited about the whole business one way or another. What happens in the English theatre leaves me so cold.

The expectant father rumors were all the bunk.[3] Between us we have four children already and find they are expensive and we are not such gluttons for punishment that we want to take on any more of these responsibilities—in bringing into the world fresh victims for the new poison gases which the lads are preparing for our children.

All best to Eddy and the children—and as ever all friendship to you from us both.

Gene

Mr. Kenneth Mac Gowan,
Mac Gowan and Reed Inc.,
122 East 42nd Street,
New York City.

P.S. Be sure and let me know exactly when you will be in London. Perhaps we will be back from the Canaries by then and perhaps the weather will be such in Tourraine by that time that I can invite a visitor without it giving me a guilty conscience, and perhaps you will find you will have time to make the trip—in which cases you must certainly hop to us. You can imagine how much I would like to have a talk with you about everything in general and how much pleasure a visit from you would give us both!

---

97 • TO MACGOWAN FROM O'NEILL. ALS 1 p.

1095 Park Avenue
Dec. 29th 1931

Dear Kenneth:

I've been laid up, most of the time in bed, practically all the interim since our return from Georgia.[1] Otherwise I'd have given you

3. Walter Winchell had erroneously reported in his September 8, 1930, syndicated gossip column that the O'Neills were expecting a baby.

1. The O'Neills returned to the U.S. on May 17, 1931. They had recently vacationed for a month at Sea Island, Georgia, and had bought property with the intention of settling there permanently.

a ring or dropped a line. Have felt too punk—head like a baloon stuffed with dough—but you know. Probably you've been enjoying a bout, too. It seems to be universal just now. Christmas appears to be my unlucky period. This time last year both Carlotta and I were groggy with "flu" at Le Plessis. So the Seasonal Cheer misses out on me! But I'm better today and hope this is final.

How are the chances for you coming up to lunch or dinner in the near future? Pick your own time and give us a ring tomorrow or next day and say when. Our secret no. is Sacramento 2-5360. I've lots to tell you—about Georgia—found a grand spot down there—wonderful bathing, boating, etc.—hated to return to this damned climate.

It's great news that you've finally got a hit that will also bring home the bacon![2] I'm damned glad! You know that. Won't this encourage friend Reed to stick by the ship? The last time I saw you you seemed to think he'd be out after this year.

I haven't looked at the second "Electra" troupe yet.[3] They tell me it's none too bad.

Well, come along and let's talk. We'll fix up the Banks[4] meeting for later. I haven't forgotten it.

All best!
Gene

---

98 • TO CARLOTTA O'NEILL FROM MACGOWAN. TL (cc) 1 p.
AUGUST EIGHTEEN
1 9 3 3

Mrs. Eugene O'Neill
Big Wolf Lake
New York

Dear Carlotta:

My apprehension about Gene's lungs was no slur on your nursing. T.B. graduates are notoriously apprehensive—about the other fellow. I am terribly glad that all is well with both of you.

2. After two flops, *Lean Harvest* (38 performances in October 1931) and *The Lady with a Lamp* (12 performances in November 1931), Macgowan and Reed's production of Benn W. Levy's *Springtime for Henry* had opened on December 9, 1931, at Broadway's Bijou Theatre, where it remained for 198 performances.
3. A second company of *Mourning Becomes Electra*, starring Judith Anderson and Florence Reed, was touring the U.S.
4. Possibly Leslie Banks, one of the stars of *Springtime for Henry*.

I wrote Gene that I'd like to return the money I owe him, when and if RKO renews my contract[1] (which comes up in a month.) I am afraid I've been visualizing him as enormously and Interludishly wealthy. Anyway, here's my check for half my debt. And by sending it I'm not writing off a tenth of the debt I owe him.

Affectionately,
Kenneth Macgowan

---

99 • TO O'NEILL FROM MACGOWAN. WIRE 1 p.

OCTOBER 2, 1933

TO:
EUGENE O'NEILL
GUILD THEATRE
WEST 52ND STREET
NEW YORK CITY

I WISH I COULD BE WITH YOU TONIGHT[1]
(SIGNED) KENNETH MACGOWAN

---

100 • TO CARLOTTA O'NEILL FROM MACGOWAN. TL (cc) 1 p.

October 7, 1933

Dear Carlotta:
See what has just come back to my desk after I don't know how many weeks! This makes me wonder if Gene got my letter about THE HAIRY APE.[1]

The news is wonderful concerning AH WILDERNESS. I only hope our company comes out on top in the bidding.[2]

Hastily,

1. Macgowan had recently become a producer at RKO Pictures.

1. O'Neill's *Ah, Wilderness!* opened on October 2, 1933, at Broadway's Guild Theatre.

1. A letter from Macgowan to one of the O'Neills (probably Carlotta) had been returned to the sender. Macgowan's note seems to be a covering letter as he sends off the undelivered letter. He had apparently written to O'Neill suggesting a film version of *The Hairy Ape*, but that letter was not delivered or returned.
2. RKO was trying to buy the film rights to *Ah, Wilderness!* MGM eventually outbid them and acquired the rights.

101 • TO MACGOWAN FROM CARLOTTA O'NEILL. ALS 2 pp. (On
stationery headed: The Madison / Hotel and Restaurant / Madison Avenue at
58th Street / New York / Telephone Volunteer 5-5000)

Oct. 11th '33

Dear Kenneth—

Thanks for letter & cheque—Gene will write soon. We're just
packing to return home (to Georgia) tonight—Hence this hasty
scrawl.

Gene & I were touched by your thought of sending a wire for the
opening of "Wilderness." It is a dear play—tender, charming &
filled with laughter. Divine for Movies—& many are trying to buy
it.—

Bob Sisk[1] talked of the "Hairy Ape" & "Desire" for Movies—&
"talk" goes on. They do such rotten jobs.—They spoiled "Jones"—

But we never see any of the them—so it doesn't matter. We sell
them for *money* to buy the babies shoes!—

We rec'd no letter from *you* re "Hairy Ape"—

Dearest love & blessings from us both—

Carlotta

You will be pleased to know the $500.00 pays for a carpet &
couch for *our home*!—

---

102 • TO CARLOTTA O'NEILL FROM MACGOWAN. TL (cc) 1 p.

October 16, 1933

Mrs. Eugene O'Neill
Sea Island, Georgia

Dear Carlotta:

It must have been a week or two before you went to the Adiron-
dacks, that I wrote Gene about "The Hairy Ape," and I sent the
letter to the old Park Avenue address, and told him a good deal
about what had been happening to me. I will sit down one of these
days and go to it again. The thing about "The Hairy Ape" was simply that I wondered if he had a copy of the treatment he once made

---

1. Robert Sisk, formerly the press agent for the Theatre Guild and in 1933 a movie
executive. Sisk was one of the very few people who retained Eugene and Carlotta O'Neill's
trust and affection.

of it with silent pictures in mind. I told him that I thought I might be able to stir up RKO.

I expected to be sending you another check, but the NRA business[1] has apparently caused the studio to back-pedal on my new contract. They want to up my salary some, but not enough, and so I am running along from week to week waiting for Merian Cooper, the head of the studio, to get back from a vacation enforced by illness.

Anyway, I will write soon.

I wish to God our studio could spend more money on plays. I am afraid that M.G.M. or one of the others will get "Ah, Wilderness!"

Ever and ever,

---

103 • TO MACGOWAN FROM O'NEILL. TLS 4 pp. (On stationery headed: Casa Genotta / Sea Island / Georgia)

[October 16, 1933][1]

Dear Kenneth,

I have been waiting to write you until the hectic period of "AH, WILDERNESS" production passed and we got temporarily put down here again.

First, many thanks for the cheque. But I hope you didn't put any strain on the bankroll to do it. You remember our agreement that you were not even to think of repaying me until all other obligations were off your chest and you felt on easy street. You know, if I were ever hard pinched, I would let out a frank howl to you for assistance. Things looked bad for a while last winter, what with the hole my "sound conservative investments" had dumped me into, and my alimony overhead (which depression leaves undepressed!) but they never quite had me completely down. And now "AH, WILDERNESS" has gone over, all's well again. I explain all this because I don't want you ever to have me on your mind—that way—and get that debtor feeling which is so fatal to old friendship. And now that's said again, let's forget it.

I hoped you liked my nostalgic adventure into comedy in "AH, WILDERNESS." I think it should hand you many reminiscent

1. President Franklin D. Roosevelt had established the National Recovery Administration in 1933 to set a minimum-wage provision and to institute a number of other "fair employment practice" guidelines.

1. The date is supplied from O'Neill's mention in the letter that this day was his 45th birthday.

grins. You will remember those good old days as well as I, and you must have known many Miller families. I had a grand time writing it—also a grand time rehearsing, for the cast, taking it all in all from bits to leads, is the best I have ever had in a play. They really make it live very close to what I imagined it. A most enjoyable experience in the theatre, all told—and how the damn thing moves young, middle-aged and old! It's astonishing. And a proof to me, at least, that emotionally we still deeply hanker after the old solidarity of the family unit.

"DAYS WITHOUT END," the mask, pseudo-Faustian, "modern miracle play" opus goes into rehearsal about December first. I want it to open as soon after Christmas day as possible because then, if ever now, you catch people in a frame of mind to remember their past or present religious background. I think this play will interest you, psychologically as well as technically, and the ending astonish you a bit, coming from me. It was an end I resisted (on personal grounds) but which finally forced itself on me as the one inevitable one.

These two plays will, I know, set you to wondering what sea change has come over me. The truth is that, after "ELECTRA" I felt I had gone as far as it was in me to go along my old line—for the time being, at least. I felt that to try to top myself in various other phases of the old emotional attitude would be only to crucify my work on what had become for the time an exhausted formula. I felt a need to liberate myself from myself, so to speak—to see and express, if possible, the life preserving forces in other aspects which I knew from experience to be equally illustrative of the fate in human beings lives and aspirations. In short, I felt the justice in the criticism that my plays in toto were too one-way and presented only one side of the picture, and that, if only to bring out that tragic side by contrast, I ought to express the others. And now, whatever the fate of "DAYS WITHOUT END," I'M damned glad I did, for I feel immensely freer inside myself and better able to digest *all* the demands that future work may entail.

Well, well, there I go again giving you an earnest, heartfelt earful. Like old times, what? But then a guy ought to have some rights to express himself on his 45th birthday. In which connection, I must assert as no self-deluding lie but as a fact, that I'm damned if I don't feel a hell of a lot younger, body and spirit, than I did at 35 or 25. And there's a reason—*Carlotta.*

Your fear that our Adirondack jaunt might have been T.B. inspired was baseless. I never felt better—and T.B. has always been the least of my worries. If that had been on the cards, I would have been just too dead ten or fifteen years ago. What happened was we had a chance to rent a beautiful camp there for almost nothing and jumped at it. You see, the climate down here is very much like Bermuda—fine for ten months but August and September are oppressively hot and hard to take. So we'll probably go North someplace every year at that time.

I hope sometime you'll get a chance to visit us here. Carlotta has designed a really beautiful home for us. She has a marvellous flair for that—and for keeping it running right. At last I know the meaning of home. And don't we both love it!

Sometime, if you're ever in the mood and have the leisure, I wish you'd write me about your experiences on the Coast, and what, if any, are your hopes that something real may finally come thro' out there.

You mention a letter re the "THE HAIRY APE." No such ever reached me.

Ever see Dr. Hamilton? If so, my warm greetings to him.

All best, Kenneth, and to your wife and the kids. I hope we'll have a chance to get together again before too long. In the meantime, drop a line.

As ever,
Gene

P.S. Bobby, of course, did a marvellous job on "AH, WILDER-NESS."[2] You should see the costumes and rooms and the beach scene.

---

104 • TO O'NEILL FROM MACGOWAN. TL (cc) 1 p.

October 25, 1933

Mr. Eugene O'Neill
Sea Island, Georgia

Dear Gene:

It was swell to hear from you, and at such length. As soon as I get a little time to myself I will try to repeat all the personal history

2. Robert Edmond Jones had designed the sets and costumes for the Theatre Guild production of *Ah, Wilderness!*

which went to you in the letter that got lost somewhere between the old Park Avenue address and Georgia.

Apropos of "The Hairy Ape," the attached clipping from the Hollywood Reporter indicates that the silent scenario which I want to get hold of has turned up in a book shop. I wonder if you have a copy.

Hastily,
Kenneth Macgowan

---

105 • TO O'NEILL FROM MACGOWAN. TL (cc) 1 p.

January 12, 1934

Mr. Eugene O'Neill
Sea Island, Georgia

Dear Gene:

I have a swell alibi this time. The head of the studio has been away sick for four months and his assistant went away a month ago and left me holding the bag. The boss is back and the assistant will be back in a few weeks and then I will stop spending my nights reading scripts and instead I will write you a letter.

I read most of the reviews of your new play[1] today and of course got a very mixed impression. I sent to the book shop for a copy and hope to be enjoying myself the moment the boss' assistant gets back.

I am sending you a copy of the scenario of "Strange Interlude."[2] I dug this up for Bob Sisk when he was out here, and it occurs to me you might like it as a curiosity.

Best luck to Carlotta, and the same to you.

Yours,
Kenneth Macgowan

1. *Days Without End*, which had opened on January 8, 1934, at Broadway's Henry Miller Theatre; the play was published by Random House in the same month.
2. MGM had produced a film version of *Strange Interlude* in 1932, starring Norma Shearer and Clark Gable.

Dear Kenneth,

Many thanks for the cheque—and for your letter which I was darned glad to receive. The tale of your labor sounds gruelling but if you're getting fat on it, and the bankroll also, what the hell? I'm more in touch with R.K.O. doings than you'd suspect. See a lot of Bob Sisk in N.Y. and he writes me down here. He told me about "The Devil's Disciple."[1] It strikes me as a grand idea. You ought to get something fine out of that—if they'll let you alone.

Did you see "Emperor Jones"?[2] I didn't. I heard too much about it—how they'd messed up the first part with a lot of old stuff, Harlem hooey, etc. Too bad. There was a chance there. And I know they started off with the best intentions of doing something original and imaginative. Also, they had a fine man for the dialogue of the new stuff—Du Bois Heyward.[3] I gave him my ideas for the silent treatment—and his own ideas were all good. But in the last stages of the making, rumour has it that everybody concerned started stepping on everyone else—and the result a shoddy compromise. However, I wail not, I got my money.

I'm glad you liked "Ah, Wilderness," I knew it would hand you a reminiscent chuckle. It's a play which seems to hit all ages and classes one way or another—even, judging from letters and talks,—the modern college youth whom I thought would be sure to be superior. The production goes merrily along—looks good for the rest of the season.

Re "Days Without End," as you've probably heard, the critical lads fair beshit themselves. I expected all along they would, and they sure lived up to expectations! Haven't run into such an idiotic storm of prejudice since the good old days of "All God's Chillun." It constantly kept reminding me of that event. I mean, everyone lined up as anti-Catholic and just too sophisticatedly modern-sceptical—and in the resultant flood of smart-crack bilge the play was drowned and lost sight of. No one saw it as a psychological study with, I think, profound implications, except a few psychologists. No one grasped

---

1. A film adaptation of Shaw's play was under consideration, but it never materialized.

2. The film version of O'Neill's play, starring Paul Robeson, had been released in the fall of 1933.

3. DuBose Heyward was coauthor of *Porgy* (1927).

its Faustian undertheme, none saw what I intended in labelling it "A Modern Miracle Play." No one saw its larger—and obvious—aspect as a play which beyond its particular Catholic foreground is a drama of spiritual faith and love in general—that is, it was only Jesuits and Catholic theologians who saw this! No one—But why go on? You will gather that no one got me except a very few exceptions. But I'm confident that in other countries this play will come into its own. (It's already on the way to production at the Abbey Theatre, for one instance). And for me personally it's very much a success. The Guild production was good—Larrimore[4] excellent—Simonson[5] did a fine job—but I doubt if it can live beyond subscriptions, so great was the hostile critical barage. Well, I certainly never expected it would be a financial success—nor did the Guild—so this is not such a blow as might be. I wish you could see it. The technique, mask, etc. would interest you and you'd be astonished the way it holds audiences tensely and silently all thro' to six to ten curtain calls nightly at the end—Guild audiences three-quarter Jewish! And yet the critical jackasses have the nerve to say the technique doesn't come off! If we could get people in the theater, I really believe now this play could be a success—but the reviewers keep too many away, that's the trouble. It's alive for those who go. I've had more letters from people about this play than any play I've ever written—which must prove something.

What am I doing now? Loafing determinedly. For twenty-two months with practically no let up—I was either writing or rehearsing—thinking nothing but plays—and I feel as stale as mousetrap cheese on the theatre. I won't start anything new for a long while. I'm fed up.

Yes, this Sea Island is good stuff. There are some lacks but, all in all I can't imagine a better place for a home—and, thanks to Carlotta, we have a grand one. Did you see pictures of it in the January HOUSE AND GARDEN? Not so good, but they'd give you an idea.

Much gratitude for the invitation but it's not likely we'll be going to the Coast—or anywhere else—for some time to come. We feel very much like staying put here now—having been away four and a

---

4. Earle Larimore, who played the lead role of John in *Days Without End*. Previously he had appeared as Sam Evans in *Strange Interlude* and as Orin Mannon in *Mourning Becomes Electra*.

5. Lee Simonson did the settings for *Days Without End*.

half months out of the last six. Why don't you come East on a vacation and fly down here?

Tell Griffith[6] I'll be only too tickled to sign Paddy's speech.[7] I always liked that and I'm glad he does. Bob Sisk was going to get us together in New York. Then I had to go to Boston on "Days Without End" and missed it.

Carlotta joins in all best.

Good luck!
As ever,
Gene

Feb. 14th 1934

---

107 • TO MACGOWAN FROM CARLOTTA O'NEILL. ALS 9 pp. (On stationery headed: Casa Genotta / Sea Island / Georgia)

Feb. 14th 1934

Dear Kenneth,—

Gene suggests *I* write to you—! I'm sure you're not interested in my life!—But if you *are*—well Gene & I never leave each other—so, if he writes of what we're doing—you know it all!—

Being the type of old fashioned female who thinks marriage really means something (if not—get out of it!)—my great joy & work & thoughts are all here.—

I worked, very hard, designing, getting built, & furnishing this house. Then there was the garden to make—on a sand dune! It is really what I most wanted. A simple, comfortable very *personal home!* Gene has every comfort & also those things to please the eye (I *hope!*)—.

I am wife, mistress, housekeeper, secretary, friend & nurse so have no time to worry about my personality being submerged or my career being ruined. We were interested & amazed at the number of women in New York, who (absolutely without one shred of real talent for anything) are eating their hearts out to *be* some one—to be talked about—to be alluring! They are rotten wives & bad mistresses & poor unhappy wretches. We have lived so much apart from others—& so

---

6. Possibly the film director-producer D. W. Griffith.

7. Probably the long speech by Paddy in scene 1 of *The Hairy Ape*, in which he recalls nostalgically the days of sailing ships.

close together & gone thro' all sorts of hurts where we found that we had *very* few friends & were surrounded by parasites—that now life is very simple for us—& "chi chi" a bit of a bore!

You dear old Scotchman—you know what loyalty means. You don't sit on the fence—& lie—& pretend.—

We'll always love you for that.—But most of those others B.C. (Before Carlotta!) do not exist for us.—

Can't you come & see us some day? We'd both love to have you.— And I know you would love it here.—

We won't go to California. I loathe the place—always have. Geographically it is marvellous (particularly North of St. Barbara!!!) but the people (generally speaking) drive me mad.—I never drank, played bridge or golf—& *loathe* the country clubs,—so that does not make for popularity.—But, I have motored over nearly every foot of that pesky state & know some lovely spots. My Mother, daughter & I own a lot of real estate there,—I wish to Heaven times would get better so we could sell it!

My daughter, now sixteen,[1] (& in Piedmont with my Mother) tells me she is engaged to be married!—(Heavens, it seems to run in our family!) But, that she will wait a year before going thro' with it! My great joy is—that the boy concerned has the same "old fashioned" ideas that I have & his ideas of life & love & marriage are those of an adult—not a prep school boy.—

And so Life goes on—Oh—thanks for the scenario of "Interlude"— you were kind to go to all that trouble. Mr. Rubin[2] had sent one to Gene years ago. This a grand place for reading. Last Winter I *reread all* of Balzac,—Gautier,—Hugo,—Flaubert,—and Colette! Now I'll get to Dostoevsky, Lermontov, Turgenev, and, perhaps, *Dickens*!

Am very interested in Jules Romain's long novel experiment,[3] aren't you?—And like Pearl Buck.—Did you read "Peter Abelard"— *excellent*—

Gene & I never go to the theatre or movies. Gene always says—

---

1. Cynthia, Carlotta's daughter by her second marriage, to lawyer Melvin C. Chapman, Jr.

2. J. Robert Rubin, Hollywood producer Louis B. Mayer's lawyer. The MGM film version of *Strange Interlude* had been delayed by the film company's refusal to buy the rights until the plagiarism suit against O'Neill was settled (see Letter 91 above).

3. *Les Hommes de bonne volonté*, published in English as *Men of Good Will*. Begun in 1932 and completed in 1944, Romains's novel eventually ran to 27 volumes in the French edition and 30 volumes in the English translation.

"They can buy 'em for Movies but they can't make me go & see them"—!

I do hope you make lots of money & invest it wisely—& that you keep well & happy & *busy*.

God bless you—
Carlotta

Am enclosing some photographs I took you might like. I have been Gene's official photographer for some time now! Am every thing but his tailor!!

Pardon this scrawl—

P.S. Gene buried both Terry Carlin[4] & Jack McGrath[5] the early part of January

---

108 • TO MACGOWAN FROM O'NEILL. ALS 1 p. (On stationery headed: Casa Genotta / Sea Island / Georgia)

Feb. 17th 1934

Dear Kenneth:

Forgot in my letter of a couple of days ago to answer your query re "Hairy Ape" treatment.[1] I have no copy. Perhaps Madden[2] has—but I doubt it. They seem to have never been returned when submitted to movie offices years ago. But I'll write Dick to send you one—there were only two—if he can dig it up.

As I remember, it was not so hot, anyway. And, if anyone bought the rights to the play I could give those doing it an outline of that scheme in ten minutes, to use or not as they saw fit—what I did with the "Emp. Jones" people when they flew down here to consult me.

All best again!
Gene

4. An old friend of O'Neill's, whom he first met at John Wallace's Golden Swan saloon (known as the "Hell Hole") in Greenwich Village in 1915–16. Carlin, an important figure in O'Neill's life throughout his Greenwich Village and Provincetown years, later was the basis for the character of Larry Slade in *The Iceman Cometh* (1946).

5. Another of O'Neill's drinking companions from days in Greenwich Village, whom he had continued to see.

1. O'Neill had prepared a scenario for a film version of *The Hairy Ape*.

2. Richard Madden.

4: Tao House

4: Tao House

What remained of the relationship can be briefly chronicled. Macgowan had a talent for friendship to which the O'Neills responded, but long physical separation was inevitable. Travel, the letters recall, was not the simple matter it has become. Macgowan's flight to Seattle to be with O'Neill when he won the Nobel Prize called for some intrepidity. Moreover, in Hollywood, Macgowan was working hard. In the O'Neill household, the way of life called for isolation and intense work, a condition that became nearly absolute as the playwright turned to the planning of "A Tale of Possessors, Self-dispossessed," the long cycle of plays on American historical subjects that he intended as his crowning achievement. Meetings between the friends could now be only circumstantial and ceremonial.

Tao House, near Danville, California, finally made the intensive work possible. O'Neill's illness brought the life there to an end, but for a time he entered on a period of creative activity that made all that had preceded it—even the writing of *Mourning Becomes Electra*—seem leisurely by comparison. In Letter 86, O'Neill wrote Macgowan that after he and Carlotta had explored exotic lands, they would come "back to California where C. and I expect to make our home for good." The California commitment was perhaps more Carlotta's than her husband's. Although she wrote in Letter 107 that she loathed California, she had been born there and perhaps felt that the San Francisco Bay area was her native earth.

For a time, they had tried to live in Georgia and in 1932 built a palatial home on Sea Island, naming it with a portmanteau coinage of their first names, Casa Genotta. The location was a poor choice. Heat, humidity, mosquitoes, and the occasional buzzing of airplanes from a nearby flying club conspired to make work difficult. In Seattle in 1936, where he had gone partly to escape from Sea Island, partly to do research on the cycle plays, O'Neill learned that he had been given the Nobel Prize for Literature. The prize money made choice possible and the O'Neills traveled south to Oakland, California, where by March 1937 they had determined to settle.

The Nobel award brought Macgowan back into their lives, and the friendship was resumed in an undemanding way. As Macgowan found ways to keep the relationship alive—the gifts of Disney drawings, Calypso records, noh masks, books—and as with some difficulty he made time to visit them, a candor and ease entered the communications that had not been there before. No one now demanded anything. Pretensions dropped away. Among the three a mutual confidence was manifested.

For the O'Neills, Tao House was a true haven. Built on 156 acres on the western rim of the San Ramon Valley, it commands a superb perspective of the massif of Mount Diablo and of the valley floor covered with orchards of walnut and almond trees. The walls of the house are thick, and the environment—even today with the encroachments of freeways and unchecked building developments—is quiet. The house itself is elegant but without pretension. O'Neill told Macgowan it was "Carlotta's masterpiece," and the term and tribute to her taste are not inappropriate.[1]

The isolation of the house betrayed O'Neill in the end. When the war came, the house proved unmanageable. Carlotta's letter of June 5, 1943 (Letter 158), describing the problems of managing a house without servants, of scrounging for gasoline, of relying on the kindness of a hardware dealer to drive them, suggests that the situation was untenable. More serious was the advent of O'Neill's tremor, initially diagnosed as incipient Parkinson's disease, which made work impossible and for many days left O'Neill in intense physical pain.

O'Neill entered Tao House with his creative energies at the full. Less than a decade later, he left it a broken, skinny, shaking invalid, entirely dependent on the care of Carlotta and his doctors—and unable to write.

The medical records contain a history of his illness and a precise indication of the care that Carlotta took of him. Carlotta's medical report for the month of August 1943, kept for the doctors' benefit, is sufficient indication:

July 30th 1943—infected molar pulled

August 6th—feels so low has coffee at 5:30 AM—has 15 drops stramonium three times during the day—after the third dose tremor better

August 7th—has three doses stramonium of twenty drops each—tremor bad in AM but better after third dose—has less tension in solar plexis after luncheon and dinner—doesn't sleep

---

1. Tao House has been named a National Historic Site and is to become a center for the performing arts.

August 8th—three doses stramonium of twenty drops each—complains of "inner" tension—about 3:30 PM has crack-up—tremor ghastly—weeping—

August 9th—stop stramonium—takes Dukes' Mixture[2] before dinner—on going to bed—(1 teaspoon—and then 2 teaspoonsful)—had to take another teaspoonful at 1 AM.

August 10th—quieter—less strained—eyes loosing their "shine"—swims—takes 1 teaspoonfull Dukes' Mixture at 6:30 PM and 2 teaspoonsful at 2 AM.

August 11th—has two men here and swims—spends much longer time then usual at the pool—and on returning to house finds two people here with whom he talks, etc.—has restless night—takes 2 teaspoonsful Dukes' Mixture at 10:30 PM—Wakes at 5 AM with bad headache—takes alka seltzer—sleeps until 11 AM—nerves bad

August 12th—doesn't feel very active—by night complains of "tightness" and discomfort in glands and bronchial tubes—put him to bed—rub his chest and put heat on—he takes 2 Alka seltzer at 10 PM and 1 at midnight—

August 13th—better—rub him again at night—he takes 2 teaspoonsful Dukes' Mixture at 11 PM.

August 14th—does not feel very energetic—begins the "water test" at 6 PM—has wretched night of coughing but can take nothing

August 15th—finishes the "water test"—has breakfast at 1 PM—feels a bit low—coughing

August 16th—wakes coughing and spits up blood—seems very worried about this—is not well—tremor bad—

August 17th—Feels wretched in morning—keep him in bed—send for Dr. Feiler who gives him sulfadiazine, cough medicine and something to make him sleep—He passes a much more comfortable night—no bad coughing fits—

2. A sedative prepared by one of O'Neill's physicians, Dr. Charles A. Dukes.

August 18th—Keep him in bed—he is glad to be there but looks better—still taking medicine and had no more bad coughing fits. He eats well of nourishing plain simple foods. Ricke comes over to massage me and prepares the inhaler for Gene. He spends the entire night coughing—is exhausted. I make him coffee at 2:30 AM.

August 19th—Gene exhausted—but eats well—at night I rub his chest and put on heat—he sleeps better—make him coffee at 5 AM.

August 20th—Gene's cough looser and he seems to be more relaxed. I rub him night and morning and use the hot pad

August 21st—Gene has a bath and his bed changed which refreshes him—Feiler comes takes his blood pressure 110/80—temperature 98.4—very nervous from barbiturates—he is low at 10:30 AM asks for strong coffee—only two coughing spells during the night—a quieter night

August 22nd—Gene's cough better—he gets up for about four hours—puts on Hitchcock's belt as his back is bothering him again—belt is painful rubbing against his vertebrae—eats well—takes Secconal and has a fairly good night

August 23rd—Tapering off Feiler's medicine (Sulfadiazine and an internal mixture with ephredine in it) also the barbiturates and cough medicine—is nervous, weak, shaky and low mentally. Give him paraldehyde (two teaspoonsful in orange juice with cracked ice) on settling for the night. At long last he goes to sleep but wakes in two hours—nervous—on the verge of cracking—Make him coffee at 5 AM—his intestines are bothering him—no bowel movement for three days—and three days before that. Asks for Carlsbad salts (early Tuesday morning)

August 24th—drinks coffee at 5:00 AM—paces the floor with pain in intestines, groin, back, rectum—nerves are "shot"—rests about quarter of an hour and wakes in the jitters—after a light luncheon (creamed soup and soft rice pudding) dresses, goes outside for about ten minutes—returns in pain and very nervous—goes to pieces at tea time—fearful of a nervous breakdown—phone Charity to tell Dr. Taylor—takes Dukes' Mixture—and one of Dukes' opium suppositories for the rectum pain. Sleeps lightly but is able to get a little rest without the nervous jitters—

August 25th—wakes very early and asks for coffee—go down and make it for him and he only drinks a few mouthsful (the first time this has ever happened in sixteen years!)—complains of bad pains in all of intestinal area—can't get comfortable—seems very ill—very low in mind—worrying about prostate and Reinle being away on his holliday making it the longest time ever without treatment—something seems to be very wrong inside—he can't get comfortable.

His weight had dropped to 138 pounds, and, as the tremor increased, his face showed signs of the rigidity of the facial muscles associated with Parkinson's disease, which physicians call a "mask." Carlotta nursed him as best she could, measuring amounts of urine, preparing special foods, providing massages, and caring for his needs at any hour. His doctors did their best, indeed tended him with devotion. One handwritten, unsigned summary of his medical history concludes with this paragraph:

These items [the medical history] have been gathered at the office and at his home. He hates to enter the hospital. He is in no sense in a critical state. We would like to help him, though, toward well-being and more active work. His wife is resplendent and has been a revelation to me: a beautiful girl with a brain. Mr. O'Neill is greatly worried at times but is marvellously understanding and tolerant. I so much want to be of help to him.

The last two sentences were originally very different and were altered, no doubt because of their tone. The doctor had written, and then deleted, "Mr. O'Neill is my idea of a latter-day knight—so patient & kind. He tried hard ⟨illegible⟩ and will be my chief concern as long as he is content with me."

The caretakers stayed with him until the end, but Tao House, so isolated during the war, was no place for a sick man. It was sold, and when he was well enough, the O'Neills moved east to oversee the premiere of *The Iceman Cometh*. Thereafter, they lived briefly in Marblehead Neck in Massachusetts, where Macgowan's association with his friends was to end, as O'Neill and his wife entered a nightmare of illness that permitted no intrusion. The words Carlotta wrote to Macgowan in 1950—"Gene is not too well"—mark the end of a relationship that had in its time been of profound creative value, but of which, at the last, the exhausted O'Neills were incapable.

109 • TO O'NEILL FROM MACGOWAN. WIRE 1 p. (At foot of WIRE
(charge Kenneth Macgown—W.L.A. 32197))

NOVEMBER 13, 1936

WESTERN UNION—DAY LETTER
MR. EUGENE O'NEILL
470 W. RUFFNER STREET
SEATTLE, WASHINGTON

OLD MAN NOBEL OUGHT TO HAVE COME THROUGH TEN YEARS
AGO[1] BUT IT IS GREAT NEWS JUST THE SAME AND MAKES ALL YOUR
OLD FRIENDS CHEER AGAIN WITH HAPPINESS GRATIFICATION AND
PRIDE MY VERY BEST TO YOU AND CARLOTTA BUT WHY NOT
TAKE A STEAMER RIDE DOWN HERE

KENNETH MACGOWAN

---

110 • TO MACGOWAN FROM O'NEILL. ALS 3 pp.

4701 West Ruffner Street,
Seattle, Wash.
Nov. 15th '36

Dear Kenneth:

The past couple of days have been pretty hectic—dodging the radio & newsreel baloney, when they refused to take no for an answer, & etc.—or I would have acknowledged your wire ere this. I needn't tell you, I hope, that your message was among the few that meant most. I know your friendship is sincerely pleased at my good luck.

And quite apart from congrats over the Nobel, I was damned tickled to hear from you again. Thought you'd forgotten me. You owe me a letter from way back—or am I wrong again? No, I'm sure I'm not. I've sort of kept in touch with your doings through Bob Sisk, and I've been damned glad to hear what a fine thing you are making of it out here. I can guess what peace of mind that must bring you, after all the years of financial worry and uncertainty, in which the so-called Legit.[1] rewarded your work so miserably and thanklessly. And this Nobel thing makes me think back—(only I often do, anyway)—and remember the days when your friendship was such a constant encouragement, and when you worked so hard and unselfishly to help put my work across, and I want to tell you now, again, of the grat-

1. O'Neill was awarded the Nobel Prize for Literature on November 12, 1936.

1. The legitimate theatre.

itude I always will feel. You are one of the finest guys and one of the best friends I have ever known, Kenneth, and I rate it a damned shame and loss that circumstances in the past few years have placed us so far apart in these U. S. that we never get a chance even to say howdy to each other, let alone work together any more. I often dream of what a grand break it would be if you and Bobby and I could get together again, and start again in New York on our own with a resurge of the old spirit to prompt us. I don't notice much of that spirit in the present New York theatre—in fact, not any. The dreams there seem to be "all wet." Maybe I'm getting aged and crabbed but there seems nothing left—outside of the Radical propaganda on 14th street—which has any definite ambition toward any goal. Of course, there are plenty of compromisers who straddle the fence, and try to be both this and that, and end up by being neither. But I don't know of one producing group that has the guts to hew to the line as we did. And so, outside of my job of writing plays, I've just about lost all interest in the theatre.

Perhaps all this strikes you as a bit too mournful and dejected. And maybe it is. Truth is, I'm worn out physically and badly need a complete rest. I worked on my damned cycle[2] constantly every day for seven months without one day off—all through an extra scorching Georgia summer—and by the end of Sept. I was a wreck and about ready to feed the hookworms. Carlotta was also climate-sunk. So we've decided to sell the Sea Island mansion and give Dixie back to Tin Pan Alley. And to look for a home in a more salubrious clime— once the Ga. one is sold. We came here for a complete climate change—and a rest—and for me to "get" the background of all this part of the country for use in cycle, But principally for a rest. And now comes the Nobel—and no chance of rest for a while, what with all plans up in the air. So it is not an unmixed blessing. In fact, so far, I'm like an ancient cab horse that has had a blue ribbon pinned on his tail—too physically weary to turn round and find out if it's good to eat, or what.

We may take that steamer ride you suggest sometime but for the nonce we can't. I'm waiting for word from Sweden and can't move

---

2. "A Tale of Possessors, Self-dispossessed," originally envisioned as five plays but then expanded to seven and eventually to eleven. O'Neill destroyed all drafts except *A Touch of the Poet* (completed 1946, produced 1958) and the uncompleted *More Stately Mansions* (completed 1938, produced 1962).

until all about that is settled. And then there's the climate. Boy, what we crave now are cold, and gray skies, and be damned to sun and warmth!

Carlotta joins me in all best to you! And my best to all the other Macgowans!

As ever,
Gene

P.S. I'm bound to be here for the next two or three weeks—so write, if you can find time, and let me know all of what's what with you.

---

111 • TO MACGOWAN FROM CARLOTTA O'NEILL. ALS 3 pp.

Tuesday—
[November 17, 1936]

Kenneth, you are a God blesséd angel.—I love you for your loyalty to Gene. He feels such a deep, warm friendship for you. I am furious that Bobby sent him no word of congratulations! However—that is what humans are!—

Couldn't you fly up here for a few days with us? We will never go to Los Angeles, for that would mean so much unpleasantness from the Hollywood angle. Which you so well understand.

I am so happy for Gene.—

God, how that man works. His whole energy & life are given to his work. I have never left him for an hour—so I *know*!—And being his secretary brings me in from the work end. It is marvellous to live so closely to the man you love—& understand his *work, ideals, & dreams,* as well as the *man* side of him. God knows we have our worries—& hellish responsibilities—but we have *us* to face them.

I wish *you* could go to Sweden with us.—And *you* are the only person I would like to go with us!—Gene would love it so. Do you ever take a holiday?

This is a crazy note—but I want you to know what your wire & letter to Gene meant to me.

Our dearest love to you.

God bless you—
Carlotta

112 • TO MACGOWAN FROM O'NEILL. TLS 1 p.

> 4701 West Ruffner Street,
> Seattle,
> Washington

Dear Kenneth,

Just a line to thank you for the photos, which I'm darned tickled to have. If I had some snaps of us here I'd reciprocate in kind, but they are all back in Sea Island and we have no kodak with us.

You sure look healthy and blooming—a good ad. for golf and the California climate! As for me, I'm from ten to fifteen pounds heavier than in the old days—even now when I feel punk and exhausted—but my puss retains its haggard hungry look. And I've a lot of hair on you still, if it is beginning to thin on the crown.

Carlotta has written re any prospect of your paying us a week-end visit. But I fear, after reading your letter, that you will never have the time. But here's hoping.

Carlotta joins me in all best,

> As ever,
> Gene

November 25th 1936

---

113 • TO THE O'NEILLS FROM MACGOWAN. WIRE 1 p. (At foot of WIRE (charge Kenneth Macgowan—W.L.A. 32197))

DECEMBER 2, 1936

WESTERN UNION TELEGRAM
MR. & MRS. EUGENE O'NEILL
4701 WEST RUFFNER STREET
SEATTLE, WASHINGTON

TRYING ARRANGE FLY SEATTLE THIS OR NEXT WEEK END WHICH IS BETTER FOR YOU

KENNETH MACGOWAN

114 • TO O'NEILL FROM MACGOWAN. WIRE 1 p. (At foot of WIRE (charge Kenneth Macgowan—W.L.A. 32197))

DECEMBER 4, 1936

WESTERN UNION TELEGRAM
MR. EUGENE O'NEILL
4701 WEST RUFFNER STREET
SEATTLE, WASHINGTON

UNLESS BAD WEATHER OR EMERGENCY ARRIVING SEATTLE SIX TEN SATURDAY EVENING UNITED AIRLINES MUST LEAVE SUNDAY NIGHT NINE PRESUME DO NOT NEED FANCY CLOTHES
KENNETH MACGOWAN

115 • TO CARLOTTA O'NEILL FROM MACGOWAN. WIRE 1 p. (At foot of WIRE (charge Kenneth Macgowan—W.L.A. 32197))

DECEMBER 7, 1936

WESTERN UNION TELEGRAM
MRS. EUGENE O'NEILL
4701 WEST RUFFNER STREET
SEATTLE, WASHINGTON

ARRIVED SAFE SLEEPY AND GRATEFUL BUCKED UP NO END
KENNETH

116 • TO MACGOWAN FROM CARLOTTA O'NEILL. ALS 2 pp.

Monday Noon
[December 7, 1936]

Dear, dear Kenneth,

Your wire just here which relieved me no end.

What an angel you were to take all that trip to see us. And what a joy it was to us!—

You improve so handsomely with the years—& I think you are *much* more attractive!!!! (To me, anyway.)—

It makes our idea to live in Northern California have another meaning now—it will give us a closeness to you. Gene & I love so few—but those few we dearly love.—And you are the dear Scot—loyal & charming.

If I go on like this—it will sound like a love letter!

Anyway, we love you. We also, were "bucked up no end" & we want to do all our 'possible' to be closer to you, in future.

Bless you—
Carlotta

Hope you weren't too tired.

---

117 • TO CARLOTTA O'NEILL FROM MACGOWAN. TL(cc) 1 p.

December 7, 1936

Dear Carlotta:

You knew of course how much it meant to me to see Gene again and talk with him about all the sort of things that are close to both of us. And I think you know that I was eager, too, to see you once more. But I want to say how happy I was not only over re-establishing these two contacts but just as much over seeing at first-hand how much you mean to Gene, how much you have done to straighten out his personal and domestic life and make it beautiful and creative.

I hate to dictate this letter, but I am afraid that is the only way I am going to get it written as quickly as I want to. Here is a check for the telephone call. In a few days you ought to receive the Viennese chocolates and the book by Max Miller.[1]

Affectionately yours,

Mrs. Eugene O'Neill
4701 West Ruffner Street
Seattle, Washington

---

118 • TO MACGOWAN FROM CARLOTTA O'NEILL. TLS 1 p.

[December 1936]

Kenneth dear,

Our letters must have crossed. But we enjoyed seeing each other! Gene and I still feel nice and warm from our all too short visit with you.

---

1. Possibly *For the Sake of Shadows* (1936). Miller's best-known work was *I Cover the Waterfront* (1932), later turned into a film.

The candy arrived. Many thanks. It is very delicious and we'll get curves! Gene asks me to thank you for the Miller book. It is very late but I am trying to finish off Gene's letters for him so I will be able to finish the packing in the morning, so we can leave here Monday early. Boxes going off to-morrow.

Yes, Kenneth, Gene and I are a thousand times closer than the day you went with us to get the passports. We paid a devil of a price but it was more than worth it. And we found out how few friends either of us really had! And *that* we will never forget! That is one of the reasons we both hold you so dear. (You weren't afraid to stick.)

I'm dead tired.

Good night, my dear—

Love from us both,
Carlotta

Hotel Fairmont
San Francisco
(confidential)

---

119 • TO O'NEILL FROM MACGOWAN. TL(cc) 1 p.

December 16, 1936

Mr. Eugene O'Neill
Hotel Fairmont
San Francisco, California

Dear Gene:

Here's a coincidence for you, and also a laugh. Yesterday I was thinking of sending you samples of our two daily trade papers, knowing you would be amused by them. Today "Variety" pulls a front page yarn implying that I went up to Seattle to try to talk you into picture work!

Hastily and affectionately,
Kenneth Macgowan

---

120 • TO MACGOWAN FROM THE O'NEILLS. TLS 1 p. (On stationery headed: Fairmont Hotel / Nob Hill / San Francisco)

December 20th 1936

Kenneth dear,
I didn't know Santa Claus was aware of my being in San Francisco!

You're a darling and I can't tell you how surprised and pleased I was about the wee earrings. Being one of those savages, with *holes* through my ears, I am going to have them arranged to wear that way!

My deep thanks, and love to you.

Always,
Carlotta

ALS

Dear Kenneth:

Thanks for the trade papers. They are darned amusing—the Variety yarn re your visit especially so. It was in New York Variety, too. Madden sent me a clipping. He seems steamed up over the mysterious possibilities! I'm thinking of writing him you offered me ten grand a week & 50% of the gross—only I'm afraid he'd believe it, and faint at the idea of my refusing such a commission for my agent! But I don't mean that, at that. Dick is really a grand guy and a good friend—but I know he thinks at times I'm hopelessly nuts and need a caretaker.

Any chance of you visiting us here? We hope so! We will be here for couple of weeks.

Gene

---

121 • TO MACGOWAN FROM CARLOTTA O'NEILL. ALS 3 pp.

Dec. 31st 1936

Dear Kenneth—

Your letter just forwarded from the Fairmont. Gene had his appendix cut out the 29th—& is getting on very well. He came here the 26th for observation—had an attack at 4.30 A.M. on the morning of the 29th & his appendix was removed at 1 P.M. on that day. He had a marvellous surgeon,[1]—a great friend of mine—who took my appendix out 17 years ago!

We are trying to keep this out of the papers & away from his friends. After he gets out of here we will go away somewhere for him to recuperate. Every thing is, thank God, going along beautifully.

I am here in the next room so I can look after him outside the nursing.

---

1. Dr. Charles A. Dukes.

Re your letter, Gene has made an iron clad rule to get mixed up—in *no* way—in politics.[2] He is an artist, *not* a politician & *never* (under any circumstances) *writes* his opinion on any subject for any paper, or any Meeting. He is asked every-day, by *some one*, to write about *something*. He always refuses. Please don't let these people think he will write anything. Try to shield him from their asking. Did you tell them he was in San Francisco? I hope *not*. When he leaves here he will be in worse condition than ever to buck against all such rackets—& people wanting something—He will be physically *weak* & I intend to look after him—& hope not to be rude. If you have already told people he is in San Francisco—can you not now tell them he has gone somewhere else? Because he must have no excitement *whatsoever* after this—until he is completely well & over the shock of the operation.—

Gene never likes meeting authors, anyway.[3] Why, I don't know. He much prefers scientists, brokers, (!) brick layers, or sea Captains! Anyone to do with the theatre or writing, he runs from! And that's that.

Pardon pencil—Am writing this in bed.—

Do hope you understand what I've tried to say.—

Dearest love to you—

Carlotta

---

122 • TO CARLOTTA O'NEILL FROM MACGOWAN. WIRE 1 p. (At foot of WIRE (charge Kenneth Macgowan—WLA 32197))

JAN. 4, 1937

WESTERN UNION
MRS. EUGENE O'NEILL
MERRITT HOSPITAL
OAKLAND, CALIFORNIA

TERRIBLY SORRY TO HEAR ABOUT OPERATION STOP MORNING TIMES CARRIED NEW STORY THIS MORNING INCLUDING YOU IN NEARBY ROOM SEVERE CASE INFLUENZA STOP YOUR LETTER JUST RECEIVED RELIEVES ANXIETY LOVE

KENNETH MACGOWAN

2. Macgowan had passed on to O'Neill a request that he lend his name in support of a candidate for the Nobel Peace Prize. See below, Letter 123.

3. Macgowan had asked if O'Neill would see German expressionist playwright Ernst Toller (1893–1939), who had been exiled by the Nazis and was in California earning a living by lecturing and working as a screenwriter.

January 4, 1937

Dear Carlotta:

I got a bit of a scare this morning when I read the enclosed story in the Los Angeles Times,[1] but your very welcome letter from the hospital put my mind somewhat at ease. I judge Gene is definitely out of the woods. Getting out the old appendix ought to put his whole system in better shape for the future.

I didn't think Gene would want to mix into the political situation as regards the Nobel Peace Prize, but I felt I ought to put it up to him since Biberman[2] asked. As to Toller, I think Gene would enjoy him very much. He is still interested in the theatre as much as he is in politics, and he really is a very stimulating and arresting person, who has been through some hellish experiences and is still vital and courageous. He wouldn't lug Gene into any political controversy. All I told him about Gene's whereabouts was that he might be in the neighborhood of San Francisco sometime this month and if I found it corresponded with Toller's speaking date up there I would let him know. Of course, the Times' dispatch has spilled the news of where Gene is.

I hope the story about your being sick too is grossly exaggerated. Give my very best to Gene, and love to you.

Ever and ever,
Kenneth Macgowan

Mrs. Eugene O'Neill
Merritt Hospital
Oakland, California

Jan. 4th '37

Kenneth dear /

Thank you for your wire. Gene is getting on quite nicely. Is comfortable—& has enough nurses & care for 3 sick men.

1. News of O'Neill's appendectomy had leaked out to the press on January 3, 1937. The dispatch also reported that Mrs. O'Neill was ill as well.

2. Herbert J. Biberman, a young director of leftist persuasion whom the Theatre Guild, turning socially conscious, had added to its Board.

The damn papers got hold of the "news" & really have been most unpleasant demanding "interviews" & "photographs."—The people of the newspaper world are either idiots or s.o.b.s!—They have no sense of decency or delicacy—& ask absurd favours. Of course, no one can bother Gene—but they drive *me* mad—as I am the bumper between him & the world that he doesn't wish contact with! A funny job!

Don't worry, Kenneth dear, all is well. And I am sure Gene will be much better with the troublesome worm out.—

I am all right—but still shakey & jittery.

Our love to you always—

Carlotta

---

125 • TO MACGOWAN FROM CARLOTTA O'NEILL. ALS 2 pp. (On stationery headed: Samuel Merritt Hospital / Oakland, California)

Jan. 6th 1937

Dear Kenneth /

Thank you for your kind letter.—

Gene getting on very nicely—Stitches come out tomorrow. He has another trouble in his insides that will need treatment—but nothing serious. He will be here for some time yet.—The Dr. warned me this morning how strict I must be with him during the recuperative period. He also told me I had just escaped pneumonia—maybe that is why I feel so terribly jittery now.—

By the way—if you ever loose track of us—mail is always forwarded from Sea Island.—

I will be here for a week anyway. But the Fairmont Hotel will reach us.—

Love always—
Carlotta

---

126 • TO MACGOWAN FROM CARLOTTA O'NEILL. ALS 3 pp. (On stationery headed: Samuel Merritt Hospital / Oakland, California)

Jan. 20th '37

Personal

Dear Kenneth—

The appendix thing forgotten. A beautiful job—But Gene had a prostate-kidney infection which meant fevers (out of his head), chills & pain. I was with him night & day.—All over now but treatment & recuperation—I had a re-currence of flu & nerve kick-up—.

We are seeing no one—

But *write,* if you like.

Am feeling pretty lousy. Gene's N.Y. doctors are so full of the "mental" they couldn't see his abused insides. This prostate has been kicking up for years—& was *not* in his head!—

Hope all goes well with you—

Love from us both—
Carlotta

---

127 • TO O'NEILL FROM MACGOWAN. TL(cc) 1 p.

January 21, 1937

Dear Gene:

In a day or so you ought to get a drawing by Walt Disney. I suppose he intended it as a Christmas card, but perhaps it is just as well that it arrives when you need entertaining more.

I haven't taken the thing apart, but I think it contains the usual painted background and on top of it a sheet of celluloid with figures drawn on it. I have never seen cut out trees added, but I suppose he is now doing it. Sometimes, you know, he has three or even four layers of celluloid with different figures on different layers in order to be able to have some of them move without having to repaint the others.

I made a funny discovery today. A Scandinavian character actor named Christian Rub, who is working in a picture here, collects masks. I haven't seen them yet, but I hear they are rather good. When affluence struck me I decided that I could collect them myself, but I have had an awful time finding any. I bought three Javanese ones from an explorer's collection that Norman Foster was selling in his book shop, and Aline MacMahon[1] brought me three from Java. I haven't run into any others except rumours of those in Seattle. (Now I suddenly remember that I must have told you about this when I was up north.)

Nothing new goes on here. Except that I am trying to put a love

1. Actress who had played Ruth Atkins in the 1926 revival of *Beyond the Horizon* produced by Macgowan's Actors' Theatre combine.

story into Robert Louis Stevenson's "Kidnapped" and am making a picture about the founding of Scotland Yard. Walter Winchell turns out to be a natural born actor.

Harry Weinberger has been here a couple of weeks and I have had a very good time with him. I really had no idea he was such a nice guy. In New York most of my contacts were purely business.

Now I have got to go to work again. My best to you and Carlotta.

Mr. Eugene O'Neill
Merritt Hospital
Oakland, California

---

128 • TO MACGOWAN FROM CARLOTTA O'NEILL. ALS 2 pp. (On stationery headed: Samuel Merritt Hospital / Oakland, California)

Jan. 26th 37

Dear Kenneth——

I *did* laugh when Gene rec'd the Krazy Kat. The expression on his face was *too* funny!—

"I" have been the Disney enthusiast in our family, & Sisk had promised *me* a drawing—but it never materialized! But Gene's did!

Please let me know *who* I can write to & *where* to thank them for Gene—as he (Gene) always gives me such things to attend to. And—*I* appreciate it! (The Krazy Kat!)

Our love to you—
Carlotta

Gene will be here at least two weeks longer.

Isn't the Middle West[1] thing *terrible.* God must have it in for the Middle West!—

---

129 • TO CARLOTTA O'NEILL FROM MACGOWAN. TL(cc) 1 pp.

February 2, 1937

Dear Carlotta:

I am awfully glad to hear that you are both out of the woods.

If Walt Disney had written me a personal letter about sending the

1. Heavy rains in the Midwest had recently caused flooding of the Ohio and Mississippi river valleys, doing extensive damage to Cincinnati and Louisville and affecting thirteen states in all.

drawing—instead of having his secretary do it—I would suggest that Gene ought to present him with his autograph, but as things stand I don't see why you shouldn't take over the job. Disney's address is 2719 Hyperion Avenue, Hollywood.

Hastily but affectionately,
Kenneth Macgowan

Mrs. Eugene O'Neill
Merritt Hospital
Oakland, California

---

130 • TO MACGOWAN FROM O'NEILL. TLS 1 p. (On stationery headed: Fairmont Hotel / Nob Hill / San Francisco)

March 30th 1937

Dear Kenneth:

This, to let you know I am at last out of the hospital—left about a week ago—and though still feeling in that convalescent state of general punkness, weakness, and mental low grade A, am at least out of the woods, though I still have to report twice weekly for treatments.

It is a great temptation, which I shall nobly resist until I see you, to go at great length into all the details of my late two and a half months in hospital. Suffice it for the nonce that my operation was the cinch part of it, taken in itself, but it did act as a sort of final straw which weakened me and left me wide open for a lot of other stuff that had evidently only been waiting for the right moment to work on me—principally an interior abcess which burst and flooded my frame with poison so that I was off my nut for a few days and had the medicos worried. But "all's well" etc. and they tell me that if I watch my step and religiously rest for eight months to a year, I will feel better than I have in many a moon. This is fine, but not such an interesting prospect for that year since it holds up my work on the Cycle[1]—and I want so much to get back on the job. But I think I will force myself to obey orders this time, because the result of my ignoring them during the past two years was undoubtedly the principal cause of the present break-up.

And that's enough of that. What I want to tell you most is that we shall be at the above address for a while—in case you happen to

1. "A Tale of Possessors, Self-dispossessed."

get up this way. We are having a devil of a time locating a place to rent, that is worth renting, to hold us for the next eight months or so until we can locate the right land to buy to build our new home. But we hope to land a rentable place within the next week or so. One or two prospects look good. I will let you know our new address as soon as we have one.

One thing I meant to write you about from the hospital. The head surgeon took me out one night with his family—this while Carlotta was in Sea Island winding up the sale there—and, on my steer, we went to "Lloyds of London."[2] I liked it a hell of a lot, Kenneth—a damned fine picture in every way, I thought—and here's my belated congratulations!

Carlotta joins in love to you and the hope we may see you again before long. She also insists I say that this lousy typing job is none of her work but done by me while she was out home-hunting. She don't want no slurs cast on her efficiency as Secretary!

As ever,
Gene

---

131 • TO O'NEILL FROM MACGOWAN. TL(cc) 1 p.

June 29, 1937

Dear Gene:

This is just a hasty note to tell you that Irving Pichel[1] is going to be up in Berkeley for some weeks. I know you will want to see him. I think you can get in touch with him if Carlotta will drop a note to him care of J. Stitt Wilson, Berkeley.

How are you feeling? And how's Carlotta?

As always,
Kenneth Macgowan

Mr. Eugene O'Neill
Fairmont Hotel
San Francisco, California

2. Motion picture starring Tyrone Power and Madeleine Carroll, on which Macgowan was the associate producer (1936).

1. Pichel, who had played the title role in the Pasadena Playhouse production of *Lazarus Laughed* (1928), was now a movie director.

August 26th 1937

Dear Kenneth /

Just a line to let you know all goes well with us. Gene seems to be on the up-grade—altho', at the moment, he has the *hives*—a silly and annoying business!—

I am in the throes of building a new home.

It reminds me of producing one of Gene's longest plays! We have bought a beautiful site in the country—(with a really amazing view) and are building. It is difficult to know, these days, whether one will be *permitted* to build! Laborers are always calling strikes—& Mr. Roosevelt smilingly approves. We, also, have to develope a water supply from springs, build a road, & do—God knows what.—But it will be a really *home*, which Gene & I find so important. We have 156 acres. Gene keeps insisting he have some pet chickens! So be prepared for anything when you arrive! We *hope* to *begin* to move in sometime in January. And then you'll have no excuse to keep you from week-ending with us—*often!*

We have a place here, in the country, about ten miles from where we are going to build. We have about 22 acres here—& a swimming pool for Gene.—He has that for exercise. He doesn't see many people—as confusion tires him. And, anyway, he never has cared to see many people. He really cares for so few. And when working, he doesn't like giving out energy that could be, & should be, kept for his work.

How are you? And are you doing anything you really like?

When I went to Georgia to sell our house, Gene's doctor took him to see "Lloyds of London" & he thought it a fine job. Did he tell you? He keeps saying he must write you—but it is hard for him to get to it. Hence this from me.

Let us have a line from you now & again.

Our love always—
Carlotta

August 26th 1937
Lafayette,
Contra Costa County,
California

Lafayette,
Contra Costa County,
California
Sept. 20th '37

Dear Kenneth:

Well, I have honestly been meaning to write you for the past three months—ever since we settled out here. We rented this place—about the only one we could find for rent that was at all right—for six months, which will probably run into seven (the 1st of the year) before our new home, now building, is ready to move into. The house here is nothing to rave about but there are twenty-two acres of garden and orchards (maintained, thank God, by the owner and not us!) which are grand. Also, principal item to me, a pool. On the whole, not bad, though much too costly. We have spent an enjoyable summer, and my health, I am glad to report, is much improved. But until the first of the year, the Docs still warn me I must go easy—and this time, believe me, I am obeying orders.

However, pending the time when I can really buckle down, I have been doing some flirting with my Cycle and find myself full of fresh angles and ideas. One of those brilliant inspirations, more's the pity, is for still another play, making nine in all, and taking the opening curtain back to 1775. It looks very good indeed in outline and I am afraid it simply can't be left out.[1] So the job ahead becomes just that much more of a job. But, given health and time, I know I can do it—and if done as it ought to be this Cycle sure will be a final something! Then I shall retire and spend my declining days composing limericks.

Our new home is going to be a beauty. The property—158 acres—is in the hill's of the San Ramon valley, with one of the finest views I have ever seen. Construction is going ahead—so far without strikes to hold it up. Roof will be on in about four weeks. Carlotta is in a whirlwind of activity doing this and that and the other and generally bossing everything. She has a wonderful flair for home making—not to mention home running—and I think this is going to be her masterpiece. She says to tell you she is fixing up a guest

---

1. This play, tentatively titled "The Greed of the Meek," does not survive.

room that will be sure to please you, and for you to remember there is always welcome for you inscribed on its threshold. So don't forget!

One of the best things about this new place is that its in absolute country and yet only three-quarters of an hour motor ride from Frisco—that is, after the new tunnel opens up through the Berkeley hills next month.

Meanwhile, if you get up to Frisco in the near future, we have no guest room here but will send the car in for you and take you back, if you can find time to visit. We are only a half hour from Frisco here.

Well, that's all my news, I guess—except that I've sent to London for a book for you—"Masks of the World" by Joseph Gregor, director of the theatrical art section of the National Library in Vienna—translation from German. It has some fine colored plates. I just got my copy and I thought, after a look, that you'd like one in your library, too. But it won't reach you for a few weeks. I'm telling you about this beautiful present so prematurely because I don't want you to go buying it yourself before you heard from me.

Bobby[2] came out here with Felton Elkins[3] three or four days ago and we had a fine visit. He looked fine and was the same old Bobby. It was grand to see him.

We have seen quite a bit of Felton and his wife. They drive over almost every week. He has been a big help to us in many ways—the same contractor who built his house is building ours—etc. I have always liked him, as you know, and, if I remember right, you did, too—and I like him even better now that he is older and has cut out booze. (There is no one detests liquor in others more than a reformed tank!)

Much affection from us both, Kenneth. I suppose you're working your head off but drop a line when you get a chance. And be sure and let us know whenever you are going to come to Frisco.

As ever,
Gene

2. Robert Edmond Jones.

3. A millionaire classmate of O'Neill's in George Pierce Baker's English 47 class at Harvard, with whom he had kept in sporadic contact since 1914–15.

November 17, 1937

Dear Gene,

Here at last are snapshots of most of my masks, though I think there are about ten more. If you want to keep them, that would be all right with me, but if they are of no real use to you after you have looked them over, I would just as soon have them back.

There is nothing very new here except that Peter[1] has grown half an inch in the last six weeks and is now just a shade shorter than I.

I hope you are feeling better and that Carlotta is as well as ever. Give her my love.

Ever and ever,

Mr. Eugene O'Neill
Lafayette
Contra Costa County
C a l i f o r n i a

Dear Kenneth,

Herewith the snapshots—and many thanks for sending them. You certainly have some extraordinarily interesting ones and I am glad of the chance to look them over. I have a few, mostly African, I bought in France. But my prize is a real Emperor Jones African drum—wonderfully carved. Covarubias[1] told me it was one of the finest he had ever seen—and he knows whereof he speaks. I'll take pride in showing it to you when you visit our new home.

The home proceeds on schedule. We expect to move in in January and be really put there by February.

No news except that I'm managing to do more and more about work. And that "Mourning Becomes Electra" is opening in London to-night—with Beatrice Lehman[2] and others. Begins at seven and

1. Macgowan's son.

1. Mexican painter and illustrator Miguel Covarrubias (1904–57), who was in San Francisco to do some murals for the upcoming Golden Gate Exposition and World's Fair.
2. Noted English actress Beatrix Lehmann, who, besides playing Lavinia Mannon in *Mourning Becomes Electra*, also played Ella Downey and Abbie Putnam in English productions of *All God's Chillun Got Wings* and *Desire Under the Elms*, respectively.

runs right through with no dinner intermission. You can imagine how the perfidious Limeys will resent an Irish-Yank demanding that from them! I anticipate the snootiest sort of condescending critical bilge. Plus a record short run and barely perceptible royalties. If I know the London theatre, these fond expectations will be exceeded, if possible.

Love from us,

As ever,
Gene

November 19th 1937

---

136 • TO MACGOWAN FROM CARLOTTA O'NEILL. ALS 2 pp.

Christmas Day—[1937]

Dear Kenneth—

You would have been delighted had you seen how pleased Gene was to receive your beautiful mask.—Altho' you sweetly included *"Mrs"* in the address I have insisted it is to be *his very own*—& will go in his new study at Tao House.[1]—(We are like that about our toys—Very possessive!)—We begin to move Monday—(God help me!)—And will be at it every day this week. Hope to get Gene in next Friday. Only the kitchen wing—our bedrooms & Gene's study will be finished—the rest will be completed while we are in residence! It will take about two months to get put.—*Then* we look forward to a weekend with *you* with us—

Our love always—
Carlotta

New address on envelope—

---

137 • TO CARLOTTA O'NEILL FROM MACGOWAN. TL(cc) 1 p.

December 27, 1937

Dear Carlotta:

I am so glad you and Gene liked the mask. I am sure it is only a modern reproduction, partly because I didn't pay much for it and partly because the old ones are treasured by Noe actors or else kept

---

1. The O'Neills had named their new home from the Chinese word *tao*, which means "the right way of life."

in museums. The Japs are frightfully clever at copying. In this case I am sure the original was so old that it had lost all its surface paint and they reproduced its actual worn state. As near as I can figure out, this is one of the many feminine types used in Noe plays.

I am glad you are at last on the eve of moving into your permanent home. Be sure and send me some snapshots of it when you get settled.

Tell Gene I had a great wind-fall on Christmas Eve and was able to buy ten very old Hopi leather masks for the ridiculous sum of $175.

Love to you both.

Mrs. Eugene O'Neill
Lafayette
Contra Costa County
C a l i f o r n i a

---

138 • TO MACGOWAN FROM O'NEILL. ALS 1 p.

Danville

new address[1] Contra Costa Co.

Cal.

Dec. 28th 1937

Dear Kenneth:

Just a line amid the furor of getting packed to move into our new home.

A million thanks for the mask! I have never had a gift that pleased me more! It's a beauty, and nothing could have been more welcome as an adornment for the O'Neill maison. And I know how it must have broken your collector's heart to part with it, which makes me all the more grateful! All I can say is, now I *do* believe in Santa Claus again!

And here's hoping you will be able to visit us as soon as we're settled.

As ever,

Gene

P.S. I was entirely and astoundingly wrong about "Mourning Becomes Electra" in London. It scored an almost unanimous artistic hit—critics so laudatory, you wouldn't believe it—and promises to

1. O'Neill circled this phrase and drew an arrow from it to the address.

do well financially, too. Altogether, a miracle! I'm tickled to death because "Electra" has never failed anywhere it has been done so far, which is going some for a Trilogy Tragedy, but I was certain London would ruin that record.

---

139 • TO MACGOWAN FROM O'NEILL. WIRE 1 p. (SF54 34- TDJD DANVILLE CALIF JAN 22 1938 1055A)

KENNETH MACGOWAN-

TWENTIETH CENTURY FOX STUDIOS-
ONLY TOO DELIGHTED BUT WRITE ME DETAILS SO I WILL KNOW EX-
ACTLY HOW PROCEED STOP YOU SEE ONLY INFORMATION I EVER
HAD FROM MADDEN WAS LUX REFUSED RENEWAL RADIO ROYALTY
AND DEAL WAS DEAD-[1]

GENE

---

140 • TO O'NEILL FROM MACGOWAN. TL(cc) 2 pp.

January 22nd, 1938

Mr. Eugene O'Neill
Tao House
Danville, Cal.

Dear Gene:

Here's what happened! My business manager and I decided I ought to budget myself on masks and not spend more than $500. a year that way. Of course, I've spent almost all of that in six months, and I decided I better make some extra money, writing. I found this pretty difficult at the distance I am both from New York and my former career with the typewriter. And, one Sunday, hearing Deems Taylor[1] talk during the Philharmonic Concert, I got the bright idea that I could make some money out of radio. I told my agent the plays I had been connected with, and I emphasized that if somebody put another of your plays on the air, I would be an ideal explainer. He said that Lux was planning to do "Anna Christie" if they could get the cast they wanted, and of course I told him that this would work out ideally. My agent saw the Lux people and they took to it very warmly. Later, however, they got the idea of having you in-

1. The Lux Radio Theatre had expressed interest in "Anna Christie."

1. American composer and critic-musicologist.

stead. Of course, in spite of my love for masks, I would like nothing better than having you go on the air down here, because we could have another pow-wow. I was pretty sure, however, that you still would fight shy of something like this, so I shot off a wire. I am sure Lux is pretty keen about doing "Anna Christie," in spite of their split with Madden over the old deal, because I know they are negotiating with M.G.M. to get Joan Crawford and Spencer Tracy for the leads. (Spencer Tracy ought to be perfectly swell.) If the Lux people go through with the deal and approach you about speaking, I think you might merely mention that there is someone down here who could fill the job ideally because of his connection with many of your plays.

If the thing goes through, I'll outline to you what I will try to say. Roughly, it seems to me, it ought to be a discussion of how you happen to be the outstanding playwright that you are. Let's stress, to begin with, the fact that you learned about life first-off and at first-hand—living over Jimmy, the Priest's,[2] for example—and that then you developed your means of expression. I would throw in as much colorful detail about your life on the water-front and in sailing ships as you would feel proper.

That's enough for now, I guess, as I am up to my ears with work, starting three pictures in three weeks.

My best to you both.

Ever and ever,
Kenneth Macgowan

---

141 • TO MACGOWAN FROM O'NEILL.[1] AL 2 pp.

[Spring 1938]

Dear Kenneth:

I am going to be absolutely frank, as I know you would want me to be. A visit *with Edie* simply would not work. Carlotta feels too bitter and enduring a resentment. She will never forgive those among my supposed friends who took the attitude, when we went off to-

2. The Fulton Street saloon and flop-house on New York's Lower East Side where O'Neill had lived—for $3 per month—in 1911–12. He later used it as the setting for act 1 of "*Anna Christie*."

1. This letter appears only in holograph form on lined, spring-binder notebook paper and may well never have been sent.

gether, that I was being hooked by an unscrupulous floosie, and believed as Gospel every rotten thing they could of her. For that matter, I don't feel very forgiving myself. And we had too many reliable reports of what Edie said, and of her great sympathy with Agnes, to have any doubts where she stood. And when you add to this the antagonism which she and Carlotta just naturally feel toward each other, anyway—No, it wouldn't be a pleasant visit. At best, there might be a faking veneer on the surface but the atmosphere would be poisoned.

And so. Its one of those things. I'm damned sorry it is—but it is. And I know you will understand and agree with me that its much wiser to be realistic about it. You also know, I hope, that Carlotta has a very genuine and deep affection for you—and you know my feeling. There is no one in the world we would rather have with us than you.

The above, of course, is strictly confidential between us. And, believe me, it wasn't easy to write.

Thanks for the mask snaps, which I enclose back to you herewith. They are damned interesting. I have no snaps of my few—and my prize drum!—but I hope you will come and see them.

It's fine news about Peter and Harvard. Shane has just been here on a visit and Eugene is coming this summer. Shane, with three years of a bookworm Southern prep. school against him, won't make a University for another year. Then, I think, he'll go to Colorado— the best in the territory between East & Coast, so Eugene assures me. He is at a combination of ranch and tutoring school at Golden, Colorado now and has gone heavily horsey, cowboy boots and all—has learned to break horses and is a fine rider. He's getting a job on a ranch this summer as a wrangler. What he will eventually choose to do, God knows, but for once in his life he's genuinely self-confident and enthusiastic—about horses and stock-raising, not scholastic pursuits, I might add.

Yes, I am hard at the Cycle again—have been ever since the neuritis that gave me hell all winter let up a month or so ago. Almost gone now. Five teeth out eventually stopped it. Thank God, I have few left now to cause trouble! Have you ever had neuritis? Well don't, if you haven't. It's the most demoralizing, nerve-wracking pain I know of.

Carlotta joins in love to you.

As ever,

Dear Kenneth,

Just a line to thank you for the opus on O'Neill from dear old
Buenos Aires.[1] I little dreamed when I slept on plaza benches down
there that I'd ever appear in any book—except the one at the police
station, maybe. It was damned kind of you to send it. I rec'd one
copy from the author—he translated "The Great God Brown" which
scored quite a success—(artistic, anyway)—in Buenos Aires a couple
of seasons back,[2] but I am glad to have another.

Feeling good, working hard. Neuritis gone—for good, I hope—
thanks to sun and swimming.

Did you take that Mexico vacation?

Here's hoping to see you here before too long.

Carlotta joins in love.

As ever,
Gene

July 25th 1938

Mr Kenneth Macgowan,
Twentieth Century-Fox Studios,
Beverly Hills,
California

Dear Kenneth,

A million of thanks for the mask! It was damned kind of you, and
Carlotta is as delighted with it as I am. We're particularly pleased
because it fills in a space in the entrance hall where my masks are
hung and completes the effect. Also, it lends variety because I have
no Indian one of any sort. So consider your Santa Clausing for us a
huge success! I wanted to send you something but I couldn't dig up
anything out of book catalogues, English or American, that interested me or I thought would interest you.

---

1. Probably *El teatro de O'Neill* by Léon Mirlas, published in 1938 by Precio in Buenos
Aires.

2. Mirlas's translation of *The Great God Brown* (*El gran dios Brown*) had been published
in 1934 by Editorial Argentores in Buenos Aires.

How is everything with you? I'm just about at the end of going over the fourth play,[1] the first draft of which I completed a couple of months ago. The job on this play has taken longer than I had anticipated. It is, I think—and hope!—the most difficult of the lot. Psychologically extremely involved and hard to keep from running wild and boiling over the play mould. But damned interesting and worth the labor. The status now is—two plays—3rd[2] and 4th—finished, and two more, 1st and 2nd[3] in first draft. I won't go back to finish these first two until I have the remainder of the Cycle done. To pull an Irish bull, they repeat a theme variation which occurs afterwards in the last plays. It's a question of how much I want of it in the first two and how much I better save for the later ones. In a week or so, when this going over of the fourth is finally done, I think I'll lay off for a spell of rest. Been working every damn single day without a miss since the middle of last April and am beginning to feel stale and fed-up mentally with this elephantine opus, which demands so much more time and labor than I had expected.

How do you like our best of all possible worlds these days? Me, I'd as soon be a native son of a sty, and maybe sooner! It's time God got plumb disgusted and unleashed a new improved Black Death. That sort of purge used to be extremely effective in cooling off hoggish high spirits in the dear dead days. Maybe it would work again. Anyway, I'm all for giving it a thoroughgoing trial. I'm getting sore exasperated with the latest stupid repetitions in the history of man's stupid greed—and particularly annoyed with the stupidity that will not recognize them as repetitions, but believes the slogans, and gapes with amazed alarm as at something new!

And so, Happy New Year!

And again much grateful appreciation—and here's hoping to see you here the first time you can make it.

Carlotta joins me in love.

As ever,
Gene

December the 28th 1938

1. *More Stately Mansions*, which survived in manuscript and unrevised form at O'Neill's death. It received its first production on November 9, 1962, by the Royal Dramatic Theatre in Stockholm. It was published in 1964 by the Yale University Press. After an initial tryout in Los Angeles, the play received its first New York production on October 31, 1967, at the Broadhurst Theatre.

2. *A Touch of the Poet*, left completed at O'Neill's death, and produced for the first time in the U.S. on October 2, 1958, at New York's Helen Hayes Theatre. It was published in 1957 by Yale University Press.

3. "The Greed of the Meek" and "And Give Me Death," both of which were eventually destroyed by O'Neill.

144 • TO O'NEILL FROM MACGOWAN. WIRE 1 p. (At foot of WIRE (charge Kenneth Macgowan—W.L.A. 32197))

MARCH 27, 1939

MR. EUGENE O'NEILL
DANVILLE
CONTRA COSTA COUNTY, CALIFORNIA

AM COMING TO SAN FRANCISCO WEDNESDAY FOR PREVIEW OF ALEXANDER GRAHAM BELL[1] AT FAIR[2] RETURNING EARLY WEDNESDAY EVENING. WOULD LIKE TO PHONE YOU IF YOU WILL WIRE NUMBER. LOVE TO CARLOTTA AND YOU.

KENNETH MACGOWAN

---

145 • TO MACGOWAN FROM CARLOTTA O'NEILL. WIRE 1 p. (SA75 10-DANVILLE CALIF MAR 27 1939 542P)

KENNETH MACGOWAN-

TELEPHONE DANVILLE 116 WE WOULD LOVE TO HEAR FROM YOU-

CARLOTTA

---

146 • TO CARLOTTA O'NEILL FROM MACGOWAN. WIRE 1 p.

[Spring 1939]

MRS. EUGENE O'NEIL,
DANVILLE, CALIFORNIA

HAVE TICKET ON DAYLIGHT LIMITED ARRIVING OAKLAND 6:07. IF PRODUCTION EMERGENCY MAKES NECESSARY CANCELLATION OR POSTPONEMENT WILL WIRE YOU AS FAR IN ADVANCE AS POSSIBLE. LOVE.

KENNETH MACGOWAN

---

147 • TO MACGOWAN FROM CARLOTTA O'NEILL. TLS 1 p. (On stationery headed: Tao House / Danville / Contra Costa County / California)

Kenneth Dear,

Bless your heart for writing me such a sweet letter. We are so happy that you know what we have up here in our house on the hill.

---

1. *The Story of Alexander Graham Bell*, 1939 film produced by Macgowan and starring Don Ameche, Henry Fonda, and Loretta Young.
2. San Francisco's Golden Gate Exposition and World's Fair.

It was a joy to see you even for that brief few hours. Would a miracle ever happen that would bring you to us for a few days? That's what we're burning candles for!

You looked well and are always the same. In fact, dear Kenneth, we think you are just about all one could wish for in the role of best friend.

Thank you for the Pacific Cultures book.[1] Maybe I'll get Gene to the Fair before it closes—I hope so.

Our love always,
Carlotta

June the 10th 1939
Joan[2] is charming and very pretty!

---

148 • TO THE O'NEILLS FROM MACGOWAN. TL(cc) 2 pp.

August 12, 1939

Mr. and Mrs. Eugene O'Neill
Tao House
Danville, Contra Costa County
C a l i f o r n i a

Dear folks:

Thanks so much for the two photographs, especially the one of the Maestro.[1]

I have had no luck at all in getting those West Indian records I told you about, but I hear that Columbia may re-press them again sometime. Meanwhile, I have asked the New York music store that specializes in these songs to send you two records. I don't know a thing about them. They are not sung by the man who did my records, but I hope they are representative. One of them is along their favorite "historical" line—"Selassie Is Held by the Police" and "The Reign of the Georges." I enclose a list because you will be amused at the names of the composers and singers—"The Caresser," "Atilla The Hun," etc.

Somebody connected with the Rockefeller Foundation's film de-

1. Probably *Pacific Cultures*, published in 1939 in San Francisco by the Golden Gate International Exposition.
2. Macgowan's daughter.

1. Carlotta often referred to O'Neill, seriously, as "the Master."

O'Neill and Carlotta in the living room at Tao House

partment has come through with what may turn out to be a swell idea for my future. This is to get the Foundation to provide the money for a three-year trek in Mexico and Central America, making a motion picture record of the ruins. If this comes through there will be a salary connected with it and I can quit here. It will probably take a year to do this. Meanwhile, I have signed up for another term.

I have lately come on the most amusing story of a drunkard's reform that I have ever heard. Ivan Kahn, our talent scout, used to be a very successful and extraordinarily drunk agent. He was such a lush that he used to end up literally in a gutter until a policeman hauled him off to jail. Every now and then he tried tapering off. On one of these occasions he went to Arrowhead Springs Hotel, taking along six bottles of gin to taper with. He drank one bottle and went out for a walk. A couple of miles along the road he came on a turkey farm. The turkeys fascinated him, one gobbler in particular. He called to the gobbler, and it came over to the fence. Then he began to talk to it and the gobbler answered him back. At last he asked the gobbler the most important question in the world, and the gobbler gave him the right answer. After this miracle, Kahn returned immediately to the hotel, poured all the gin down the toilet and hasn't touched a drop since. His only sorrow is that he can't remember what the question and the answer were. Also, he immediately became a failure as an agent.

I hope everything is going swell.

Affectionately yours,
Kenneth Macgowan

---

149 • TO MACGOWAN FROM O'NEILL. TLS 1 p. (On stationery headed: Tao House / Danville / Contra Costa County / California)

Dear Kenneth,

I should have written long since to thank you for the records, which I am delighted to have in the collection. But August was a hectic month with us. A family month. First came Eugene on a visit with a new bride.[1] A stalwart stout young woman. All right in her way—which is all-too-familiar Connecticut small city type—but, from my angle, a rather disappointing daughter-in-law. (Boy, you

1. Eugene O'Neill, Jr., at this time a classicist at Yale University, had recently married for the third time.

don't know the half of the family racket yet! Wait till the progeny begin introducing their brides and their bridegrooms!) On the top of their leaving us, Carlotta's son-in-law[2] (a hell of a nice guy) became seriously ill and had to be taken to the hospital. Lastly, Oona[3] flew out for a visit. This turned out to be a bright spot. I was very apprehensive, not having any idea what she might be like. But Carlotta and I were both delighted with her. She is really a charming girl, both in looks and manners. And she has intelligence, too. So, (knocking on wood) hurrah for that!

Then came the War and ears glued to the radio. And all the time I've been trying to keep on with the job.

I imagine this European tragic mess has got your goat as badly as it has mine. Jesus, the incredible, suicidal capacity of men for stupid greed! That's about the only comment I can find to make, remembering all that has been done from 1918 to date.

Your tale of Ivan Kahn's reformation is damned amusing. I envy him his turkey gobler. In those Ridgefield winters, apple jack, hard cider and acidocis frequently lead me into intimate converse with a rat in the wall regarding cosmic matters. But the bastard didn't know any answers. He only asked questions.

I hope to God this war business will not ruin that Rockefeller Foundation opportunity!

Love from us, Kenneth, and let us hear from you.

As ever,
Gene

Sept. 10th 1939

---

150 • TO O'NEILL FROM MACGOWAN. WIRE 1 p. (At foot of WIRE (charge K. Macgowan, WLA 32197))

DAY LETTER   JULY 18, 1940

MR. EUGENE O'NEIL
DANVILLE
CONTRA COSTA COUNTY
CALIFORNIA

MADALYN OSHEA WHO DIRECTED PROVINCETOWN PLAYHOUSE UNDER FEDERAL THEATRE PROJECT ASKS ME TO WIRE YOU AS FOL-

2. Roy Stram, Cynthia's second husband.
3. O'Neill's daughter by his marriage to Agnes Boulton and later the wife of Charles Chaplin.

LOWS QUOTE PROVINCETOWN THEATRE TO BE FORECLOSED AND
TORN DOWN. CAN YOU HELP? MRS. BELARDE[1] STILLS OWNS IT AND
WILL CONTINUE TO DO SO IF IT CAN BE SAVED BY RAISING FIVE
THOUSAND DOLLARS. THEATRE IS IN EXCELLENT CONDITION HAV-
ING BEEN COMPLETELY REPAIRED AND RECONDITIONED DURING
FEDERAL THEATRE MANAGEMENT UNQUOTE I AGREED TO FOR-
WARD THIS MESSAGE WITHOUT COMMENT. LOVE TO YOU BOTH.

KENNETH MACGOWAN

---

151 • TO MACGOWAN FROM O'NEILL. TLS 1p. (On stationery headed:
Tao House / Danville / Contra Costa County / California)

Dear Kenneth,

My reply to the O'Shea wire will be to ignore it. I am extremely
sour on that outfit. Last summer I let them do my stuff without royalty, as an old times sake gesture, and I never even received a word
of thanks, or Madden either. Furthermore, their publicity gave out
a wire, supposed to come from me but which I knew nothing about,
and it was even quoted in New York papers. I don't love that kind
of stuff. Anyway, even if I had no cause for complaint, I am all for
that theatre being torn down. It has lived shabbily and meaninglessly
too damned long on a dead past which once meant something.

Any chance you may get up this way this summer? We'd love to
see you. There's a lot I'd like to hear, and a lot I'd like to tell you—
about a certain new play[1] I've done since I saw you last, etc. So here's
hoping!

A very beautiful world it's getting to be, isn't it? I've been sunk
for months in the lowest brackets of pessimism with no interest in
work—this state being intensified by a spell of poor health—low
blood pressure stuff, which doesn't fill you with enthusiasm even in
normal times.

Much love from us both, Kenneth!

As ever,
Gene

July the 21st 1940

1. Jennie Belardi, who owned the building at 139 MacDougal Street that had been the
first New York home of the Provincetown Players in 1916.

1. *The Iceman Cometh*, which O'Neill had finished in late November 1939; it was not
produced until 1946.

Dear Kenneth,

Many thanks for the copy of your "open letter." I'm damned glad you sent it because I quit clipping bureaus many years back—except foreign, to keep cases on production over there (when there was an over there!)—and I might never have seen it.

I liked it a lot. I agree with you on the general excellence of the picture[1] and with the exceptions you take to that general excellence. The opening sex wallop of Hollywood bumboat tarts rubbing their prats agin the tropic palms left me faintly nauseated. And there were a few other touches that struck me as not belonging. But they are not important and I haven't, and wouldn't, mention them to Ford[2] or anyone but you, because the picture as a whole is so damned good, and such a courageous thing for a producer to do, especially at this time.

Nichols[3] work, as you say, is a grand job. He deserves equal credit with Ford. And the photography is splendid. All in all, I was enormously pleased.

So much for the picture part of your open letter. The memory of the old P.P.[4] days part moved me to a sad nostalgia. There was a theatre then in which I knew I belonged, one of guts and idealism. Now I feel out of the theatre. I dread the idea of production because I know it will be done by people who have really only one standard left, that of Broadway success. I know beforehand that I will be constantly asked, as I have been asked before, to make stupid compromises for that end. The fact that I will again refuse to make them is no consolation. The fact that I will have the final say on everything is also no consolation. The fact that I like these people personally and the relationship is always friendly and considerate, is no consolation. The big fact is that any production must be made on a plane, and in an atmosphere to which neither I nor my work belongs in spirit, nor want to belong; that it is a job, a business within the Showshop, a long, irritating, wearing, nervous, health-destroying ordeal, with no

1. The movie version of *S.S. Glencairn*, released in the fall of 1940 under the title *The Long Voyage Home*. Macgowan had apparently written an "open letter" to some newspaper regarding the film.
2. John Ford, director of the film.
3. Dudley Nichols, who wrote the screenplay.
4. Provincetown Playhouse.

creative enthusiasm behind it, just another Broadway opening—the Old Game, the game we used to defy in the P.P. but which it is impossible for me to defy now, except in my writing, because there is no longer a theatre of true integrity and courage and high purpose and enthusiasm. There are just groups, or individuals, who put on plays in New York commercial theatres. The idea of an Art Theatre is more remote now, I think, than it was way back in the first decade of this century, before the Washington Square Players[5] or the P.P. were ever dreamed of.

The above is not the usual beef of fifty-two years old against the decadence of the times. It seems to me plain simple fact. After all, the times *are* obviously decadent, and the condition of the theatre reflects them. To have an ideal now, except as a slogan in which neither you nor anyone else believes but which you use out of old habit to conceal a sordid aim, is to confess oneself a fool who cannot face the High Destiny of Man!

The above all sounds much too pessimistic. I don't mean too pessimistic about the times. One couldn't be that, God knows. But about my own mood. So long as I shun production and live here with Carlotta, doing my job of writing plays, I rate myself the most fortunate of men. Especially since I am certain the two plays[6] I've done outside the Cycle in the past year and a half belong among the very best things I've ever written. In some ways I believe they are better than anything I've done before. The last of them "Long Days Journey Into Night" I finished quite recently. It isn't even typed yet.

Would you like to read "The Iceman Cometh"? If so, I have a script I can send you. I certainly want you to read it because I know it will interest you. But pick your own time. If you are being harassed and overworked right now so that you're worn out at the end of each day, I know you won't want to tackle it. And I wouldn't want you to, because it's long and it needs close to three hours concentration. I want you to read it when you can give all to it, so to speak. Which I know is what you would wish. I've been hoping you might be able to pay us a visit and stay a couple of days. Then when you were rested I would have dumped the script in your lap.

5. Theatre group founded in the winter of 1914, dissolved in 1918, and brought to life a year later as the Theatre Guild by Lawrence Langner, Philip Moeller, Lee Simonson, and others.

6. *The Iceman Cometh* and *Long Day's Journey into Night* (the latter completed in September 1940 in first draft but not produced until 1956).

It's rotten luck about your Five Year Plan, and I realize from my own experience that it is hard to take it philosophically as a part of a general fate which everyone shares. Me, I've abandoned the idea of future security, and stopped thinking beyond a few months ahead, because if this country escapes with the best break on the inevitable, we are all certain to be taxed out of a great part of whatever income we get. Even tax exempt securities won't be exempt in a few years. They can't be, and ought not to be.

The best news in your letter is that you hope to quit Hollywood within a year. I don't want to butt in with any unsolicited opinion but it seems to me you ought to do that—at any cost, even if you have to gamble on the future, and use part of your capital each year. After all, capital can no longer be regarded as capital in any security meaning it used to have, while individual freedom is becoming more valuable and rare every day, especially when one is over fifty and the horizon begins to creep up on you. "Shoot the piece" should be the motto of all us Fiftyites—shoot it before it's too late!

Well, I began this feeling I owed you two letters but it looks now as if I felt I owed you five! That's what comes from writing trilogies and cycles. You get so damned long-winded.

Make yourself come up for a visit, darn you! It would do you good. And do me good. Tell the bastards you're sick or something! After all, it's only two hours or so by plane.

Much love from us.

As ever,
Gene

November the 29th 1940

---

153 • TO MACGOWAN FROM O'NEILL. TLS 1 p. (On stationery headed: Tao House / Danville / Contra Costa County / California)

Dear Kenneth,

A line to tell you the script[1] is being sent, registered, today. One of the best things I've ever done, I think. Have I written you this self-gratifying judgement before? I've forgotten, but anyway the enthusiasm I feel for it can't be too emphatic.

The dump in the play is no one place but a combination of three

1. *The Iceman Cometh.*

in which I once hung out.[2] The characters all derive from actual people I have known—more or less closely or remotely—but none of them is an exact portrait of anyone. The main plot is, of course, imaginary.

Here's hoping the reading gives you something of what I got from it in the writing.

Your news about the possibility that you may become assistant and general supervisor with Jock Whitney[3] in the film end of the government's Spanish American bureau sounds like a grand way out for you. I'm hoping like hell it goes through all right!

Love from us,
Gene

December the 15th 1940

P.S. Please be sure NO ONE else sees this (the script) and return as soon as is convenient.

---

154 • TO MACGOWAN FROM O'NEILL. TLS 2 pp. (On stationery headed: Tao House / Danville / Contra Costa County / California)

Dear Kenneth,

(The following letter was written before Christmas. Right after I wrote it I came down with bronchitis and have been in bed ever since, feeling rottener than rotten, and forgot to have the letter typed.)

I'm delighted "The Iceman Cometh" made such a deep impression on you. I was confident it would. And I'm grateful for your frank critical suggestions. I wanted them, and will keep them in mind when it is time to give the play a final going over, which it hasn't had yet. I know when this is done I will find that a general pruning is needed, but I'm sure I won't agree with you on the advisability of any drastic condensation of the first part. I see what you're driving at, but I honestly believe if I did it you would be the first to see afterward it was wrong because it had changed the essential character and unique quality of the play. After all, what I've tried to write is a play where at the end you feel you know the souls of the seventeen

---

2. Harry Hope's bar was modeled on the Golden Swan saloon (the "Hell Hole") in Greenwich Village, on Jimmy the Priest's, and on the taproom of the Garden Hotel on New York's Madison Avenue.

3. Millionaire philanthropist John Hay Whitney.

men and women who appear—and the women who don't appear—as well as if you'd read a play about each of them. I couldn't condense much without taking a lot of life from some of these people and reducing them to lay figures. You would find if I did not build up the complete picture of the group as it now is in the first part—the atmosphere of the place, the humour and friendship and human warmth and *deep inner contentment* of the bottom—you would not be so interested in these people and you would find the impact of what follows a lot less profoundly disturbing. You wouldn't feel the same sympathy and understanding for them, or be so moved by what Hickey does to them.

It's hard to explain èxactly my intuitions about this play. Perhaps I can put it best by saying The Iceman Cometh is something I want to make life reveal about itself, fully and deeply and roundly—that it takes place for me in life not in a theatre—that the fact it is a play which can be produced with actors is secondary and incidental to me and even, quite unimportant—and so it would be a loss to me to sacrifice anything of the complete life for the sake of stage and audience.

That doesn't say it, but never mind. You'll get what I mean. Take for example your point about the part near the end where each character tells his face-saving version of his experience when he went out to confront his pipe dream. *I* don't write this as a piece of playwrighting. *They do it. They have to.* Each of them! In just that way! It is tragically, pitifully important to them to do this! They *must* tell these lies as a first step in taking up life again. Moreover, their going through with this pathetic formula heightens by contrast the tension of Larry's waiting for the sound of Parritt hurtling down to the backyard, and the agony he goes through. If our American acting and directing cannot hold this scene up without skimping it, then to hell with our theatre! You know as well as I that the direction and acting of the old Moscow Art Theatre, or Kamerny,[1] could sustain the horrible contrast and tension of this episode and make it one of the most terrible scenes in the play, as it is to me now.

Well, I seem to be vociferously objecting to your objections. That doesn't mean I'm dismissing them. As I said before I'll keep them in the old bean when I come to read over the play. I'm going on my memory of it now, which is pretty vivid still.

1. The Kamerny Theatre of Moscow, whose productions of *Desire Under the Elms* and *All God's Chillun Got Wings* O'Neill had seen in Paris in the spring of 1930.

What you wonder about Hickey: No, I never knew him. He's the most imaginary character in the play. Of course, I knew many salesmen in my time who were periodical drunks, but Hickey is not any of them. He is all of them, you might say, and none of them.

Parritt is also almost entirely imaginary. His betrayal of the Movement derives from a real incident, but I never knew the guy, or anything about his mother, so Parritt's personal history is my own fiction.

I'm not discussing the minor matters you bring up because I'd have to read the play again first, and I don't feel up to that now. I've felt like hell for the past five weeks—insomnia, stomach gone blooey, nervous exhaustion, etc.—one of my periodic sinking spells, complicated by flu. On top of all this our dog, Blemie, died a few days ago. He was thirteen, growing feeble, blind and deaf, and death was a mercy for him. But he had been with us ever since we were married. We loved him and his passing has knocked both of us out. Christmas is not going to be merry in Tao House.

Love from us and much gratitude for your letter.

As ever,
Gene

December the 30th 1940

---

155 • TO O'NEILL FROM MACGOWAN. TL(cc) 1 p.

MARCH
Tenth
1 9 4 1

Eugene O'Neill
Danville, Calif.

Dear Gene:

Here are a couple of stories from the Hollywood Reporter that alarm me.[1] I hope there's really nothing in them. Please let me know how you are.

I was away in New York last week getting set on this government job under Jock Whitney. Now it all seems to be straightened out,

1. O'Neill had suffered from a series of minor but debilitating ailments during the first three months of 1941; apparently, the *Hollywood Reporter* had run a story indicating that the playwright was too ill to go to New York to oversee a planned production of *The Iceman Cometh*—a production that did not materialize.

and I'm going back to New York in three weeks on a leave of absence from the studio. The job is more or less what I outlined to you about trying to promote better understanding between Spanish America and the United States through distribution of various sorts of films of a non-theatrical nature. I've got a whale of a funny title. Director of Production in the Motion Picture Division in the office of Coordinator of commercial and cultural relations between the American republics under the Council of National Defense. First off New York scared me—I haven't lived in the city for so long—but after I put in a week in and around the Film Library of the Modern Museum, through which most of the work will be done, I felt pretty happy about it all.

This is a pretty hasty note, but anyway, my best to you and Carlotta.

Ever and ever,
Kenneth Macgowan

---

156 • TO MACGOWAN FROM O'NEILL. TLS 1 p. (On stationery headed: Tao House / Danville / Contra Costa County / California)

Dear Kenneth,

There's this much truth in the report. I have been laid up a lot since last Fall with one ill or another—the worst Winter for me in several years. And it's true I'm not letting the Guild make plans to produce "The Iceman Cometh." Health is one good reason for this. As I guess I've told you before, I've been warned that any excessive strains which drain the old nervous vitality might land me where I was several years ago—to wit, on my back in a hospital. Even living quietly here, I get recurrent woozy upsets when my blood pressure drops in my boots and I have to take a course of shots to buck it up again. Going to New York where I'm always below par, for the ordeal of putting on a play under existing conditions, when I cannot feel the slightest interest or enthusiasm for the game, would be quite likely to knock me out. So why take the chance until finances force me to? Production isn't that important. It can always wait. Writing can't.

There is nothing new in the above health dope. Except for the extra low Winter, my general condition is the same now as in the other years since my break-up in 1937. Nothing dangerous, so long as I watch out and follow a careful routine. If I didn't, it could be. That's the whole situation, and it is due to endure for the rest of my life, but what the hell, there's nothing very unpleasant about it.

It's fine to know you landed that job. It ought to be damned interesting in itself, and a welcome escape from the Hollywood grind besides—even if, with that title of yours, you have to use eight-sheets for business cards!

I suppose there's no chance of your getting up this way before you move East? If there is, let us know. We'd love to see you.

Love from us,

As ever,
Gene

March 15th 1941

---

157 • TO CARLOTTA O'NEILL FROM MACGOWAN. TL(cc) 1 p.

JUNE
Second
1 9 4 3

Mrs. Eugene O'Neill
Tao House
Danville, Calif.

Dear Carlotta:

I happened to run into Buck Crouse[1] the other day and he alarmed me quite a bit by what he said about Gene's general state of health. I do want to know more from you.

But the immediate point of this letter is that I think I can find a legitimate excuse for using up railroad transportation to the north. In two weeks I shall have a picture shooting on location at Santa Rosa and Healdsburg. Irving Pichel is directing and I think I can make this the occasion of a fairly legitimate trip to San Francisco. If I can do this, can you put me up over night? I could come up on the daylight train, spend the night with you, go back to San Francisco

---

1. Playwright Russel Crouse (1893–1966), who had served as press agent of the Theatre Guild in the early 1930s, coauthor, with Howard Lindsay (1889–1968), of *Life with Father* (1939), among other plays and musicals.

the next day and then up to Santa Rosa. I presume that taxis can be had from the end of the electric car line or bus.

My love to you both.

Affectionately,
Kenneth Macgowan

---

158 • TO MACGOWAN FROM CARLOTTA O'NEILL. ALS 4 pp. (On stationery headed: Tao House / Danville / Contra Costa County / California)

June 5th 1943

Dear Kenneth:

A joy to hear from you—but a surprise to learn you are again in Hollywood.

My dear Kenneth, Gene has Parkinson's disease, a progressive disease, so each day makes it worse. With it, goes days of nerve upset—&, if he does too much, a sort of (what we term) sinking spell. All this breaks my heart—but I *must* keep going no matter what—for he needs me more than ever, now. In spite of an arthritic back I am taking care of this entire house—& *cooking!* The cooks we've had this past year were all sixty or over, lazy, stupid, ill mannered & knew nothing of cooking. Two were mentally unbalanced, seriously so. So,—I had to take over. I have never cooked before—but got out the books & went to it. I *loathe* it as I loathe hell—but, *who cares?* Gene must eat—&, funnily enough, he eats more than he has for years! It must be simply because he doesn't want to discourage me in my effort. All this leads to your asking us to put you up for a night. Considering how close you are to the O'Neill household I *will* put you up. (I wouldn't cook for another soul in the world, but Gene. Maybe you'll wish I hadn't!) But it must be a definite date—because rationing, & living in the country, makes house keeping very difficult. Don't ask to bring anyone else—or don't tell anyone you stopped for the night, etc.—Russel Crouse hired a car in San Francisco, & came over with Lindsay[1] & Miss Curtis[2] for tea, & then motored back. Freeman[3] is in the Marines you no doubt know. The hardware man

---

1. Howard Lindsay.
2. Actress-playwright Margaret Curtis, author of *Highland Fling*, which Lindsay and Crouse were considering producing. The production never materialized.
3. Herbert Freeman, the O'Neills' chauffeur and utility man, an important figure in their lives for more than ten years.

in Danville drives us to town for the doctor, etc. There is a bus to *Walnut Creek,* if you could get that far, & then phone, I'd get the car there for you. Or, if you will know exactly when you'll arrive in *Oakland*—I could save gas & make arrangements for Mr. Haskell[4] to go in & pick you up there. Please figure it all carefully & let me know in plenty of time so I can make decent arrangements at this end. We'll love seeing you—& it will do Gene good to have a gossip with you. So do try to come.

I feel so befuddled by the strange things that are happening to the *mind* (?) of America. After the war is over it will be *ghastly*. But I'll be so damned old it won't matter.

Gene joins me in love—

As ever,
Carlotta

Write as soon as you *can* about days, dates, hours, stations, & we'll be looking forward to seeing you with great happiness!—

---

159 • TO CARLOTTA O'NEILL FROM MACGOWAN. TL(cc) 1 p.

J U N E 2 6
1 9 4 3

Mrs. Eugene O'Neill
Danville, California

Dear Carlotta:

I was just getting squared away to write you a letter when yours arrived. I talked with our cook as soon as I got back, but found that she wouldn't be in contact with her friends in the negro quarter until Sunday. So I'll tell her to lay off a couple and look for a cook.

That's good news about Mr. Haskill. Despite all the very real miseries that seem to be descending on Tao House just now, you might take rueful satisfaction from the situations of Messers Haskill, Roberts[1] and Freeman. When Roberts was driving me to the bus, he did nothing but talk about what swell people you were. He said that you were much too generous to everyone, and certainly to him.

4. Curtis Haskell, the town constable and owner of a hardware store in Danville, who occasionally drove for the O'Neills after Freeman left.

1. Charlie Roberts, chauffeur for the owners of the Blackhawk Ranch near Lafayette (west and north of Danville), who, like Curtis Haskell, helped drive for the O'Neills in Freeman's absence.

How very, very fortunate for Gene that he has you with him in this time of his life! I wouldn't have missed being with you for anything, and yet it was so tragic to know how Fate, in various guises, is blocking the outlet of Gene's creative genius. But perhaps if you can only get a cook, you can find some way to break through the dam.

The trip was really beautiful, and I had quite a lot of fun up at Santa Rosa. Their beef steaks are really fabulous. Irving Pichel asked about you both.

A San Francisco bookstore with the amazing name of 'Newbegin' or something like that, is going to send you the two New England joke books. They had only one in stock. If both don't come, please let me know.

Affectionately,

---

160 • TO MACGOWAN FROM CARLOTTA O'NEILL. ALS 1 p.

Sunday—
[1944–45]

Dear Kenneth:—

We look forward, with great pleasure, to seeing you Saturday, the twenty-seventh, at lunch.

Lud, doesn't that sound formal! We'll *adore* seeing you! Hope we can give you something decent to eat!

Our love,
Carlotta

Lunch at one!
Apt. 1006—
1075 California St.,

---

161 • TO MACGOWAN FROM O'NEILL. ALS[1] 6 pp. (On stationery headed: The Barclay / New York 17, N.Y.)

Jan. 1st 1946

Dear Kenneth:—

It was grand to get your letter and here is a belated Happy New Year back to you.

---

1. The letter was written by Carlotta and signed by O'Neill.

As you see, we *are* East and we are busy planning ahead for the production of three plays. We meant to let you know before this of our return home, that is, the East—but things happened suddenly in San Francisco. Railroad accommodations, etc.—and we jumped at the chance to grab the offered accommodations.

It is almost impossible to get a room in New York. But we managed, through friends, to get a living-room, & bed & bath here.

We are delighted that your retirement from pictures is really set this time. And I think the job of Director of the University Museum in Philadelphia could be just the thing for you. Here's hoping that it comes through.

I also believe it's time for you to do a book, and certainly the subject of "Early Man in America" should interest every intelligent person.[2] For one thing it will show us how far we have slipped since the good old Cro Magnon days.

No, you can't grab my sound scriber.[3] I have simply *got* to learn how to use it when I start being creative again, which probably means when we go to Sea Island for four months May first.

Re productions:—"The Iceman Cometh," with Eddie Dowling playing Hickey & directing, will begin rehearsals in September. It will be followed, around the first of the year, by either "A Moon for the Misbegotten" or "A Touch of the Poet"—and the third play the beginning of next season.[4] Which of these plays comes first all depends on the casting.

Here's hoping we'll soon meet here.

Carlotta joins me in love.

As ever,
Gene

2. Macgowan's *Early Man in the New World*, published by Macmillan in 1950.

3. The dictating machine that Lawrence Langner had given to O'Neill after the Parkinson's disease from which he suffered caused his hands to tremble so much that he could not write. O'Neill was never able to use it.

4. *The Iceman Cometh* opened at Broadway's Martin Beck Theatre on September 2, 1946, directed by Eddie Dowling and starring James Barton. *A Moon for the Misbegotten* and *A Touch of the Poet* did not receive their first productions until 1947 and 1958, respectively.

162 • TO MACGOWAN FROM O'NEILL. TLS 1 p. (On stationery headed:
Point O'Rocks Lane Marblehead Neck, Massachusetts)

[1948–50]

Dear Kenneth:

Congratulations on Random House publishing your "Primer of
Playwrighting."

As for the dedication I like "To Eugene O'Neill and Robert E.
Jones and the theatre we worked for."[1] And Carlotta agrees with me.

I will be glad to take a look at a manuscript or set of proofs. Don't
expect any keen comment. My memory is blurry, and the worse
curse of this disease is that it makes it so difficult to concentrate.

The idea of your next book sounds grand. Good luck to it!

All best to you and yours—

Gene

P.S. I had a very nice letter from your daughter-in-law.

163 • TO MACGOWAN FROM CARLOTTA O'NEILL. ALS 2 pp. (On
stationery headed: Point O'Rocks Lane / Marblehead Neck, Massachusetts)

Dear Kenneth:

Thanks for your note—we'll love seeing you.

As to "living in a shack in Provincetown"—?—We are still where
you saw us,—& mama Carlotta took her nest egg to rebuild the hut,
that is tied to a rock on the Atlantic, & it cost *over* $85,000.00!!!
Believe it or not!!

So it goes. Perhaps now old friends will be sorry for us & not want
to borrow money!

It will be a joy to see you!

Love to all the children & grandchildren from us old folk!

As always,
Carlotta

Dec. 6 / 1950
Gene is not too well.—

1. *A Primer of Playwriting* was published in 1951 with the dedication "To Eugene
O'Neill and Robert Edmond Jones and the theatre we worked for."

164 • TO O'NEILL FROM MACGOWAN. TLS 2 pp. (On stationery headed: 10737 Le Conte Avenue / Los Angeles 24, California)

Feb. 8, 1951

Dear Gene:

The paper says a broken kneecap. That's a hell of a note. Ask Carlotta to write me how long this will keep you in the hospital. Maybe they can set it and send you home. I hate hospitals since my last adventure with kidney stones that turned out not to be there. It was a Catholic joint—the best in the city. I came in the afternoon to wait for an "exploration" the next morning. Two men had appendectomies that evening from nearby beds, and a priest—a young one—came in to do the honors. Then he turned to me and said: "Are you a Catholic, son?" "No, Father," said I dutifully. "Well, I wish you the best of luck just the same." I didn't know whether he meant in the operation or in getting to heaven unshriven.

The nearest I came to kneecap trouble was bursitis in the right knee joint. Pretty painful, but it could be baked out in time. What rotten luck for you!

When we were with you at Xmastime and you seemed to enjoy the talk that was going on, I thought that it was a pity you weren't in some slightly more accessible place, for you might get a lot out of such young people as at UCLA or some of the saner screen-writers. And what they'd get out of you! Pete[1] knew you, of course, from way back, but Barbara[2] was enormously thrilled.

I saw Mary Morris[3] at the American Educational Theatre Conference and gave her greetings from you. She seems hale and hearty, as well as bit plump—as who isn't except you?

Saxe[4] has been swell about the book.[5] I finished up revisions in two weeks, and went over everything with him in New York on Jan. 29th. It's being rushed into galleys and they're going to get out sample copies to the teachers in early spring.

By the way, I've come on two quotes that will interest you:

Writing for the theater is a peculiar business. . . . It involves a craft that you have to learn and a talent you must possess.

1. Macgowan's son.
2. Probably Macgowan's daughter-in-law.
3. Actress who had created the role of Abbie Putnam in *Desire Under the Elms* (1924).
4. Random House editor Saxe Commins, one of O'Neill's closest friends for many years.
5. *A Primer of Playwriting.*

Neither is common, and you have to have both of them if you want to succeed.—Goethe.

I tried to keep in mind that in a play, from time to time, something should happen; that the audience should be kept in constant expectation that something is going to happen; and that, when it does happen, it should be different, but not too different, from what the audience has been led to expect.—T. S. Eliot.

I didn't think much of Eliot's "The Cocktail Party." The first act was warmed up Pinero-Shaw-Wilde. The second act went High Church mystical in a nauseating way. As for the "verse"—Eliot says in a rather modest article in the current Harper's that each line has "a caesura and three stresses," "there must be one stress on one side of the caesura and two on the other." I can't find caesuras or stresses in lines like these:

If there happened to be anyone with you
I was going to say I'd come back for my umbrella. . . .
I must say you didn't seem very pleased to see me.
Edward, I understand what has happened
But I could not understand your manner on the telephone.

Eliot has the decency to say, "it is perhaps an open question whether there is any poetry in the play at all." And yet the purpose of the article is to argue that he had at last worked out a "metric" for the modern poetic play—and he prints the play as if it *were* poetry. I prefer Christopher Fry's gay, extravagant show-off of verse in "The Lady's Not for Burning." (That play was superbly acted in New York.)

I saw two of Ibsen's in New York. Arthur Miller did a good colloquial adaptation of "An Enemy of the People"—barring a few phrases such as "I feel like I was," that sound too "Amurican." "Peer Gynt" in Paul Green's adaptation and condensation still seemed to me an undramatic and slightly pretentious bore. Ye Olde Doll's House still stands up damned well in performance as well as reading. I wish I could see some Strindberg. I think back to "The Spook Sonata"—and a lot of other things.

Give my love to Carlotta. Be of as good cheer as you can these days. A hell of a world.

Kenneth

Index